THE WORD
ON HEALTH

A Biblical and Medical
Overview of How to Care
For Your Body and Mind

THE WORD
ON HEALTH

DR. MICHAEL D.
JACOBSON

MOODY PRESS
CHICAGO

To my parents, Gerald and Jean,
who from my youth have taught me to love the Scriptures,

To my children, Joshua and Nathan,
through whom God has brought immeasureable joy and hope for a heritage
that will last beyond my lifetime,

To my wife Susie,
my closest friend and companion.

All Scripture quotations, unless indicated, are taken from the King James Version.

Scripture quotations marked (NIV) are taken from the *Holy Bible: New International Version*®. NIV®. Copyright © 1973, 1978, 1984 by International Bible Society. Used by permission of Zondervan Publishing House. All rights reserved.

The "NIV" and "New International Version" trademarks are registered in the United States Patent and Trademark Office by International Bible Society. Use of either trademark requires permission of International Bible Society.

Scripture quotations marked (NASB) are taken from the *New American Standard Bible,* © 1960, 1962, 1963, 1968, 1971, 1972, 1973, 1975, 1977 by The Lockman Foundation, La Habra, Calif. Used by permission.

Scripture quotations marked (NEB) are taken from the *New English Bible* © 1961, 1970 by the Delegates of the Oxford University Press and the Syndics of the Cambridge University Press. Used by permission.

Quotations attributed to Archibald Hart are excerpted from Archibald C. Hart, *Adrenalin and Stress* © 1986, Word Publishing, Nashville, Tennessee. All rights reserved. Used by permission.

Library of Congress Cataloging-in-Publication Data

Jacobson, Michael D.
    The Word on health / by Michael D. Jacobson.
        p. cm.
    Includes index
    ISBN 0-8024-6496-3 (trade paper)
    1. Medicine--Religious aspects--Christianity. 2. Health--Religious
aspects--Christianity. I. Title.

BT732 .J33 2000
261.8'321--dc21

99-057990

1 3 5 7 9 10 8 6 4 2

Printed in the United States of America

CONTENTS

LISTING OF
FIGURES AND TABLES

Figure

Table

LAYING THE FOUNDATION

Therefore whosoever heareth these sayings of mine, and doeth them, I will liken him to a wise man, which built his house upon a rock: and the rain descended, and the floods came, and the winds blew, and beat upon that house; and it fell not, for it was founded upon a rock. And every one that heareth these sayings of mine, and doeth them not, shall be likened unto a foolish man, which built his house upon the sand: and the rain descended, and the floods came, and the winds blew, and beat upon that house; and it fell: and great was the fall of it.

—Jesus Christ (*Matthew 7:24–27*)

1

A HEALTH CARE
WAKE-UP CALL

In A.D. 1348, approximately 100 million people inhabited Europe, northern Africa, and the Near East.[1] One year later, 25 million were dead, victims of the bubonic plague.[2] Throughout the Middle Ages, the plague repeatedly swept through Europe, decimating a large percentage of the population. During one three-month period, five to ten thousand people died every day in Constantinople alone.

During a later sweep, in 1603, 23 percent of the population of London died. England was estimated to have lost up to one half of its people to the dreaded disease, as entire villages were completely destroyed.[3] All told, estimates range from 60 million deaths to 75 percent of the entire populace.[4]

As the plague continued its scourge, it became apparent that the Jewish people were somehow escaping its death grip. This led many to persecute them. People concluded that it was the Jews who were responsible for the plague, since they were the only ones who were not dying.

The truth is that, hundreds of years prior to the discovery of bacteria, the Jews were protecting themselves from the deadly *Yersinia pestis* microbe by practicing cleanliness and good hygiene. Why? Because more than three thousand years before man discovered bacteria, the Creator had given detailed instructions that, if followed, would prevent the spread of such a deadly communicable disease. Had these instructions, as recorded in the book of Leviticus, been generally implemented, God's guidelines would have minimized the rat population, which carried the plague. They also would have limited the plague's spread through requiring strict cleanliness and quarantines, and cleansing following contact with the sick or dead.[5]

He that dwelleth in the secret place of the most High shall abide under the shadow of the Almighty. I will say of the Lord, He is my refuge and my fortress: my God; in him will I trust. Surely he shall deliver thee from the snare of the fowler, and from the noisome pestilence. He shall cover thee with his feathers, and under his wings shall thou trust: his truth shall be thy shield and buckler. Thou shalt not be afraid for the terror of night; nor for the arrow that flieth by day; Nor for the pestilence that walketh in the darkness; nor for the destruction that wasteth at noonday. A thousand shall fall at thy side, and ten thousand at thy right hand; but it shall not come nigh thee. Only with thine eyes shalt thou behold and see the reward of the wicked. (Psalm 91:1–8)

Centuries later, Ignaz Semmelweiss (1818–1865), a Hungarian obstetrician, was walking through the lobby of Vienna General Hospital when he noticed a near-term pregnant woman weeping inconsolably. When he asked why, he was informed that the distraught expectant mother had just been assigned to the obstetrics ward serviced by the medical students. To her, this was a death sentence, because—in contrast to midwife care—the medical student ward had a horrible reputation for postpartum infection. In fact, one out of every six women died.

Semmelweiss pondered. What was the difference between the practice of the medical students and that of the midwives? Then, as if a blindfold had just been removed from his eyes, he thought, *The anatomy lab!*

In his day, it was common practice for medical students to dissect cadavers in the anatomy lab while expectant mothers labored in a nearby ward. Periodically, a student would leave the lab to check the progress of his obstetrical patient with an internal exam.

Semmelweiss suspected a connection, and he ordered that all his students rinse their hands in a bowl of limewater prior to doing internal examinations on the laboring women. Within one month, the death rate had dropped to one in eighty-four.

But when Semmelweiss announced his discovery to the medical profession, he was confronted with disbelief and scorn. Instead of embracing his findings, doctors viciously attacked him. Eventually he went insane and died at the age of forty-seven, the same year that Joseph Lister performed the first antiseptic surgery.[6]

And whoso toucheth any thing that is unclean by the dead . . . shall not eat of the holy things, unless he wash his flesh with water. (Leviticus 22:4, 6, excerpts)

He that toucheth the dead body of any man shall be unclean seven days. He shall purify himself with it on the third day, and on the seventh day he shall be clean: . . . because the water of separation was not sprinkled upon him, he shall be unclean; his uncleanness is yet upon him. This is the law, when a man dieth in a tent: all that come into the tent, and all that is in the tent, shall be unclean seven days. And every open vessel, which hath no covering bound upon it, is unclean. (Numbers 19:11–15)

Many have dismissed such Old Testament commandments related to uncleanness as no longer relevant. They are considered just ceremonial and designed only for the nation of Israel. But could they be relevant?

Today we understand the transmission of bacteria that was taking place from the cadavers to the ladies-in-waiting. Back then there was no knowledge of microbiology. But how many deaths could have been avoided had the Word been carefully considered and followed *by faith!*

The problem is that medicine has a long history of ignoring the Word of God. Countless theories and practices have been proposed and implemented that are contrary to biblical teaching or principle. And medicine stubbornly clings to these until overwhelming evidence forces it to change.

The "best" medicine of just one hundred and fifty to two hundred years ago would be considered nothing less than barbaric today. Broussais (1772–1838) assumed that most diseases were due to engorgement and inflammation in the digestive tract. That assumption led him to vigorously advocate the use of leeches and venesection (draining the patient's blood). Hoffman (1742–1788) believed that most illnesses arose from degenerate acid humors that must aggressively be eliminated from the body. Stoll (1742–1788), once referred to as "the greatest living clinician," taught that most diseases were due to gastric impurities, especially bile, and "hidden inflammations." These, he said, must be eliminated by the use of emetics (drugs to induce vomiting) and purgatives (drugs to induce diarrhea).

The Scotsman John Brown (1736–1788) claimed that all generalized diseases were due either to an excess of excitability (sthenic) or lack thereof (asthenic). As with the theories of Hoffman and Stoll, the treatments were usually severe. For sthenic diseases, "irritability reducers" were needed: venesection, emetics, purgatives, sudorifics (to eliminate "evil humors"), starvation, cold water, vegetable diet, or bodily and mental rest. Asthenic diseases required warmth, alcohol, raw meat, spices, musk, camphor, ether, opium, and physical and mental exercise. Beck recommended calomel, a toxic mercury compound, "in as large doses as the system will bear."[7]

The net results of such massive amounts of drugs were salivation, loosening of the teeth, falling out of the hair, and other symptoms of acute mercuric poisoning. Medicine became so notorious for its drastic "heroic" treatments that it was mocked in popular songs such as "A Dose of Calomel."

> Physicians of the highest rank,
> To pay their fees would need a bank,
> Combine all wisdom, art and skill,
> Science and sense in—*calomel.*
>
> The man grows worse quite fast indeed!
> Go, call the doctor, ride with speed;
> The doctor comes, like post with mail,
> Doubling his dose of—calomel!
>
> The man in death begins to groan;
> The fatal job for him is done!
> He dies, alas! And sad to tell—
> A sacrifice to—calomel![8]

Today, in order to avoid side effects and toxicity, emphasis is placed on giving patients the lowest dose of medicine necessary to accomplish the therapeutic effect. But just two hundred years ago, drugs were given several grams at a time because the toxic side effects were actually seen as *necessary* to the medicine's accomplishing its purpose (e.g., the induction of vomiting, diarrhea, etc.).

> This was the medicine; the patients died,
> And no one thought of asking who recovered.
>
> So 'mongst these hills and vales our hell-broths wrought
> More havoc, brought more victims to the grave
> By many than the pestilence had bought.
>
> To thousands I myself the poison gave:
> They pined and perished; I live on to hear
> Their reckless murderer's praises far and near.[9]

Even dedicated Christian physicians such as Benjamin Rush (a signer of the Declaration of Independence) were strong proponents of these harsh treatments. Rush had such confidence in bloodletting that he proclaimed, "I would sooner die with my lancet in my hand, than give it up while I had breath to maintain it or a hand to use it." And use it he did, removing up to four-fifths of the patient's blood. Similarly, Dr. A. Twitchell stated that he began treatment "by bleeding *ad dilgerium or* till a very sensible impression is made upon the system."[10]

Sadly, America's beloved first president also fell victim to the hands of misguided physicians. On December 14, 1799, George Washington came down with a severe sore throat. It was inflamed and gave him some difficulty in breathing. His overseer removed a pint of blood, but that provided no relief. A physician was called, who applied a blister to the throat and let another pint of blood. At three o'clock that afternoon, two other doctors came to consult with the first one. By a vote of two to one they decided to let more blood and removed a quart that time. They reported that the blood flowed "slow and thick." By then the president was dehydrated, and it would seem that the doctors must have had to squeeze out the final drops. Washington died sometime between ten and eleven that same night.[11]

If only Rush and others would have heeded the word from Scripture stating that the life is in the blood, the lives of Washington and many others may not have been cut short. Modern medicine rejects venesection almost completely, realizing that even modest blood losses can be devastating to any patient, particularly to one already weakened by illness.

Many believe that science has now advanced to such a level that it is not to be questioned. This is most unfortunate and is the same mistake that each generation has made in the past. Philosopher George Santayana was correct when he said, "Those who cannot remember the past are condemned to repeat it."[12]

On the first day of medical school, the dean of the college of medicine introduced our educational experience by informing us: "In the next four years, 50 percent of what you are about to learn will be incorrect! However, we do not yet know where the inaccuracies are. So, you are going to need to learn it all, and master it, then continue to study after you leave here so that, as new discoveries are made, that which is no longer relevant will be discarded." Unfortunately, my experience was not unique. Physician colleagues who attended other schools have shared similar experiences with me.

Now I realize that the reason for the dean's statement was to challenge us to be learners the rest of our lives. However, it certainly did not inspire confidence in the medical profession when one heard that half of what he was about to learn was probably false.

Today, when science appears to conflict with the Scriptures, it is science that is given the benefit of the doubt. But how can we put such blind faith in a profession that gets it right only half the time? God's Word is revealed truth. And though the Bible is not a medical textbook, it does have a great deal to say about medicine and health. Furthermore, it is the testimony of One who was there when it all began—an eyewitness. Therefore, when the Word speaks, it is science that needs to do the yielding.

> The captain of the ship looked into the dark night and saw faint lights in the distance. Immediately he told his signalman to send a message: "Alter your course 10 degrees south."
> Promptly a return message was received: "Alter your course 10 degrees north." The captain was angered; his command had been ignored. So he sent a second message: "Alter your course 10 degrees south—I am the captain!"
> Soon another message was received: "Alter your course 10 degrees north—I am Seaman Third Class Jones."
> Immediately the captain sent a third message, knowing the fear it would evoke: "Alter your course 10 degrees south—I am a battleship!"
> Then the reply came: "Alter your course 10 degrees north—I am a lighthouse."[13]

When the Word conflicts with science, history has repeatedly proven that it is science that must make the change of course. When the Creator speaks, we should listen. Hosea 4:6 says, "My people are destroyed [perish needlessly] for lack of knowledge." Let us not perish needlessly by making the same mistake as many previous generations. Let us carefully examine the Scriptures. And take God at His word.

THE ROLE OF THE CHURCH IN LAYING
A BIBLICAL FOUNDATION FOR HEALTH CARE

Why should we take Him at His word? Maybe we should ask, Why not? After all, God is our Inventor, Engineer, and Great Physician. But how many of us have even thought to consider asking for His input in the critical area of health and medicine? The sad fact is that many of God's people have not done so. I believe a major reason we are in a health care crisis today is that the church has failed to look to God's Word for direction about our health matters.

"What would the Bible have to do with health, disease, and medicine?" you might ask. But think about it for a moment. Can you imagine the earthly ministry of Christ without any miraculous healing? Ministering to the sick was central to Jesus' earthly ministry and the spread of the gospel. When messengers from John the Baptist asked if Jesus was the Christ, He answered by pointing out His healing power and concern for the sick and the poor.

> *Go your way, and tell John what things ye have seen and heard; how that the blind see, the lame walk, the lepers are cleansed, the deaf hear, the dead are raised, to the poor the gospel is preached.* (Luke 7:22)

When Jesus sent out the disciples, He commanded them to heal the sick (Luke 9:2; 10:9). Furthermore, following the example of Christ and the apostles, it was the early church that established the first hospitals as a means of caring for the sick. Their testimony of love for people was so powerful that it was perceived as a major threat to the Roman Empire and prompted fourth-century Emperor Julian the Apostate to complain:

> Now we can see what it is that makes these Christians such powerful enemies of our gods; it is the brotherly love which they manifest towards strangers, and the sick and the poor.[14]

Julian then proposed that Rome build its own hospitals as a counterpropaganda device.

Throughout most of history since the time of Christ, the church has been known for its concern for and care of the sick and poor. Today, a major tool of evangelism has been lost, for *government* has become the major provider of health care in most Western nations. In addition, health care has become big business and a major expense—so major that it is draining the financial lifeblood of our families, church, and nation.

In the United States, health care expenditures have outpaced inflation every year since 1945, the year the federal government decided there was a shortage of hospital beds and began providing matching funds for communities through the Hill-Burton Act.

Just how bad is the crisis? In 1994, the U.S. spent $1 trillion on health care. That is $3,800 annually for every man, woman, and child, regardless of whether or not they were sick. Recently, costs have been rising by 13 or 14 percent each year. By the year 2000, they were expected to exceed $2 trillion (that's $2,000,000,000,000, in case you want to see how many zeros that is). That means that in just six years—from 1994 to 2000—costs of health care are expected to have doubled—during a time when inflation rates have been at a constant record low.[15]

We can graphically illustrate this rise in health care expense by looking at the gross domestic product (GDP). In 1960, health, defense, and education each took 6 percent of the nation's GDP. But by 1994, while defense and education each dropped to 5 percent of the GDP, health care more than doubled to 13 percent. In other words, health care is taking a bigger and bigger slice of the GDP pie. The question is, How long can we continue to allow that slice to grow before it consumes the entire pie?

Many now suggest that the only solution to the current crisis is to implement a government-run system such as is used in Canada.

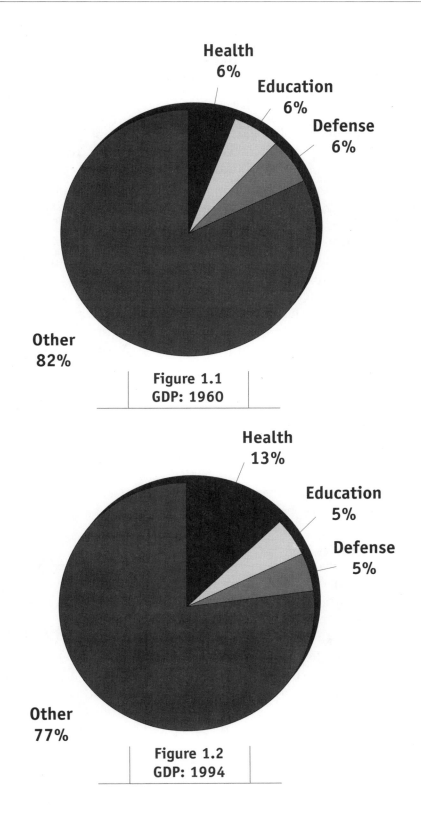

Health
6%

Education
6%

Defense
6%

Other
82%

Figure 1.1
GDP: 1960

Health
13%

Education
5%

Defense
5%

Other
77%

Figure 1.2
GDP: 1994

But an examination of the Canadian health care system reveals that they struggle with the same root problems that are experienced in the United States.[16] And, as one would expect, medical services have been curtailed in some instances in order to control costs. Hospitals have begun to look at substituting physician services with lower skilled, less expensive personnel, for certain services. More than 50 percent of breast cancer patients awaiting radiation therapy experience significant delays in treatment.[17] Likewise, heart patients are often delayed in their ability to obtain standard cardiac procedures.[18] As a result, Canadians in one year spent more than $1 billion on health care in the United States.[19] And a growing number of voices are now calling for a private option to the Canadian health care system.[20]

Yes, the church has abdicated its role in selflessly caring for the sick, and we are definitely in a cost-of-health-care crisis as a result.

But I believe that there is an even more serious crisis at hand—a crisis that is present because of the failure of the church to teach sound doctrine. We all know that the church has an obligation to proclaim the truths of salvation, godly character, spiritual growth, and so on. But health care and medicine? Aren't they a little outside the church's domain?

However, sound doctrine should be taught regarding *any* area of life to which the lordship of Christ applies. Health care and medicine are no exception. When was the last time you heard a sermon that dealt with health care, or some medical treatment, or what to do when you get sick? The sad fact is that the church is almost completely silent in the vital area of health and medicine.

A void has been created by this silence, and into that void have come philosophies with pagan traditions and unbiblical pretexts. Many Christian physicians, myself included, have been exposed to these false ideas.

I was born into a Christian family, became a Christian at a young age, and went through Bible college and a Christian liberal arts university. I completed medical school at an institution that has a strong Christian heritage. But my fellow Christian physicians and I have, nevertheless, been trained to approach medicine in a secular way, almost completely devoid of the Scriptures.

Consequently, I am sure that if Jesus Christ were to lecture in the classroom of a modern-day medical school, many Christian physicians would be stunned by what they would hear. How greatly the medical profession needs sound doctrine: principles that do not change with time, because they are truth revealed by our Creator, "in whom are hid all the treasures of wisdom and knowledge" (Colossians 2:3).

But the void is not just in the medical profession; it exists inside the church as well. As a result, believers have felt like ships aimlessly adrift without rudders, unsure of the route they should take through the minefield of health care. Some place blind faith in their physicians, too afraid to consider that there might be a better way. Others spurn orthodox medicine and have plunged into any of a number of questionable alternatives. But perhaps most commonly has been a tendency to ignore the subject of health altogether.

CONCLUSION

Ron had just come home from the mission field where he had served for several decades. His ministry had been incredibly successful. He had built it from the ground up—from nothing to a major evangelistic force in the region. He had an outstanding staff, excellent materials, and exceptional financial support. But he had been taken out of the battle in an unexpected way: His health failed.

One statement he made summarized his feelings: "I have served God for forty-three years, and now this." "This" referred to an incurable, terminal illness. Prior to now, Ron had never given his health a thought. All of his energy was devoted to "ministry." He took for granted the health he would need in order to accomplish it.

Likewise, many Christian workers have gone into the ministry thinking that since they are "doing God's work," they don't have to concern themselves with matters of health; God is going to take care of them. Their lives and ministry seem to go along smoothly until they hit forty or fifty years of age, when suddenly disease strikes. Then, despite the fact that they have been violating God's natural law all of their lives, they often ask, "Why?" and may even question God's character for allowing them to get sick.

A bumper sticker says it this way, "Ignore your health . . . and it will go away!" That is just what we have done in the church: we have ignored our health . . . and it has gone away.

2

THE WORD ON WHY PEOPLE GET SICK

These wait all upon thee; that thou mayest give them their meat in due season. That thou givest them they gather: thou openest thine hand, they are filled with good. Thou hidest thy face, they are troubled: thou takest away their breath, they die, and return to their dust. (Psalm 104:27–29)

I thank the Lord for eyeglasses. I was born with such significant eyesight problems that I had to have eye surgery at the age of three. How different life would have been for me and millions of others had we been born prior to the 1700s, when the principles of optics were refined. Many like myself would have been declared blind. But with the use of corrective lenses, our vision is essentially normal.

Although many people have perfect physical eyesight, every human being is born spiritually blind. Adam's original sin has produced in us a fallen nature and has corrupted our ability to see and understand reality and truth. Man is in need of "corrective lenses." Without them, he develops his own vain philosophies to answer the questions that constantly plague his heart, such as, Who am I? Where did I come from? Why am I here? Why do we get sick, suffer, and die? How can I live forever?

Our Creator knows the answers to these questions. He is the First Cause. He made life happen. He is why we are here. And He has given each of us "corrective lenses" with which to properly understand life: the Holy Scriptures. The Bible tells who we are, where we came from, and why we get sick, suffer, and die. It tells us how we can live forever.

In order to know the truthful answers to these questions, we need to put on the eyeglasses of Scripture so that our fallen vision can be corrected and we can see clearly from the Creator's perspective. What we think and believe determines what we do. Therefore, if we are going to make the right choices when it comes to health and medicine, we need to have the right understanding, or worldview.

WHERE IT ALL STARTED

The foundation for our understanding of health, disease, death, and healing is found in the "book of beginnings," Genesis. In the first few chapters of the Bible, we learn several critical things about ourselves.

- Life comes from the Creator, who is the only true God (Genesis 1 and 2).
- Man was created in the image of God, in His likeness: yet he is separate and inferior (Genesis 1:27; 2:7).
- Man was created "very good" (Genesis 1:31).
- Man was created immortal; he would never die (Genesis 2:17).
- Man is to live in submission to His Creator ("divine right by creation").
- God and man have an adversary who opposes them (Genesis 3:1).
- Man (Adam and Eve) sinned: they listened to Satan and violated God's only restriction (not to eat the fruit of the forbidden tree; Genesis 3:6).
- Death (and disease) entered the world as a result of Adam's sin (Romans 5:12; 6:23).
- Due to man's potential for great wickedness, God limited his life span (Genesis 6:3).

Here then, we have the essential elements of a biblical worldview of health and disease. We know we will all die, because that's what God's Word says. Why do people spend their lives chanting a mantra or looking for the Fountain of Youth or some other magic formula to make them immortal? Because they have not allowed the Word of God to correct their vision.

THE PROMISE OF LONG LIFE AND HEALTH IF . . .

Shortly after God miraculously brought the nation of Israel out of Egypt, He spoke to the people through Moses, giving them an awesome promise:

If thou wilt diligently hearken to the voice of the Lord thy God, and wilt do that which is right in his sight, and wilt give ear to his commandments, and keep all his statutes, I will put none of these diseases upon thee, which I have brought upon the Egyptians: for I am the Lord that healeth thee. (Exodus 15:26)

The promise was that He would put none of the diseases of the Egyptians on the Israelites. And what were the diseases from which God would protect Israel if they followed Him?

We have a clear idea of the Egyptian diseases from radiographs and autopsies performed on mummies by paleopathologist Marc A. Ruffer and others. These studies show that many Egyptians had the same diseases that still cause illness today.[1]

Heart disease, cancer, stroke, arthritis—those were the diseases of the Egyptians, and those are the diseases of our day.

Wouldn't it be wonderful if the threat of heart disease, cancer, and stroke were gone? According to Moses, that was possible through God's protection. But—like many of God's promises—there were conditions attached. Let us take a brief look at the conditions that were to be met in order for God's promises of health and long life to become a reality.

Keep God's Commandments

We saw this in Exodus 15:26. In addition, we read:

I have set before you life and death, blessing and cursing: therefore choose life, that both thou and thy seed may live. (Deuteronomy 30:19)

My son, forget not my law; but let thine heart keep my commandments: for length of days, and long life, and peace, shall they add to thee. (Proverbs 3:1–2)

The fifth commandment promised long life to those who *honor their parents* (Exodus 20:12). The commandment and promise are repeated in Ephesians 6:1–3:

Children, obey your parents in the Lord: for this is right. Honour thy father and mother; (which is the first commandment with promise;) that it may be well with thee and thou mayest live long on the earth.

Did you know that honesty in business transactions could prolong your life?

A perfect and just measure shalt thou have: that thy days may be lengthened. (Deuteronomy 25:15)

David tells us that *watching what we say* can prolong life:

What man is he that desireth life, and loveth many days, that he may see good? Keep thy tongue from evil, and thy lips from speaking guile. (Psalm 34:12–13)

In Proverbs, Solomon repeatedly links the pursuit of wisdom with long life:

Hear, O my son, and receive my sayings; and the years of thy life shall be many. (Proverbs 4:10)

Similarly, Solomon links the *fear of God,* and its corresponding *humility,* with good health:

Be not wise in thine own eyes: fear the Lord, and depart from evil. It shall be health to thy navel, and marrow to thy bones. (Proverbs 3:7–8)

Finally, keeping the heart contented and merry can have a dramatic effect on one's health (Proverbs 14:30; 16:24; 17:22). In a later chapter, we will examine some fascinating new research that demonstrates the significance of this.

ROOT CAUSES OF SICKNESS

Since keeping God's commandments is associated with His promise of health and long life, it should come as no surprise that illness and death may be associated with failure to follow His requirements:

> *But it shall come to pass, if thou wilt not hearken unto the voice of the Lord thy God, to observe to do all his commandments and his statutes which I command thee this day; that all these curses shall come upon thee, and overtake thee. . . . The Lord shall smite thee with a consumption, and with a fever, and with an inflammation, and with an extreme burning, and with the sword, and with blasting, and with mildew; and they shall pursue thee until thou perish. . . . Then the Lord will make thy plagues wonderful [i.e., incredible—not the kind of wonderful you or I would want!], and the plagues of thy seed, even great plagues, and of long continuance, and sore sicknesses, and of long continuance. Moreover he will bring upon thee all the diseases of Egypt, which thou wast afraid of; and they shall cleave unto thee. Also every sickness, and every plague, which is not written in the book of this law, them will the Lord bring upon thee, until thou be destroyed. . . . And among these nations [to which you have been scattered] shalt thou find no ease, neither shall the sole of thy foot have rest: but the Lord shall give thee there a trembling heart, and failing of eyes, and sorrow of mind: and thy life shall hang in doubt before thee; and thou shalt fear day and night, and shalt have none assurance of thy life. (Deuteronomy 28:15, 22, 59–61, 65–66)*

In other words, if Israel turned her back on God, there would be a rise in the frequency and severity of disease. The nation would experience the dreaded "diseases of Egypt." Those diseases would be degenerative in nature, since they would be "of long continuance" and would "cleave" to them. Is this not a picture of what we see happening in our day?

People who are diagnosed with heart disease, cancer, diabetes, arthritis, hypothyroidism, high blood pressure, emphysema, lupus, multiple sclerosis, or many, many others have a diagnosis that tends to stay with them for the rest of their lives—their disease "cleaves" to them.

Now we may tend to discount these warnings as given only to Israel. But they appear to have relevance to our nation today. Remember that, though the Old Testament is primarily the story of God's dealings with Israel, there are numerous accounts of His addressing other nations. Jonah was sent to Nineveh. Pronouncements were made against Tyre, Babylon, Assyria, and Sodom. Consider God's words spoken through the prophet Jeremiah:

> *At what instant I shall speak concerning a nation, and concerning a kingdom, to pluck up, and to pull down, and to destroy it; if that nation, against whom I have pronounced turn from their evil, I will repent of the evil that I thought to do unto them. (Jeremiah 18:7–8)*

Now, I do not believe that God sits on His heavenly throne, observes nations rejecting His commandments, and then orders plagues and diseases sent upon them. Though He certainly has the right to do so, He does not need to. Whenever people reject the ways of the One who created them, they also reject wisdom, and certain consequences are engaged, with disease and death as a natural result.

We have already seen clear examples of this in the opening chapter, such as the Jewish people being protected from the bubonic plague and Dr. Semmelweiss's patients being protected from postpartum infection. As we examine Scripture for the root causes of disease, we will see numerous cause-and-effect sequences that we may have never considered before. But like Dr. Semmelweiss, let us put on the corrective lenses of God's Word and allow Him to let us see that which, at least in some cases, may not yet be comprehended by the mind of man.

A study of the Word indicates that there are at least six root causes of illness:

- Sickness unto death
- Sickness to glorify God through healing
- Sickness for the purpose of testing or developing character
- Sickness due to chastisement
- Sickness due to a broken spirit
- Sickness due to purely physical causes

Regardless of the root cause, there are, in general, three *ways* in which illness can come upon us. (1) God can bring disease upon us. (2) Sickness can be due to demonic (Satanic) influence. (3) Or we can bring sickness upon ourselves, such as through a violated conscience or a broken spirit. Now let us look at each one in detail.

Sickness Unto Death

> *Now Elisha was fallen sick of his sickness whereof he died.* (2 Kings 13:14; see also Deuteronomy 32:48–50)

This is the easy one. Since Adam, death has been the rule; only two individuals have escaped death. So, unless you are on a par with Enoch and Elijah, or unless the Lord returns soon, death will be your ultimate sickness. I recall a lecture in which the statement was made that half of all of our health care dollars are spent in the last two weeks of life. Now, if one's sickness is "unto death," wouldn't it be prudent to seek that discernment and avoid expensive tests, treatments, and hospitalizations that will not affect the outcome?

But oftentimes we don't want that kind of discernment. We are afraid of death. We fear it either for ourselves or for the one we do not want to lose. So, despite the fact that we may know an illness is terminal (a sickness unto death), as soon as our loved one takes a turn for the worse, we rush him back to the hospital and lay him at the feet of the physicians, hoping that they will somehow be able to forestall the inevitable.

Remember King Hezekiah? It was said of him that he trusted God more than any king ever to rule Judah. But when Isaiah informed the king that his sickness was unto death, Hezekiah turned toward the wall, "wept sore," and begged God to extend his life. God heard Hezekiah's prayer and gave him another fifteen years (see 2 Kings 20:1–6).

Isn't that exciting? Not really. Very little is said about the last fifteen years of Hezekiah's life, except for two things: (1) He blundered by boasting of his wealth to the visiting Babylonians. As a result, Isaiah predicted that his riches would be carried off to Babylon. (2) Three years after he should have been dead, Hezekiah had a son, Manasseh, who became the most wicked king to sit on the throne of Judah. Manasseh practiced occult worship, sacrificed his own son to a pagan god, and "filled Jerusalem from one end to another" with innocent blood. Manasseh was the "straw that broke the camel's back" and resulted in the entire nation of Judah's being condemned to captivity for seventy years (2 Kings 21).

If the Lord says it's time to go, don't you think we should listen? After all, we're going to die eventually anyway. There are some things that are worse than death.

> *I am torn between the two: I desire to depart and be with Christ, which is better by far.* (Philippians 1:23 NIV)

This is in no way to be interpreted as an endorsement of the growing practice of euthanasia. Apart from self-defense (including the defense of one's nation) and capital punishment as a due process of the law, God did not give man the right to take the life of himself or another human being.

Sickness to Glorify God Through Healing

However, not every sickness is unto death. Some illnesses may actually be there in order to demonstrate God's power and love through His healing. Such was the case with Lazarus. When Jesus was told that Lazarus was sick, He said:

> *This sickness is not unto death, but for the glory of God, that the Son of God might be glorified thereby.* (John 11:4)

The first time I met Pastor Larry Cornett, he had a serious, debilitating problem with pain in his neck from two herniated discs. He had been suffering for some time, and a neurologist had just informed him that he had two weeks to have decompression surgery or he would lose the function of his left arm.

But Pastor Cornett did not believe God wanted him to go through the surgery. So he prayed, asking for God's will and help, and was anointed by the elders of his church.

Through a series of circumstances, he was referred to me for a special injection procedure in which I had been trained. These injections, referred to as prolotherapy, were made into his damaged supporting ligaments in order to induce an inflammatory response. (This sends a signal to the body that an injury has occurred, and it kick-starts the repair process). After receiving prolotherapy, Pastor Cornett was restored completely—without the surgery.

Two months later, he invited me to speak at his church. The Lord used that experience to give guidance to our family. As a result, several months later, we moved two hours north to Cincinnati, where we have lived and served ever since. Not until later did I learn that Pastor Cornett had been praying that God would bring a doctor to minister at his church. The Lord both heard his prayer and gave our family direction, but it required that the pastor herniate two discs in his neck to bring it to pass.

Sickness to Test or Develop Character

That is not to say that the only way that God will be glorified is through healing our diseases. Sometimes He is glorified even more if our faith and character are purified in the midst of suffering. Consider the life and ministry of Joni Eareckson Tada, who through a diving accident was paralyzed from the neck down. Despite her affliction, Joni developed incredible skill in artistry, using her mouth to hold her instruments. Today, she has an international ministry, largely *because* of her affliction.

Soon after the apostle Paul's conversion, God gave this new believer an unprecedented look into the third heaven. What a temptation to pride! So, according to Paul,

> *Lest I should be exalted above measure through the abundance of the revelations, there was given to me a thorn in the flesh, the messenger of Satan to buffet me.* (2 Corinthians 12:7)

We don't know what Paul's "thorn in the flesh" was. Some have said it was near blindness. Others say a speech impediment. Nevertheless, it was difficult. Three times, probably through extended prayer and fasting, Paul asked the Lord to heal him. But God's answer was no. Our Lord felt it necessary for Paul to remain afflicted in order to remain most usable to Him. And Paul, even today considered one of the most influential people of all time, had to agree. He said, "Most gladly therefore will I rather glory in my infirmities, that the power of Christ may rest upon me" (2 Corinthians 12:9).

Job was inflicted with disease *because* of his blameless, godly character. The adversity he experienced was actually to demonstrate to the invisible spirit world that his righteousness was not simply for personal gain.

> *And the Lord said unto Satan, Hast thou considered my servant Job, that there is none like him in the earth, a perfect and an upright man, one that feareth God, and escheweth evil? and still he holdeth fast his integrity, although thou movedst me against him, to destroy him without cause. And Satan answered the Lord, and said, Skin for skin, yea, all that a man hath will he give for his life. But put forth thine hand now, and touch his bone and his flesh, and he will curse thee to thy face. And the Lord said unto Satan, Behold, he is in thine hand; but save his life. So went Satan forth from the presence of the Lord, and smote Job with sore boils from the sole of his foot unto his crown.* (Job 2:3–7)

Sickness Due to Chastisement for Sin

Unfortunately, our sicknesses are not always borne out of our excellence in character and spiritual maturity. Sometimes we are sick because we have done something wrong and we are under chastisement.

Failure in leadership. Affliction may come even though we may have done nothing wrong personally but those in leadership have broken God's law. David took an illegal census of Israel's military. As a result, 70,000 men lost their lives (1 Chronicles 21; 2 Samuel 24).

Now, lest we become too critical of David, it appears that the nation had done something to incite the taking of a census. According to the account of this event in 2 Samuel 24:1, "the anger of the Lord was kindled against Israel," and He moved David to take a census.

Immorality. Second, chastisement may come as a result of immorality. Proverbs abounds with strong warnings against such a lifestyle:

> *For her house inclineth unto death, and her paths unto the dead. None that go unto her return again, neither take they hold of the paths of life.* (Proverbs 2:18–19)

Paul warned that those who live an immoral lifestyle will receive in their own bodies the just penalty for their perversions (Romans 1:27). Unfortunately, mankind often fails to listen, as is evidenced by the ages-old battle with sexually transmitted diseases (STDs). Today we hear of epidemics of human immunodeficiency virus (HIV), human papillomavirus (HPV), herpes, and chlamydia. Even the STDs of yesteryear, syphilis and gonorrhea, are returning with strains resistant to nearly every available antibiotic. Virtually all STDs could be completely prevented if sexuality were kept within its biblical confines.

Taking Communion unworthily.

> *Wherefore whosoever shall eat this bread, and drink this cup of the Lord, unworthily, shall be guilty of the body and blood of the Lord. But let a man examine himself, and so let him eat of that bread, and drink of that cup. For he that eateth and drinketh unworthily, eateth and drinketh damnation to himself, not discerning the Lord's body. For this cause many are weak and sickly among you, and many sleep. For if we would judge ourselves, we should not be judged.* (1 Corinthians 11:27–31)

It was Sunday morning. After taking care of a few things, I quietly slipped into the back of the church. To my dismay, the Lord's Supper was laid out on the altar. *Oh no,* I thought, *not today!*

I knew I had a problem. Just the day before, I had become infuriated with someone, and I had not resolved the problem before the close of the day (despite the fact that I knew I should), primarily because I was convinced that I was totally right.

But as I stared at the Communion table, I wasn't so sure. The warning "He that eateth and drinketh unworthily, eateth and drinketh damnation to himself" kept running through my mind. What was I to do? As a deacon, I was not only going to have to serve the elements but also partake of them in front of everybody, including other pastors and deacons.

The time came for the sermon. Pastor Cornett quietly approached the pulpit. Then he paused and said, "This morning I had a message all prepared. But I feel that the Lord would have me to postpone that sermon in order to focus this morning's message on Communion and what it means to partake of the body and blood of our Lord Jesus Christ."

OK, Lord, I prayed. *That settles it. I see what You're doing here, and I realize that I have been terribly wrong.* I quietly confessed my sin to Him and committed to correcting my wrong at the soonest possible opportunity.

How merciful our God is! He knew that I would be jeopardizing my health and ministry if I were to take Communion without self-examination. He didn't have to intervene, but He did. And I am grateful.

I wonder how many come to the Lord's Table and, having failed to examine themselves properly, are ill because of it. According to Paul, the answer is *many,* and his letter was written to a Gentile church. Could it be that many of us fail to judge ourselves, partake of Communion unworthily, and at some later time come down with a disease but never see the connection? We need to take a very close look, "for if we would judge ourselves, we should not be judged."

Lying. Had Ananias and Sapphira been given a second chance to examine themselves, they would most certainly have used the opportunity. Their lie seemed a small thing at the time, especially in light of the great deal of good they were doing—or so they thought. They had sold some land in order to give money to the church and had decided to keep part of it for their own use.

As Peter would later affirm, there was nothing wrong with that. The land was their land to do with as they chose. But apparently they wanted others to believe they were even more generous than they were. They told the apostles that they were giving the church *all* the proceeds. Unfortunately, their "little white lie" cost them their lives. What they had done was more than just a small thing, Peter informed them. They had actually lied to the Holy Spirit.

Aletheia, the Greek word for truth, means "the unveiled reality lying at the basis of and agreeing with an appearance [denoting] the reality clearly lying before our eyes as opposed to a mere appearance, without reality."[2]

Ananias and Sapphira were trying to make it appear to the church that they were giving *all* the price of the land when, in reality, they were giving only part. What they did didn't seem particularly significant, but it was a misrepresentation of the truth. Have we ever misrepresented ourselves to others in the church? To do so, according to Peter, is to lie to God Himself. This may happen more often than we realize. Perhaps illnesses indeed have occurred with this as the cause, and we had no idea of the spiritual connection.

Rebellion. Not only are we to be truthful with the Lord and with the authorities He has ordained, but we are also to humbly submit to their leadership. Miriam, along with her brother Aaron, was lifted up with pride and spoke against their ruler-brother Moses. As Numbers 12 explains, "the Lord heard it," and, after a dramatic confrontation with the sibling rivals, Miriam was struck with leprosy. In an instant, she had gone from self-proclaimed coleader to social outcast. Rebellion, another possible cause of sickness, is costly.

Bill Gothard, founder and president of the Institute in Basic Life Principles, explains that authority acts as an "umbrella of protection." As long as we remain under God-ordained authority, we experience His divine protection from Satan, our adversary. But when we rebel, we step out from under that umbrella of protection and expose ourselves to Satan's power. Rebellion is dangerous.

Such was the case with Israel's first king. Saul had been commanded by God to attack the Amalekites and destroy them completely, taking no prisoners and no spoil. But Saul decided not to follow the instructions he had been given. He spared King Agag's life and kept back the best of the animals. Saul defended his actions by stating that the animals were kept for a sacrifice to God. His excuse is what prompted the prophet's great response: "To obey is better than sacrifice. . . . For rebellion is as the sin of witchcraft, and stubbornness is as iniquity and idolatry" (1 Samuel 15:22–23).

An evil spirit came to Saul then and tormented him to such an extent that David was called in to drive it away through playing melodious music with his harp.

It is important to note that, whatever the *root* cause of their ailments, Jesus healed numerous individuals whose diseases were attributed to demonic influence. One was blind and unable to speak, being "possessed with a devil" (Matthew 12:22). Another was unable to either hear or speak (Mark 9:17–27). Then there was the woman who was bent over with such severe arthritis that she "could in no wise lift up herself." Jesus said that Satan had bound her for eighteen years. He healed her, and she immediately "was made straight" (Luke 13:11–17).

From testimonies received in our office there is evidence that demonically incurred illness is present today—as well as the power of Christ to heal.

Multiple complaints, apparently brought on by Satan, were resolved when a woman learned to pray in the power of Jesus' name:

A bad eye infection flared up. . . . We prayed for healing, but I still had my problem. One evening I was desperate; I said, "Lord, what will I do?" In my heart I heard the Lord say, *Use your authority in My Name!* So I put my hands on my bad eye and said, "In the Name of Jesus, every spirit that bothers this eye, I command you in the Name of Jesus to leave. . . . The pressure behind my eye was back to normal, my dry eyes became moistened, and I was very, very surprised at all this. My eye had no more pain, and until today I never needed to see an eye specialist. Praise God!

Since that time I pray daily for myself, lay [a] hand on my forehead and keep saying in the Name of Jesus, "Every oppression of the enemy leave my body." . . . I'm glad to report that my allergy is gone, my dry eyes returned to normal, insomnia is greatly improved, my bronchial asthma cleared up. Also, spots appeared in my face that did not heal. I prayed and they healed up too.[3]

Frequent infections, leg cramps, fear, and behavioral disorders in children cleared up after homeopathic books and remedies were destroyed because of their suspected connection to the occult. (An in-depth discussion of homeopathy and other questionable health care philosophies is beyond the scope of this book. I merely mention them here as an example so that this possibility may be considered for those to whom it may apply.)[4]

Bitterness (unforgiveness).

Then came Peter to him, and said, Lord, how oft shall my brother sin against me, and I forgive him? till seven times? Jesus saith unto him, I say not unto thee, Until seven times: but, Until seventy times seven. Therefore is the kingdom of heaven likened unto a certain king, which would take account of his servants. And when he had begun to reckon, one was brought unto him, which owed him ten thousand talents. But forasmuch as he had not to pay, his lord commanded him to be sold, and his wife, and children, and all that he had, and payment to be made. The servant therefore fell down, and worshipped him, saying, Lord, have patience with me, and I will pay thee all. Then the lord of that servant was moved with compassion, and loosed him, and forgave him the debt. But the same servant went out, and found one of his fellowservants, which owed him an hundred pence: and he laid hands on him, and took him by the throat, saying, Pay me that thou owest. And his fellowservant fell down at his feet, and besought him, saying, Have patience with me, and I will pay thee all. And he would not: but went and cast him into prison, till he should pay the debt. So when his fellowservants saw what was done, they were very sorry, and came and told unto their lord all that was done. Then his lord, after that he had called him, said unto him, O thou wicked servant, I forgave thee all that debt, because thou desiredst me: Shouldest not thou also have had compassion on thy fellowservant, even as I had pity on thee? And his lord was wroth, and delivered him to the tormentors, till he should pay all that was due unto him. So likewise shall my heavenly Father do also unto you, if ye from your hearts forgive not every one his brother their trespasses. (Matthew 18:21–35)

A woman was suffering from nightmares in which she was repeatedly followed by someone and strangled. The dreams stopped when she forgave an offender.[5]

Similarly, a woman with osteoporosis saw her bone density increase 50 percent over a matter of weeks after she forgave offenders toward whom she had become embittered.[6]

A violated conscience. One form of chastisement does not really require that either God or Satan do the chastising. We can do it to ourselves through a violated conscience. Has wrong been done toward God or others and never been confessed or made right? I have heard my father, a retired chaplain, and others state that many who are in mental institutions are there because of their inability to cope with guilt. A violated conscience exacts a heavy toll on our physical well-being.

For my life is spent with grief, and my years with sighing: my strength faileth because of mine iniquity, and my bones are consumed. (Psalm 31:10)

In Numbers 5 there is a fascinating Old Testament version of the lie detector test. A woman wrongfully accused of adultery could clear her name by drinking a cup of water containing dirt scraped from the tabernacle floor. If she was guilty, her thigh would "rot and [her] belly would swell" (v. 21). But if she was innocent, neither would happen, and she would conceive children. Same water, same dirt, opposite results. The difference: a clear conscience. Later in this book, you will learn precisely how the stress of a guilty conscience can result in a "rotting of the bones" or a host of other illnesses.

When I kept silence, my bones waxed old through my roaring all the day long. For day and night thy hand was heavy upon me: my moisture is turned into the drought of summer. (Psalm 32:3–4)

Sickness Due to a Broken Spirit (e.g., Depression)

Scripture tells us that when Abigail told her husband that she had interceded for his life before David, Nabal's heart "became as a stone," and he died ten days later (1 Samuel 25:37–38).

A pastor in Georgia related how he asked God for wisdom to help a woman who had such a weakened immune system that she literally lived in a sterile bubble to protect her from the environment.[7] While on his way to see her, the answer came to him through Proverbs 17:22: "A merry heart doeth good like a medicine: but a broken spirit drieth the bones."

When he arrived, he inquired into the woman's background, asking if anyone had ever hurt her deeply. Not only was this the case, but the emotional trauma had preceded the onset of her devastating illness. As he helped her deal with the hurt by forgiving her offenders, her health was restored.

Soon others came to this pastor for help with similar immune-system-related illnesses: chronic fatigue, multiple chemical sensitivity/environmental illness, fibromyalgia, and so on. In each case, he was able to identify a "broken spirit," a person who had been deeply hurt through one or more of four ways:

- Physical abuse
- Sexual abuse
- Emotional or verbal abuse
- Being raised in a very strict environment with many rules but little or no love and affection

Others have made similar observations. A psychologist attending one of our seminars reported that in a hospital support group for patients with serious illness, every single patient indicated that a serious emotionally or spiritually traumatic event immediately preceded the onset of his illness.

Similarly, a study of men recovering from a heart attack indicated that those who had major depression were eight times more likely to die of sudden cardiac death than those who came out of the experience happy to be alive.[8]

The spirit of a man will sustain his infirmity; but a wounded spirit who can bear? (Proverbs 18:14)

Sickness Due to Physical Causes/Natural Law

Finally, some illnesses seem to be due simply to the fact that we are physical beings living in a physical world. These ailments have no apparent underlying cause other than perhaps the function of natural law. Isaac became blind in his old age, with no reason given as to why (Genesis 27:1). Paul advised Timothy, "Use a little wine for thy stomach's sake and thine often infirmities" (1 Timothy 5:23). Here is Paul, who possessed the gift of healing (Acts 14:9–10), essentially telling his beloved son in the faith to employ a little home remedy —actually a change in diet—because he was frequently sick.

Many, many diseases of our day are strongly associated with what we put into our mouths. When we discuss nutrition, we will find that God's Word contains enduring, time-tested, and scientifically established principles that, if followed, can greatly reduce sicknesses that are due to physical causes.

CONCLUSION

Scripture has a great deal to say about health and illness. A study of the Word reveals six root causes of disease:

- Sickness unto death
- Sickness to glorify God through healing
- Sickness to test or develop character
- Sickness due to chastisement for sin either in our own lives or in the lives of those whose failures affect us, such as those in authority. (This can come by way of divine judgment, demonic influence, or a violated conscience. Chastisement may stem from immorality, taking Communion unworthily, misrepresenting the truth, unforgiveness, or rebellion.)
- Sickness due to a broken spirit
- Sickness due to physical causes

God couples numerous promises of health and long life with the following conditions:

- Diligently and carefully keep God's commandments.
- Honor your father and mother.
- Be honest in business.
- Do not speak evil.
- Pursue wisdom.
- Fear God.
- Keep a merry heart.

I used to wonder why the Hebrews so often associated disease with sin and the need for sacrifices. Now, with the observation that five of the six root causes of illness are directly related to the spirit, I instead wonder why we see so little place for the spiritual. Why is medicine the exclusive domain of scientists, doctors, and nurses? Scripture indicates that the spiritual is of primary importance to our physical well-being. Our eyes need to be opened to the possibility that many physical ailments may involve a significant spiritual component.

3

DIETARY
HERESY (1)

Be not carried about with divers and strange doctrines. For it is a good thing that the heart be established with grace; not with meats, which have not profited them that have been occupied therein. (Hebrews 13:9)

God told the nation of Israel that, if they followed His commandments, they would not suffer from the diseases that Egypt incurred (Exodus 15:26). Since there is a definite connection between diet and disease, one might wonder if God intended His people to remain free of disease by following a dietary plan. It only makes sense that our loving Creator would provide instructions to mankind as to how to nurture the physical body that He had given him. Indeed, when we look at the biblical record, we see that He did give man explicit dietary instructions.

But before we look at those instructions, we need to pay heed to a serious warning. Throughout the pages of Scripture, the people of God are warned about false prophets—teachers who *appear* to be from God but whose instruction is not from Him. Paul warned in 1 Timothy 4:1–5 that such false prophets will come "in the latter times." He even told us what they would teach: they will forbid marriage and command us not to eat certain foods. As Paul said, the source of this teaching is not from God but is demonic. It is contrary to Scripture, sound doctrine, and the spirit of the gospel.

Now the Spirit speaketh expressly, that in the latter times some shall depart from the faith, giving heed to seducing spirits, and doctrines of devils; speaking lies in hypocrisy; having their conscience seared with a hot iron; forbidding to marry, and commanding to abstain from meats [food], which God hath created to be received with thanksgiving of them which believe and know *the truth. For every creature of God is good, and nothing to be refused, if it be received with thanksgiving: for it is sanctified by the word of God and prayer. (1 Timothy 4:1–5)**

I believe that we live in these "latter times" and that the teaching of which Paul spoke is coming into the church today. Instead of recognizing the error behind this doctrine, many in the church are embracing it with open arms, often with devastating consequences.

ANATOMY OF A HERESY: A TRUE STORY

"Have Duane take her to the emergency room and tell him that I'll meet them there in a few minutes." As I raced to the hospital, fearing the worst, my thoughts scanned the events leading up to that fateful day.

Everyone at church loved Beth and Duane. She was always full of energy and joy. She had a reputation for gracious hospitality, not letting more than a few days go by without taking people into her home for a nutritious meal. Duane, a retired missionary and pastor, was Mr. Steady. Nothing ever seemed to ruffle him. Both had walked consistently with God since their early youth. Together, they had raised four children, all of whom were faithful in their attendance at church.

As they both neared seventy, their concern for preserving their excellent health continued to grow, despite the fact that they had faithfully followed a prudent diet for more than thirty years. About a year earlier, while visiting a health food store, Duane's attention was drawn to a newsletter promoting a "biblical diet for the prevention and treatment of disease." The newsletter was filled with articles and testimonials extolling the benefits of following "God's Ideal Diet" as outlined in Genesis 1:29. Upon his return home, Duane shared the newsletter with his wife. After a few phone calls, they made plans to attend a weekend seminar at the headquarters for the Christian ministry that published the newsletter.

Soon the day for the seminar arrived, and the excited couple went off with high hopes for gaining the secrets to a long, healthy life. They were not disappointed and later described that weekend as a highlight of their lives.

There they heard that our Creator has given us our dietary instructions in Genesis 1:29 and that He has designed us to live on plant food alone, especially raw fruits and vegetables. Daniel was mentioned. He had purposed not to "defile himself" with meat. The attendees also learned that man's life span averaged more than 900 years until he began to eat meat, but that once flesh was introduced into his diet, his days on earth had become progressively shortened.

Scientific evidence was cited as to how man's intestinal tract is unsuited for the digestion of animal products. Finally, the weekend featured the testimonies of numerous individuals who, suffering from a variety of debilitating diseases, had been completely healed through following "God's Diet." Even the founder of the ministry had been cured of colon cancer, which had led him to start this crusade against disease.

---

* When the King James Version uses the word "meat," it is usually the Greek *broma,* which means "food," especially the food that was allowed or prohibited in the context of Jewish dietary law. When the KJV speaks of the way we use the word *meat* today to refer to animal meat, it uses the word "flesh."

Duane and Beth returned home with renewed zeal for a lifestyle centered on a diet that they were convinced was not only totally compliant with their Creator's design but which was also the answer for every physical malady. Enthusiastically, they shared their discovery with family, friends, and any others who would listen.

Before long, they arranged to have the ministry founder, himself a pastor-now-turned-diet-evangelist, to come and speak at their church. Many attended, and the message was well received by most. However, though the speaker made a great deal of sense and there were numerous validating testimonies, a few listeners had questions. Something didn't seem quite right. But they didn't really know what it was, so they remained silent while they quietly began a study of Scripture and its references to diet.

Meanwhile, the teaching began to have its effects. As several followed the diet, they noticed significant benefits. Kidneys that had been spilling protein into the urine for years returned to normal function. Colds, sore throats, and earaches became rare in children who had had them often during previous years. The number with exciting testimonies grew. (And the skin of several individuals took on an orange hue, indicative of the many glasses of carrot juice they were consuming.)

But the benefits came with a painfully high price tag. Families became divided as well-meaning parents shared the "dietary gospel" (along with books, tapes, juicers, etc.) with their adult wayward children. Close family ties that had endured years of challenges were unable to handle this new assault and were torn apart over the food one eats. Duane and Beth seemed to suffer the most. Although they spearheaded the entire movement, their own children sought to convince them from the Scriptures that they were off balance. Women hesitated to have others over for meals, worrying that their food selection or preparation would not please the critical eye of their nutrition-minded guests.

Fellowship cliques began to form. In the one camp were the "biblical vegetarians," who believed it was wrong to eat meat or "dead food," such as that which was processed or cooked. They tried not to make food an issue, but privately they hoped that by their own excellent health they would win over the doubters to their new lifestyle. In the other camp were the junk food, "hot dogs and Ho Ho's" crowd. They ate whatever they wanted but felt looked down upon and judged by the diet elitists.

If anyone got sick, he didn't want to admit it. It was too embarrassing. If one from the junk food crowd fell ill, that would only strengthen the other camp's contention that "if you would just follow God's Diet you wouldn't get sick." On the other hand, if illness ever struck any of the diet zealots, the explanation was that they were just "detoxifying," a supposedly good sign that they were well on their way to blissful health. The elitists refused the services of physicians, considering their advice to be foolishly misguided and lacking in the true understanding of the cure for all diseases.

The church struggled on. Some families left. The pastor did his best to resolve the situation, prayerfully and carefully addressing the church in private conversations as well as through discreetly worded sermons. But healing of the soul was to finally come in a very unexpected way.

This spring morning, Beth had paid a visit to her beautician. After some friendly conversation, she was seated in a reclining chair in front of the sink where her hair was to be washed. As she leaned her head backward into the sink, everything suddenly went dark. Although she could still hear, Beth could not see. She tried to cry out for help, but no sound came. Like a bolt from the blue, Beth had suffered a massive stroke, leaving her blind and unable to talk or swallow properly.

The blow was devastating. How could this happen when she had been following "God's Ideal Diet"? Was not The Diet supposed to protect her from this? Stunned, she realized that she had transferred her confidence from the Lord to a dietary lifestyle, and her heart broke.

Miraculously, Beth recovered most of her stroke-related losses, and in a letter read before the church, she confessed her failure to keep Christ the focus of her faith.

This story is true. I know, because I observed it firsthand. But unfortunately, it is not unique. The rampant escalation of many diseases and the skyrocketing costs of health care have made the church ripe and vulnerable for such false teaching. Failing to get good answers from either the medical profession or the church, many are looking elsewhere. And into the void have come numerous "wolves in sheep's clothing" who have plundered, scattered, and destroyed the flock with their philosophies.

Three false doctrines concerning health are being brought into the church today. Our story touched on two of them and serves as a real-life lesson on the warning signs of deception. By taking a fairly detailed look at these modern-day false teachings and their related warning signs, it is hoped that you will protect yourself, your family, and perhaps even your friends and church from experiencing the tragedy that I have witnessed.

HERESY NO. 1: GOD'S IDEAL DIET IS VEGETARIAN

And God said, Behold, I have given you every herb bearing seed, which is upon the face of all the earth, and every tree, in the which is the fruit of a tree yielding seed; to you it shall be for meat. And to every beast of the earth, and to every fowl of the air, and to every thing that creepeth upon the earth, wherein there is life, I have given every green herb for meat: and it was so. (Genesis 1:29–30)

Based upon this first mention of diet in Scripture, "biblical vegetarians" draw the conclusion (and rightly so) that mankind was originally designed to be vegetarian. That is, his food was to be only plant food—fruits, vegetables, nuts, and grains. This diet has variously been referred to as "God's Original Diet," "God's Optimum Diet," "God's Ideal Diet," the "Genesis 1:29 Diet," and the "Biblical Diet." Despite any concerns that some may have about the nutritional adequacy of a vegetarian lifestyle, prior to the Flood this diet resulted in an average human life span of more than 900 years!

In Genesis 4, we learn that the first family were farmers and ranchers. Cain was a "tiller of the ground" and Abel a "keeper of sheep." Note that there is no record of their eating any animal flesh. In fact, the few references to food in the early chapters of Genesis seem to indicate that, prior to the Flood, all of mankind ate only plant food.

And of every living thing of all flesh, two of every sort shalt thou bring into the ark, to keep them alive with thee; they shall be male and female. Of fowls after their kind, and of cattle after their kind, of every creeping thing of the earth after his kind, two of every sort shall come unto thee, to keep them alive. And take thou unto thee of all food that is eaten, and thou shalt gather it to thee; and it shall be for food for thee, and for them. (Genesis 6:19–21)

Notice that Noah was to bring two of every living thing on board the ark *to keep them alive, not to eat them.* Furthermore, once the animals were all on board, he was to go and *gather* all of the food for his family and the world's greatest zoo ever.

Unfortunately, some modern nutrition prophets tend to stop somewhere between Genesis 1 and 9, claiming that, since plant food is what God originally gave to Adam and Eve, plant food is what He intends us to eat today and nothing else. But Scripture has much more to say about diet than what we find in the first six chapters.

The Flood ends on page 9 in my Bible; there are still 1,314 pages of Scripture left. Does the Word have anything more to say about diet? Absolutely. Do these later references confirm that God intends that we be vegetarian today? Absolutely not. In fact, within just three verses of the completion of the Flood story, the Creator gave animal flesh as food to mankind.

Every moving thing that liveth shall be meat for you; even as the green herb have I given you all things. (Genesis 9:3)

From then on, we see animal products as a common and significant component in the diet of God's people.

- The meal that Abraham served his angelic visitors included butter, milk, and meat from a slain calf (Genesis 18:8).
- Isaac loved venison and had his hunter son, Esau, prepare it for the meal in which Isaac was to bless him (Genesis 27).
- When the Israelites complained of a lack of food, God sent quail to cover the camp (Exodus 16:13).
- God's Law, as given to Moses, lists clean and unclean animals, and says,

  Speak unto the children of Israel, saying, These are the beasts which ye shall eat among all the beasts that are on the earth. (Leviticus 11:2)

- Under the Mosaic covenant, animal sacrifices were commanded by God and were to be *food* for the priests along with the grain offerings. Furthermore, meat was the main course at special feasts, which were held several times annually and were mandated by God (Leviticus 6:24–26; Exodus 12:1–8).
- John the Baptist ate honey and locusts—a "clean" animal, though unsavory sounding (Matthew 3:4). Perhaps if they were dipped in chocolate?
- Jesus Christ, the Son of God, ate animal products and gave them to others. Isaiah prophesied that the Messiah would eat "butter [an animal product] and honey" (Isaiah 7:15). At the miraculous feeding of the five thousand, Christ gave barley bread *and fish* to all to eat (Matthew 14:19). Later, Jesus proved His bodily resurrection through

the eating of fish (Luke 24:36–43) and gave fish to His fishermen disciples to eat on the shore (John 21:12–13).

The biblical definition of sin is to "miss the bulls-eye" of God's perfect standard. It has nothing to do with intent. In fact, the word implies that we are doing our best to hit the mark. If being vegetarian is God's ideal for man, then vegetarianism is His standard for us and it must be *sin* to eat animal products. But if that were the case, then Christ Himself would have sinned, for *He* ate animal products. If Christ sinned, then He is not the spotless Lamb who was slain for the sins of the world, and we would be lost in our sins and without hope. Thank God this is not the case (Isaiah 53).

Even if Scripture were silent on the matter, common sense would indicate that God's intent for man since the days of the Flood has not been that he totally abstain from eating flesh. For one thing, a vegetarian diet has been virtually impossible to follow for some cultural groups. In some regions of the globe, one cannot grow fruits and vegetables at all. In many other areas, these foods are only seasonal and are unavailable year-round. Only in this century, due to the employment of refrigeration and the development of airfreight, has such a universal dietary program become even a remote possibility.

To summarize, it is clear that, from Genesis 9 on, God has not expected us to abstain from animal products. Therefore, to eat meat cannot be sin, and the doctrine of God's Ideal Diet cannot be true. Given the overwhelming evidence from Scripture, one must conclude that God does not have vegetarianism as His ideal for man.

HERESY NO. 2:
GOD INTRODUCED MEAT INTO MAN'S DIET TO SHORTEN HIS LIFE

If God's ideal diet for man is that he eat only plant food, then why would He give meat to man in Genesis 9? The answer, according to some proponents of vegetarianism, is that God was and is using animal products to shorten man's life span.

Their reasoning goes something like this: Prior to the Flood, the genealogical records in Scripture indicate that man's average life span was more than 900 years. But man's wickedness reached such incredible proportions that God was grieved and vowed to limit his life to 120 years. Within a dozen generations of meat's being introduced into man's diet, his life span was averaging less than 120. Therefore, the reasoning goes, God introduced meat into man's diet to shorten his life.

> *And the Lord said, My spirit shall not always strive with man, for that he also is flesh: yet his days shall be an hundred and twenty years.* (Genesis 6:3)

Some scholars believe this meant that God would allow man 120 more years before He would destroy the earth with a flood. (And that is precisely how long it took Noah to build the ark and prepare for the Great Deluge.) In addition, it appears that God was also declaring a shortened life span for man *after* the Flood, and, indeed, this is what we see. After Jacob, only one man on record in Scripture exceeded this limit of 120, and that was the chief priest Jehoiada, who lived to be 130 (2 Chronicles 24:15). Even Moses died at age 120, although Scripture specifically states that his vision was perfect and there was nothing physically wrong with him (Deuteronomy 34:7).

From genealogies in Genesis 5 and 11, a time line for the generations from Adam to Jacob can be constructed as appears in figure 3.1 on page 42. According to the specific ages given through these first twenty generations of man, Noah's Flood (represented by the bold vertical line) occurred in the year 1656, counting from the date of Creation. Some scholars believe that these dates are not to be taken literally. However, if one examines the genealogies, I don't see how they can be taken any other way.

Again notice that, prior to the Flood, the typical life span of man was more than 900 years. The Flood occurred in Noah's 600th year of life, and he lived 350 years after the Flood, for a total of 950 years. However, by the very next generation a dramatic shortening of the life span was already evident. Shem lived 602 years. He was followed by three generations whose average life span was 445 years. This trio was followed by another that had an average age at death of 206. Then came Nahor with a life span of only 138 years; Terah, who died at 205; Abraham, who died at 175; and Isaac, at 180. The last individual whose life span we can precisely plot is Jacob, who lived 147 years. Thus we see that within twelve generations after the Flood, the average length of man's life dropped nearly 800 years.

At first glance, it seems reasonable that it was indeed meat's being introduced into the diet at the time of the Flood that led to man's shortened life. However, there are several important reasons for rejecting the concept that God deliberately introduced meat into man's diet to shorten his life span.

First of all, the only evidence is circumstantial. Nowhere does Scripture state that meat was introduced into man's diet for this purpose. Certainly, if this were the case, one would think that it would be indicated somewhere.

Second, it stands to reason that if meat in the diet is the key factor to a shortened life span, then multigenerational vegetarians should reapproximate the pre-Flood life span. That is, if a family or culture were to practice a strict vegan diet for several generations in a row, their average individual life spans should increase. Since it took only about twelve generations to go from 950 to 147 years, one should expect that a grandson or great-grandson vegetarian ought to be hitting at least the 200-year mark.

But this is not the case. No matter how purely vegetarian their diet, nowhere on the face of the earth does one find a people group whose average life span exceeds 120 years. Seventh Day Adventists, while having reduced incidences of some diseases, do not come anywhere close to 120 years of age in average life span. Likewise, tribes in the Himalayan region, despite their practice of vegetarianism for *many* generations, do not have an average life span that extends beyond the 120-year range.

Third, and most important, the proposal that God introduced meat into man's diet in order to shorten his life implies that God is not someone to be trusted.

Recently, our Sunday school invited a local law enforcement officer and his award-winning dog to give a presentation on the character quality obedience. The dog's training and performance were impressive, and the lessons of faithful obedience made a deep impression upon many. In response to a question from the audience, however, we were told

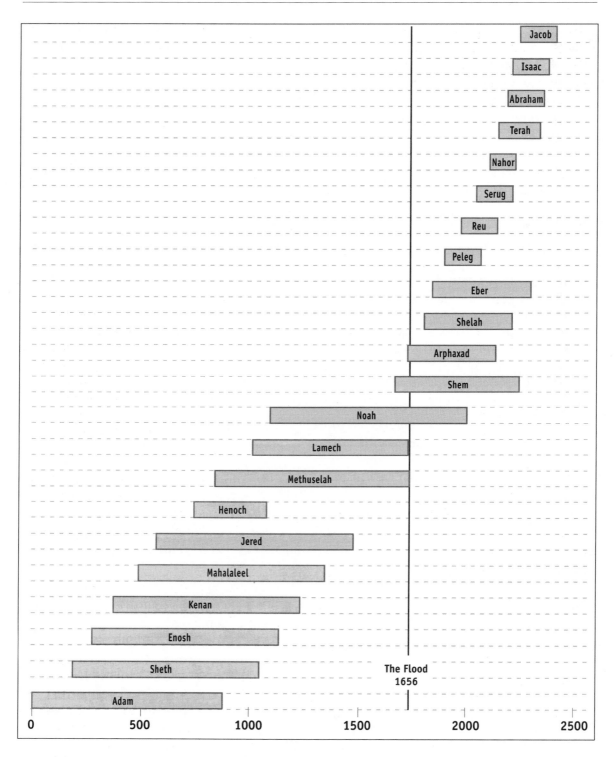

Figure 3.1
Generations from Adam to Jacob

that despite the years of expert training, police dogs retain one weakness that is common to all dogs: trusting those who feed them. Someone with malicious intent could easily give such a dog meat that was poisoned, and the dog would accept it, trusting that since it was food, the giver must be a friend.

Accepting the premise that God gave us meat to shorten our lives would force us to view Him just as we would view a villain who would poison a police dog. Rather than as our heavenly Father who gives us life, we would see God as one who slips flesh to man in order to poison him and shorten his life. Can we believe that, when Jesus fed the five thousand, He was secretly trying to shorten their lives by feeding them fish? As many have said before, if you can't trust God, who can you trust?

How Man's Life Span Was Shortened After the Flood

No, God did not introduce animal products into man's diet in order to shorten his life. There are other, better, explanations available for a post-Flood shortened life span. Let's look at them.

> *And God made the firmament, and divided the waters which were under the firmament from the waters which were above the firmament: and it was so. And God called the firmament Heaven. And the evening and the morning were the second day. And God said, Let the waters under the heaven be gathered together unto one place, and let the dry land appear: and it was so. And God called the dry land Earth; and the gathering together of the waters called he Seas: and God saw that it was good. . . . And every plant of the field before it was in the earth, and every herb of the field before it grew: for the Lord God had not caused it to rain upon the earth, and there was not a man to till the ground. But there went up a mist from the earth, and watered the whole face of the ground. (Genesis 1:7–10; 2:5–6)*

Based upon these Scriptures, as well as other evidence, many Creation Scientists believe that prior to the Flood there was a vapor canopy over the earth that produced several beneficial effects. First, it probably shielded the earth from excess solar radiation, which has been linked with changes at a genetic/cellular level that promote aging and cell death. Second, the vapor canopy produced a uniform, subtropical climate throughout the entire earth, making vegetation lush and food easy to find. In support of this, giant mammoths have been found frozen in polar ice with tropical grasses still in their digestive tracts. Obviously, there must have been tropical grasses growing there at the time of the sudden death of these animals. Additional evidence has led geologists to conclude:

> With respect to climate, the fossils show that there was a uniformly mild climate in high and in low altitudes of both the northern and the southern hemisphere. That is, there was a perfectly uniform, non-zonal, mild, and spring-like climate in every part of the globe.
>
> What a marvelous world this must have been! Our imagination is inadequate to reconstruct for ourselves a picture of the world which God had given as a possession to Adam and his descendants. . . . The world of Adam, Methuselah, of Enoch and Noah, was a wondrous world. A world rich in plant and animal life. A world which yielded food of every kind for man and beast without any great effort on the part of either, a world which could therefore support a population many times greater than our present population. A world which was made delightful by a

uniform climate of spring-like loveliness like that of Paradise itself. In short, the whole world was a garden of God, or as Luther said, "a veritable paradise," compared with the world which followed. This was the golden age in the history of the earth.[1]

Scripture indicates that in the six hundredth year of Noah's life, the springs of the earth ruptured and the windows of heaven opened. For the first time, it rained on the earth, forty days and forty nights, until all life died except for that which was aquatic or in the ark (Genesis 7:11–12, 21–22). After the floodwaters receded, the earth and life upon it were totally changed forever.

What we see today is not the same earth our early ancestors enjoyed. Life totally changed. Gone was the protective vapor canopy, the lush vegetation, the ease with which one could live literally anywhere on the globe where there was land. Things would never be the same. And it stands to reason that with all this change, man's life span would be affected as well.

Scientists have recently discovered that our cells are actually preprogrammed to die. A report on research by L. Myers states:

> The theory is that we die not because we wear out, but because we're programmed to at a certain point. [Studies] . . . looked at a segment of DNA called the telomere—the heart of the molecular clock. The telomere controls genetic reproduction when a cell divides to create a new cell.
>
> Studies in the past few years have shown the telomere is shortened slightly each time a cell divides until it is nearly gone and the cell can't replicate itself.[2]

In other words, as the cell goes through its life cycle of division and multiplication, it actually "commits suicide." It eventually dies, having lost its ability to divide further. There is nothing we can do about it. Our cells are programmed that way. And research gives no indication that meat content in the diet has anything to do with this mandatory shortening of the telomere.

Why Meat Was Introduced into Man's Diet After the Flood

So then, if man did so well on a vegetarian diet before the Flood, then why *did* God give meat for food to Noah and his descendants? The answer appears to be very straightforward. Recall God's original command to Adam at the time of Creation:

> *And God blessed them, and God said unto them, Be fruitful, and multiply, and replenish the earth, and subdue it: and have dominion over the fish of the sea, and over the fowl of the air, and over every living thing that moveth upon the earth. And God said, Behold, I have given you every herb bearing seed, which is upon the face of all the earth, and every tree, in the which is the fruit of a tree yielding seed; to you it shall be for meat. And to every beast of the earth, and to every fowl of the air, and to every thing that creepeth upon the earth, wherein there is life, I have given every green herb for meat: and it was so.* (Genesis 1:28–30)

Immediately after the Flood, this command was repeated to Noah.

And God blessed Noah and his sons, and said unto them, Be fruitful, and multiply, and replenish the earth. And the fear of you and the dread of you shall be upon every beast of the earth, and upon every fowl of the air, upon all that moveth upon the earth, and upon all the fishes of the sea; into your hand are they delivered. (Genesis 9:1–2)

But there was now a huge obstacle before Noah and his offspring. As a result of the Flood, all vegetation upon the face of the earth was destroyed. Once the waters abated, it took some time for plant life to be reestablished, as suggested by the twice return of Noah's dove (Genesis 8:8–12). With reduced vegetation and the loss of a uniform, subtropical climate, there were now regions of the earth that would be devoid of plant food, such as above the Arctic Circle and in the deserts.

All told, the regions of the world unsuitable for human habitation comprise about 40 per cent of its land surface. . . . But this is not all. The earth after the Flood was not only reduced considerably in land area, but even in this shrunken earth the fertility of the soil and the natural resources necessary for human progress are now unequally distributed.[3]

And yet, just as He had commanded Adam, God instructed Noah and his descendants to replenish (fill to overflowing) the earth. What would people eat who eventually moved into the Arctic regions where no substantial plant growth was now possible? And what about the rest of the earth, where now there were distinct seasons with temperature extremes; with no refrigeration available as of yet and an inability to have adequate fresh fruits, vegetables, and grains year-round? The answer is seen in the very next verse.

Every moving thing that liveth shall be meat [food] for you; even as the green herb have I given you all things. But flesh with the life thereof, which is the blood thereof, shall ye not eat. (Genesis 9:3–4)

Thus we see that *at the same time* God repeated His commandment to man to multiply and fill the earth, He provided him with the latitude in diet that he would need in order to carry out that directive. Is it not more consistent with God's character and His covenant with Noah that He would give flesh to man for food in order to provide for *man's new dietary needs* rather than as a secret means of shortening his life? And so we see people groups such as the Eskimos, who subsisted for centuries on a total fish-based diet and no fresh fruits and vegetables. Yet they had virtually no heart ailments, cancer, or a host of other degenerative diseases prior to the modernization of their diets.

Animal products are not the problem in themselves and therefore should not be banned on the basis of Genesis 1:29.

But is there any other connection between animal products and degenerative disease? Indeed there is. And, as we will see later, the problem is not with God's giving flesh to man *but with what man has done with God's gift.*

CONCLUSION

There is no such thing as "biblical vegetarianism." In fact, vegetarianism was gone from biblical history before Moses ever wrote the first books of the Bible. Animal products are not the problem in themselves and therefore should not be banned on the basis of Genesis 1:29 or any other Scripture. Yes, there is a connection between animal products and degenerative disease. Again, the problem is not with God's giving flesh to man *but with what man has done with His gift.*

4

DIETARY HERESY (2)

HERESY NO. 3: WE MUST FOLLOW MOSES

*T*here is no question that the typical Western high-fat, low-fiber, high-processed-food diet is a great contributor to the development of many of the diseases of our day. And yet, most Christians in Westernized nations eat such a diet. So it comes as no surprise that they suffer from the same diseases as the rest of the world.

Perhaps for this reason, many Christians are taking a second look at the Old Testament dietary laws and wondering if they are still applicable or relevant. They begin to wonder if believers today are obligated to abide by these dietary laws, particularly when they learn of the benefits of following them. Should we too abstain from the eating of blood and things strangled, and from the fat of the ox, sheep, or goat, and in particular from the flesh of animals that are classified as "unclean" in Leviticus 11? To answer that question, let us first understand just what is meant in Scripture by "clean" and "unclean."

The word "clean" is derived from the Hebrew *taher* (taw-hare), which means "to be bright." That is, by implication, to be pure, physically sound, clear, unadulterated; by Levitical law, it meant uncontaminated, morally innocent, or holy. The first time in Scripture this word is used was not with the giving of the Law of Moses but *eight hundred years earlier,* before the Flood.

Of every clean beast thou shalt take to thee by sevens, the male and his female: and of beasts that are not clean by two, the male and his female. Of fowls also of the air by sevens, the male and the female; to keep seed alive upon the face of all the earth. (Genesis 7:2–3)

This is the same word that is used in Leviticus 11 to identify those animals that were "clean" and acceptable for food to the Israelites. And so we see that the distinction between clean and unclean animals was clearly known for at least eight centuries before the giving of the Law to Moses—even before animal flesh was given to man for food! Obviously, there were no moral or religious connotations associated with this distinction at the time of Noah. It was merely a statement of fact—that God had already made a division among the animals.

Later, with the giving of the Law at Mount Sinai, God set apart the nation of Israel to be His own, a people separate and distinct from the rest of the peoples of the earth. At that time, the dietary laws were established as a means of making a division among *people*—between His people and the rest of the world—between Jew and Gentile.

> *Ye shall therefore put difference between clean beasts and unclean, and between unclean fowls and clean: and ye shall not make your souls abominable by beast, or by fowl, or by any manner of living thing that creepeth on the ground, which I have separated from you as unclean. And ye shall be holy unto me: for I the Lord am holy, and have severed you from other people, that ye should be mine.* (Leviticus 20:25–26)

The dietary laws were part of the practice of a life that was holy (separated unto God). Even today, the Jews consider the dietary laws a principal means of reminding themselves, as well as communicating to the world, that they are unique.

> Faithfully observed, these customs help one to find himself a Jew from childhood on. At every meal he has to think of his allegiance to his faith. . . . Failure to observe Kashrut [the Jewish Dietary Laws] has been considered an act of disloyalty, even of apostasy, for these laws and customs have proven an important factor in the preservation of the Jewish race, and they are indispensable for maintaining Jewish identity in the present.[1]

In other words, the Jewish dietary laws were designed to bring a division between God's people Israel and the rest of the world. But when the Messiah came, things were to be different. This division was then to be abolished. The sacrificial death of Jesus Christ on the cross would bring an end to the enmity between Jew and Gentile.

> *But now in Christ Jesus ye [Gentiles] who sometimes were far off are made nigh by the blood of Christ. For he is our peace, who hath made both one, and hath broken down the middle wall of partition between us; having abolished in his flesh the enmity, even the law of commandments contained in ordinances; for to make in himself of twain one new man, so making peace; and that he might reconcile both unto God in one body by the cross, having slain the enmity thereby. . . . For through him we both have access by one Spirit unto the Father.* (Ephesians 2:13–16, 18)

Thus, no longer was there to be a distinction between Jew and Gentile upon the basis of diet. With the coming of the Messiah, who fulfilled the Law of Moses and removed the curse associated with man's inability to keep it, diet and other religious externals such as animal sacrifice were no longer to be the distinguishing mark of God's people. Instead, the followers of Christ, whether Jew or Gentile, were to be identified by two major characteristics: salvation by faith in the finished work of Christ on the cross (Isaiah 53; Ephesians 2:8–9) and genuine love for one another ("By this shall all men know that ye are my disciples, if ye have love one to another" John 13:35).

All substitutes for saving faith and anything that would unnecessarily divide God's people had to be removed. Therefore, the religious observance of dietary laws had to be abolished. If not, they would once again bring between God's people a division that He had resolved at the cross. This abolishing of *religious* dietary practices was an important part of God's plan for the spread of the gospel and the growth of the church.

Peter's Vision of Clean and Unclean Animals (Acts 10–11)

In Acts 10 and 11, Peter experienced a vision in which God told him not to call "unclean" that which He had declared "clean." Some have concluded that God was telling Peter through this vision that He had removed the distinction between clean and unclean meat. Later, however, on two separate occasions, Peter explained that the interpretation of this vision was that *Gentiles* were not considered common or "unclean" in God's eyes. Those Gentiles who came to faith in Christ were to be accepted into the church just as Jewish people were (Acts 10:28, 34; 11:1–15).

In other words, Peter did not interpret the vision as proof that unclean meats were no longer forbidden (he is silent on this point). And neither should we. Other Scriptures shed much additional light on this question.

Apostolic Council Did Not Require the Gentiles to Keep the Law of Moses

In Acts 15, the apostles convened to discuss the "problem" of Gentile converts to Christianity. Some Jews who were converted out of the Pharisee sect said, "Except ye be circumcised [and keep the Law of Moses], ye cannot be saved" (Acts 15:1, 5).

However, in the wake of the lesson God taught him through his vision and the subsequent conversion of the Gentile Cornelius, Peter argued that God had proven that Gentiles were not saved by keeping the Law but by grace, just as Jewish converts were. He admonished his brethren not "to put a yoke [the Mosaic Law] upon the neck of the disciples, which neither our fathers nor we were able to bear" (Acts 15:10). In conclusion, the council sent a letter to the Gentiles, saying,

> *Forasmuch as we have heard, that certain which went out from us have troubled you with words, subverting your souls, saying, Ye must be circumcised and keep the law: to whom we gave no such commandment: it seemed good unto us. . . . to lay upon you no greater burden than these necessary things; that ye abstain from meats offered to idols, and from blood, and from things strangled, and from fornication.* (Acts 15:24–25, 28–29)

Food Is a Disputable Matter

In Romans 14, Paul got to the heart of the issue by explaining that diet, as well as the day of worship, was a disputable matter. Now this is remarkable, because both of these were extremely important religious practices of the Jews. Remember that even today Jews consider the kosher diet as the major distinctive of their people. However, Paul stated that now that the Messiah had come, dietary regulations were no longer to be the focus of fellowship or worship.

> *Him that is weak in the faith receive ye, but not to doubtful disputations. For one believeth that he may eat all things: another, who is weak, eateth herbs [plant food]. Let not him that eateth despise him that eateth not; and let not him which eateth not judge him that eateth: for God hath received him. Who art thou that judgest another man's servant? to his own master he standeth or falleth. Yea, he shall be holden up: for God is able to make him stand. . . . I know, and am persuaded by the Lord Jesus, that there is nothing unclean of itself: but to him that esteemeth any thing to be unclean, to him it is unclean. . . . For the kingdom of God is not meat and drink; but righteousness, and peace, and joy in the Holy Ghost. (Romans 14:1–4, 14, 17)*

Several observations can be made based on this passage. According to Paul,

- Believing one needs to restrict his diet as a matter of faith is not an indication of spiritual maturity. Rather, it may be evidence of weak faith. For example, someone who is a vegetarian for health purposes may be putting his faith in his diet and be weak in his confidence toward God to protect and preserve his health.
- No food, in and of itself, is unclean (quite a statement for a Jew of Jews to make!).
- True righteousness has nothing inherently to do with one's food choices: "For the kingdom of God is not meat and drink; but righteousness, and peace, and joy in the Holy Ghost."

Dietary Laws Intended to Be in Effect Only Until the Coming of the Messiah

The writer of the letter to the Hebrews explained that the Jewish dietary laws, like other Jewish practices such as animal sacrifice, were terminated when the Messiah came.

> *The Holy Ghost this signifying, that the way into the holiest of all was not yet made manifest, while as the first tabernacle was yet standing: which was a figure for the time then present, in which were offered both gifts and sacrifices, that could not make him that did the service perfect, as pertaining to the conscience; which stood only in meats [food] and drinks, and divers washings, and carnal ordinances [or rites, ceremonies], imposed on them until the time of the reformation [i.e., the time of the Messiah]. (Hebrews 9:8–10)*

Thus, the religious prohibition of unclean meat was a practice that was intended to be in effect only until the coming of the Messiah, at which time a more complete understanding of true righteousness would come.

All Food Declared Clean by Jesus

Food does not defile, but the heart does. Christ Himself explained to His disciples that true righteousness has nothing inherently to do with what one puts in the mouth.

> *Then came together unto him the Pharisees, and certain of the scribes, which came from Jerusalem. And when they saw some of his disciples eat bread with defiled, that is to say, with unwashen, hands, they found fault. . . . And [Jesus] said unto them, Full well ye reject the commandment of God, that ye may keep your own tradition. . . . There is nothing from without a man, that entering into him can defile him: but the things which come out of him, those are they that defile the man. . . . Do ye not perceive, that whatsoever thing from without entereth into the man, it cannot defile him; because it entereth not into his heart, but into the belly, and goeth out into the draught, purging all meats? . . . That which cometh out of the man, that defileth the man. For from within, out of the heart of men, proceed evil thoughts, adulteries, fornications, murders, thefts, covetousness, wickedness, deceit, lasciviousness, an evil eye, blasphemy, pride, foolishness: All these evil things come from within, and defile the man.* (Mark 7:1–2, 9, 15, 18–23; also see Matthew 15:11-20)

We know that washing hands is a very good idea. Certainly Jesus knew that as well. The problem was that this ceremonial tradition of men had become equated with a "commandment of God." It was not. In the same way, although certain dietary practices may be a good idea, they are not to be taught as biblical doctrine.

The Mark 7 passage is also significant from another important standpoint. In verse 19, we read the phrase "purging all meats." The *literal* translation of these words into English would read "purifying all food." The *Interlinear Bible,* which bases its New Testament on the Greek Received Text, reads "purging all the foods."[2] Other translations render the wording "Thus He declared all foods clean." This is the exact wording found in the *New American Standard Bible,* the *New English Bible,* the *Jerusalem Bible,* and the *Revised Standard Version.* In the *New International Version,* the phrase is translated "In saying this, Jesus declared all foods 'clean.'"

Be Prudent, But Not Divisive

God mandated dietary laws as a means of separating His people from the rest of the world. When Christ "purified all food," He declared that diet was no longer to be a religious practice, that is, a means of separating His people from others. Like animal sacrifice, the dietary law is fulfilled in Christ, who removed the distinction between Jew and Gentile in order to make the two one in Himself through the cross. Christ abolished the division between *people.*

> *There is neither Jew nor Greek, there is neither bond nor free, there is neither male nor female: for ye are all one in Christ Jesus.* (Galatians 3:28)

However, just because we are all one in Christ does not mean that God's inherent design for human beings has changed. Men are still different from women, and there are still physical differences between those of various ethnic origins.

Likewise, when Jesus "purified all foods," He did not change the division that God had made among the animals from the time of Noah or before. Turkey vultures did not stop feasting on dead and diseased carcasses. Puffer fish did not lose their poisonous tentacles— being pricked by one was just as deadly after the Messiah as before. Oysters, shrimp, clams, and swine were still scavengers and carriers of disease. God's *inherent design* for the animal kingdom did not change with the cross. Praying with thanksgiving over one's food certainly "sanctifies" it—makes it "clean" in a spiritual sense (1 Timothy 4:4–5), but it does not change the physical characteristics of the food. Arsenic will still poison you even if it is received with thanksgiving.

Therefore, I do believe that we should still abstain from eating blood and things strangled, from eating the fat of the ox, sheep, and goat, and from "unclean" meat. We should do so because the division in the animal kingdom still exists, and it does not appear that God designed "unclean" animals to be food for man. To continue to respect this distinction is something that you would be wise to do for your own health.

However, abstaining from these foods should be a personal matter and not bring division between people. When Jesus sent His disciples out two by two, He commanded them to "eat such things as are set before you" (Luke 10:8). All food given to you is to be "received with thanksgiving" and sanctified (i.e., set apart as "clean") with prayer (1 Timothy 4:4–5). Beliefs about food are to be kept to oneself (Romans 14:22) and not to be an issue between you and others. If they are, that is a cardinal sign that you have been deceived by a "seducing spirit" (1 Timothy 4:1).

Since these three heresies (and others) are flooding into the church, let us look at further warning signs of spiritual deception and how to insure that teaching on diet is presented with truly biblical foundation and balance.

THE THREEFOLD TEST OF SOUND TEACHING

And devils also came out of many, crying out, and saying, Thou art Christ the Son of God. And he rebuking them suffered them not to speak: for they knew that he was Christ. (Luke 4:41)

It has always intrigued me that Jesus commanded demons to be silent with regard to His being the Son of God and the Messiah. He did not want their testimony. Why? Perhaps because truth is more than just words. Jesus said, "I am the way, the truth, and the life" (John 14:6). Truth is embodied in a person: Jesus Christ. In Him we not only find perfection in word, but also in character and spirit.

It is possible for teaching to sound scriptural but contain error. Likewise, it is possible for the words spoken to be without error but the attitude, or spirit, behind what is taught to be false. So it is important to look beyond what is being taught to the spirit behind the teaching—and to the result of the teaching—to determine if it is of God.

There are three tests of sound doctrine, not just one: (1) testing the actual statements, (2) testing the spirit of the teaching, and (3) testing the teaching's fruit.[3]

Test the Statements

Does what is taught line up with Scripture? If it does not, then the teaching is false and must be rejected. I have heard people say, even after realizing that a teaching was a misrepresentation of Scripture, that they still accepted it because of the "health benefits" associated with what was taught. Unfortunately, those who would accept a little evil in order to enjoy some good do not see the big picture—including the spiritual devastation that can result from the acceptance of false doctrine.

"The blessing of the Lord, it maketh rich, and he addeth no sorrow with it" (Proverbs 10:22). God's ways are not only consistent with His Word, but they work, and they don't bring the unnecessary grief with them that our adversary intends to bring.

Test the Spirit

Beloved, believe not every spirit, but try the spirits whether they are of God: because many false prophets are gone out into the world. (1 John 4:1)

When we examine a teaching, we must examine not only the words themselves but also the life of the person behind the words. Even teachers who appear on the surface to be ordained by God Himself may actually be of a very different nature.

For such are false apostles, deceitful workers, transforming themselves into the apostles of Christ. And no marvel; for Satan himself is transformed into an angel of light. Therefore it is no great thing if his ministers also are transformed as the ministers of righteousness; whose end shall be according to their works. (2 Corinthians 11:13–15)

Does the character of the individual, to the best of your knowledge, line up with the character of Christ? Jesus said that His sheep recognize His voice. They therefore follow Him and not a stranger (John 10:4–5; 1 John 4:1–6). Does your spirit recognize Christ speaking through this teacher? Does the Holy Spirit "bear witness" with yours that he is of God (1 John 5: 6)?

Test the Fruit

Finally, we must look to the results of the teaching. Does the individual or his teaching lead to unity and the edifying of the body of Christ or to division in the church? Does what is taught glorify God or a product or program? Does it promote faith and confidence in Christ, or is He left out of the picture?

Several questions follow that can be used to test the statements, spirit, and fruit of any dietary teaching. If the answer to any of these questions is "yes," one should seriously consider the possibility that deception is present.

WARNING SIGNS OF DECEPTION

1. *Are people taught that God's ideal for man today is found only in Genesis 1:29, that is, that man is to be vegetarian?*

From Paul's letter to the Romans, as well as from our overview of Scripture, we have seen that the Christian is free to eat meat or free to be vegetarian. Vegetarianism should not be taught as God's design for man's diet today. If it is, the teaching carries "a spirit of error."

2. *Do people think or feel that they are not biblically free to eat flesh, animal products, or even "unclean" meat?*

If so, this is a sign of deception. According to the words of Jesus in Mark 7, it is clear that the Christian should not be forbidden to eat meats that are "unclean" according to the Old Testament definition.

3. Do people believe that certain foods defile the body?

Jesus specifically stated that what goes into the mouth *cannot* defile the body. Do people believe that if they eat a particular item, it will defile their body, the temple of the Holy Spirit? If so, this too is a sign of deception.

4. Do dietary practices interfere with fellowship or relationships?

Have diet and nutrition become a divisive issue between or within families? Are families or individuals no longer completely free to fellowship with one another because of some difference in dietary beliefs? This is strong evidence of false doctrine, since the very essence of demonic influence is to bring division and disharmony, which God detests.

> *These six things doth the Lord hate: yea, seven are an abomination unto him . . . a false witness that speaketh lies, and he that soweth discord among brethren.* (Proverbs 6:16, 19)

> *Now I beseech you, brethren, mark them which cause divisions and offences contrary to the doctrine which ye have learned; and avoid them. For they that are such serve not our Lord Jesus Christ, but their own belly; and by good words and fair speeches deceive the hearts of the simple.* (Romans 16:17–18; see James 3:16–18; Ephesians 4:1–6)

5. Is diet a common focus of conversation?

A wise person once said that you can tell in what a man's heart delights by what it is that he always talks about. Is the focus in the church or in the home upon Christ, the Scriptures, and what is eternal? Or is it always on some temporal subject—in this case, diet, nutrition, and health? Your thoughts and conversation will constantly be drawn to what is really important to you.

Paul instructed us in Romans that, when it comes to disputable matters, such as what one eats, we should keep our beliefs to ourselves (Romans 14:22). They should not be shared with others unless we are asked for them or we are given a position of responsibility to teach.

6. Is diet constantly promoted as the answer to anyone's health problem?

Diet is one of six possible causes of disease mentioned in Scripture. But a person who is deceived will lack discernment and balance. In fact, he may even believe that if you follow a particular diet program, you will never get sick. This will result in the belief that if someone is ill, he must have broken God's commandments regarding diet. The deceived individual will have a critical and prideful spirit and think, *If he only did thus and so, he would not be sick.* Furthermore, he will tend to be critical of pastors and other leadership for their lack of focus on diet and other lifestyle-related matters.

Ken Copley is a biblical counselor who has dealt with those who have been deceived by such dietary doctrine. He has observed that when Christians become seduced by such teaching, their faith is transferred from God to their diet.

7. Is diet given the credit when healing takes place?

Since diet is believed to be all there is to maintaining health, it should come as no surprise that it is diet that is given the credit when someone is made well. This may seem logical enough: a person changes his diet and he gets well, so credit is given to the diet. But as author and biblical counselor Jim Logan says, "The purpose of Satan's attacks is to get us to take our focus away from Christ."[4]

A popular Christian teacher concerning diet told this story. A prominent Christian editor developed prostate cancer. The editor followed the counsel of this teacher and went on a special diet. His cancer totally cleared up. In response, the editor wrote an article in which he glorified God, giving Him the credit for his healing. This was quite upsetting to the teacher, who remarked, "It wasn't God who healed him. It was the diet." Perhaps it is true that God *used* the diet to heal the man of his cancer. But how dare we rob God of the credit and "worship and serve the creation more than the Creator" (Romans 1:25)?

Recall the account of King Hezekiah. God heard the king's prayer to extend his life (2 Kings 20). When God told the prophet Isaiah that He would do this, Isaiah applied a poultice of figs and the king was healed. As things are today, Hezekiah would have been encouraged to patent the fig poultice and establish a multilevel marketing system to promote the cure for his ailment. Yes, diet (in this case, the poultice) may be the instrument God uses to bring healing, but let Him receive the glory, not the treatment.

> *Because that, when they knew God, they glorified him not as God, neither were thankful; but became vain in their imaginations, and their foolish heart was darkened. Professing themselves to be wise, they became fools. . . . Who changed the truth of God into a lie, and worshipped and served the creature more than the Creator, who is blessed for ever. (Romans 1:21–22, 25)*

8. Is there a critical spirit toward others, such as the medical profession?

Paul warned, "Be not wise in your own conceits" (Romans 12:16). No one other than God Himself understands all there is to know about health and disease. That includes physicians. And it certainly includes those who have never thoroughly studied the health sciences. I have seen physicians who fell ill and could not be helped by their colleagues but were healed through the advice of a non–health professional. And there are those who think they have no need for doctors, only to be humbled through an illness that they cannot master and finally find help when they go to a medical professional. We need one another.

9. Is there other evidence of involvement in deceptive practices?

The alternative health care movement is filled with practices that are not only unscientific but are based upon pagan religious teachings. Is there involvement in therapies such as iridology, applied kinesiology, reflexology, homeopathy, psychic imagery, therapeutic touch, and so on? Not all of these are occult in and of themselves, but because of their origin, there is that distinct possibility.

Conclusion

We should take Paul's advice from 1 Timothy 4 and be alert to false doctrine in this important area of diet. Heresy in dietary teaching is flooding into our families and churches today—with devastating consequences. Vegetarianism is not biblical. Its practice went out of biblical history prior to the Scriptures ever being written. God did not introduce meat into man's diet in order to "poison" him, and we are not bound to follow the dietary laws of Moses.

Because of the cross and a "better covenant," the Christian does indeed have liberty in the area of diet. However, after understanding this, many believers have totally abandoned Old Testament dietary law and have chosen to eat without discretion. This is a grave mistake, for to do so is contrary not only to common sense but also to the very spirit of liberty the gospel proclaims.

Be not deceived; God is not mocked; for whatsoever a man soweth, that shall he also reap. (Galatians 6:7)

5

LIBERTY—
NOT LICENSE

Stand fast therefore in the liberty wherewith Christ hath made us free, and be not entangled again with the yoke of bondage. . . . For, brethren, ye have been called unto liberty; only use not liberty for an occasion to the flesh, but by love serve one another. (Galatians 5:1, 13)

Herb Titus, former dean of Regent University's College of Law and Government, used to explain to his class that freedom is not the right to do whatever we want but rather the opportunity to do what is right. "You can take your lawn mower and use it to vacuum your living room carpet, but that's not freedom," he would explain. "Freedom is being able to take that lawn mower outside and use it for what it was designed—to mow your grass."

Similarly, when it comes to eating, just because we are at liberty to no longer follow dietary laws does not mean that we have license to eat just what we want. Instead, through Christ we now have the power, the opportunity, to do what we ought.

WHEN EATING IS SIN

After all that has been said about our liberty in Christ, it may come as a surprise to hear that a Christian *can* sin through what he eats. It is possible. After all, the first sin ever recorded took place when people ate something they weren't supposed to (Genesis 3). We have clearly established that there is no food in and of itself that, when eaten, causes the eater to sin. Remember the words of Jesus, "There is nothing from without a man, that entering into him can defile him: but the things which come out of him, those are they that defile the man. . . . For from within, out of the heart of men, proceed[s] evil" (Mark 7:15, 21).

In other words, sin is a matter of the heart. Nothing that a person eats can defile him or her. What does defile is what is in the heart. *Therefore, eating is sin when it is associated with sin in the heart.* Romans 14 gives us three such situations.

Let us not therefore judge one another any more: but judge this rather, that no man put a stumblingblock or an occasion to fall in his brother's way. I know, and am persuaded by the Lord Jesus, that there is nothing unclean of itself: but to him that esteemeth any thing to be unclean, to him it is unclean. But if thy brother be grieved with thy meat, now walkest thou not charitably. Destroy not him with thy meat, for whom Christ died. Let not then your good be evil spoken of. For the kingdom of God is not meat and drink; but righteousness, and peace, and joy in the Holy Ghost. For he that in these things serveth Christ is acceptable to God, and approved of men. Let us therefore follow after the things which make for peace, and things wherewith one may edify another. For meat destroy not the work of God. All things indeed are pure; but it is evil for that man who eateth with offence. It is good neither to eat flesh, nor to drink wine, nor any thing whereby thy brother stumbleth, or is offended, or is made weak. Hast thou faith? have it to thyself before God. Happy is he that condemneth not himself in that thing which he alloweth. And he that doubteth is damned if he eat, because he eateth not of faith: for whatsoever is not of faith is sin. (Romans 14:13–23)

When One Judges Another for What He Eats

No further explanation should be needed on this point.

When One Eats Without Faith

Eating is sin when it is not done "in faith." Although we are no longer bound to follow Old Testament dietary law, what if one still believes that he should not eat meat? Then, according to the apostle Paul, he should not eat it, "for whatsoever is not of faith is sin."

When One Eats with Offense (Without Being Sensitive to Others)

Even if one believes that he is perfectly free to eat meat, he should not exercise that freedom in the presence of a brother who lacks the faith to do so. This self-sacrificing love that is willing to give up one's own freedom for the benefit of another is at the heart of the gospel. Paul said that all the Law can be summed up in one command, "Love thy neighbour as thyself" (Galatians 5:14). In fact, for the benefit of his weaker brother, Paul was willing to go without meat entirely.

Wherefore, if meat make my brother to offend, I will eat no flesh while the world standeth, lest I make my brother to offend. (1 Corinthians 8:13)

However, there is one exception to this principle. If someone insists on teaching that righteousness comes through what one eats, then it is appropriate to refute that false doctrine through eating with offense.

Paul refused to have Titus circumcised when certain Christian teachers insisted that it had to be done to keep the Law (Galatians 2:3–5). On the other hand, when lack of circumcision was interfering with Paul's ability to communicate the gospel to non-Christian Jews, he had Timothy circumcised in order to win a hearing (Acts 16:3).

> *Let no man therefore judge you in meat, or in drink, or in respect of an holyday, or of the new moon, or of the sabbath days: which are a shadow of things to come; but the body is of Christ.* (Colossians 2:16–17)

When One Breaks a Promise (Ecclesiastes 5:4–6)

Often, due to health problems or the desire to avoid them, people make promises. For example, someone with heart problems may make a commitment never to eat "fast food" again. Now, it may be morally fine for anyone else to eat such food, but God places a high premium on keeping our word. If you have made a promise, keep it.

In the early 1990s, the Christian community was stunned to hear that the founder of Focus on the Family, psychologist and author James Dobson, had suffered a heart attack. Some time later, I spoke with Dr. Dobson about his recovery and what had since transpired. I remember being impressed with the fortitude and self-control of this man, who had made a commitment to radically change his diet in the wake of his heart attack. It appears, even years later, that he has kept that commitment ever since the day he made it.

Many of us are not so diligent to keep our word. How often, when faced with a crisis, we make a commitment but fail to keep it. We "go on a diet" to reduce our body weight or lower our cholesterol but cheat on it repeatedly until we give up trying. We joke about unfulfilled New Year's resolutions. Yet, Ecclesiastes 5:4–6 says,

> *When thou vowest a vow unto God, defer not to pay it; for he hath no pleasure in fools: pay that which thou hast vowed. Better is it that thou shouldest not vow, than that thou shouldest vow and not pay. Suffer not thy mouth to cause thy flesh to sin; neither say thou before the angel, that it was an error: wherefore should God be angry at thy voice, and destroy the work of thine hands?*

Although we may have liberty to eat, we can voluntarily give up that liberty. When we say we are going to do something but fail to do it, this is sin. Promising is a serious matter. We need to keep our word.

When Food Is an Idol

Food can become an idol when it is "worshiped" for its benefits. Since it is true that God designed our bodies to be nourished with food, it only makes sense that eating good food will be of benefit. But how many are the voices that claim almost magical properties for a dietary program, medicinal herb, or supplement? Worship Christ, not the food He has made.

> *Who changed the truth of God into a lie, and worshipped and served the creature more than the Creator, who is blessed for ever. Amen.* (Romans 1:25)

When Food Becomes an Addiction (One Becomes Enslaved to Appetite)

To eat well and to enjoy the food has been considered both necessary and desirable. But one should eat moderately, for the purpose of eating is to maintain good health. Gluttony has been strongly condemned.[1]

Our Creator designed us with certain physical drives. These are triggered by built-in sensors that motivate us to provide our bodies with what they need. For example, after a long day of work we become tired—the body's signal that it needs rest. Likewise, the body's constant need for oxygen causes us to breathe more rapidly when this precious vital nutrient becomes scarce. With regard to food, God gave us taste buds by which we enjoy eating.

The fact that we are designed to find pleasure in satisfying these physical drives is a blessing. Imagine what would happen if eating food was not enjoyable. Probably we would never eat. This is indeed what happens when the control center for appetite stimulation is destroyed in the brains of laboratory mice—they lose all interest in food, even to the point of starving to death.[2] Likewise, if physical intimacy were not pleasurable, the human race would likely perish.

But our physical drives can, through our fallen nature, push us too far. We may "cross the line" and go beyond our needs to the point of excess. Thus, getting needed rest can be taken to excess and become slothfulness. Physical intimacy, when it crosses the bounds of marriage, becomes immorality—even to the point of lasciviousness, where all self-restraint is abandoned and one does whatever his fleshly caprice dictates. Similarly, just as the enjoyment of wine can become drunkenness (an addiction to alcohol), so also a natural delight in food can become gluttony (enslavement to appetite).

Appetite is not the same as hunger. Hunger is a physiological signal that the body needs food. Appetite, on the other hand, is a craving; it is not governed by a true physical need. A cocaine addict craves the illicit drug, but his body does not need it. In fact, what his body really needs is to abstain from cocaine.

True physical needs can be satisfied. For example, God says that the mouth of the righteous will be satisfied with good things (Psalm 103:5). Likewise, He promises to provide bread that satisfies the poor (Psalm 132:15) and the one who works his land (Proverbs 12:11). To the meek, one who has entrusted himself to God, the Lord promises that he will "eat and be satisfied" (Psalm 22:26). By contrast, the appetite of the flesh, much like the craving of a cocaine addict, can never be quenched (Proverbs 27:20).

And just as the blessing of the Lord brings satisfaction from food, so also the failure of food to satisfy can be a sign of God's judgment (Leviticus 26:26; Micah 6:14).

THE UNBIBLICAL SILENCE ON APPETITE CONTROL

For the flesh lusteth against the Spirit, and the Spirit against the flesh: and these are contrary the one to the other. . . . Now the works of the flesh are manifest, which are these; adultery, fornication, uncleanness, lasciviousness, idolatry, witchcraft, hatred, variance, emulations, wrath, strife, seditions, heresies, envyings, murders, drunkenness, revellings [banquets in which the flesh was indulged with anything it craved, including alcohol, immorality, and food], and such like. (Galatians 5:17, 19–21)

The church has had a long tradition of speaking out, and rightfully so, against many of the works of the flesh listed above. All of them represent a lack of—and indeed are totally contrary to—the fruit of the Spirit, which is identified in the succeeding verses. But perhaps in an effort to avoid promoting a judgmental spirit and offending those who are overweight, appetite control is conspicuously absent from nearly any modern-day sermon on the works of the flesh.

This is understandable, since we tend to judge others by their outward appearance. We often assume that an individual who is significantly overweight must have a problem with gluttony and consume more food than an individual of normal weight. This is unfortunate, because thin people can have the same failures in the areas of self-discipline, proper food selection, and exercise. But since they don't show it in their body weight, they are often not motivated to address those deeper needs. When we judge those who are overweight, sometimes we are guilty of the same root failures.

For wherein thou judgest another, thou condemnest thyself; for thou that judgest doest the same things. (Romans 2:1)

God wants His children to focus on character. "The Lord seeth not as man seeth; for man looketh on the outward appearance, but the Lord looketh on the heart" (1 Samuel 16:7). Thus, in order to speak with authority and to help those with such needs, it is essential that we apply the same principles and standards to our own lives that we would encourage in others.

Whatever the reason, the church's silence on gluttony has led many Christians to conclude that God has no limitations on what and how much one eats. But from the beginning, He has always placed restrictions on man's diet.

- Before sin entered the world, Adam and Eve were forbidden to eat from the Tree of Knowledge of Good and Evil. This, along with the implied prohibition against eating animal flesh, was the *only* restriction placed upon them (Genesis 2:16–17).
- After the Flood, man was given animal flesh to eat; however, he was forbidden to eat blood (Genesis 9:4).
- When Israel wandered in the wilderness, God provided manna for them on a daily basis. But He commanded them to gather only what they needed for the day (Exodus 16:16).
- With the giving of the Mosaic Law, Israel was restricted from eating blood, the "hard" fat of animals, animals that died of natural causes, animals that were strangled, and animals that were "unclean" (discussed in future chapters).
- Even after the coming of Christ, the apostles commanded the new Gentile believers to abstain from eating blood and from animals that had been strangled or sacrificed to idols (Acts 15:20).
- Gluttony and drunkenness were a major cause of offense, illness, and even death in the early church at Corinth (1 Corinthians 11:21).

Failure to live within God's dietary restrictions was associated with severe consequences:

- Sin and death entered the world through Adam's dietary transgression (Romans 5:12).

- When Esau was hungry, he forsook his birthright, something of lasting significance, in exchange for a little food (Genesis 25:34; Hebrews 12:16).

- When the wandering Israelites ignored God's warning against gathering too much manna, the extra they hoarded bred worms (Exodus 16:20).

- When ungrateful Israel craved flesh over heavenly manna, God brought so many quail upon the camp that they stacked up three feet high and a day's journey in every direction. Some of the people were such gluttons that they harvested quail for thirty-six straight hours, not even taking a break to sleep. Their excess so displeased the Lord that even while they were chewing on it, He smote them with "a very great plague" (Numbers 11:31–33).

- In the Old Testament, gluttony was connected with drunkenness and rebellion (Deuteronomy 21:20; Proverbs 23:20–21). In the New Testament, in addition to drunkenness, gluttony is a characteristic of those who are enemies of Christ (Philippians 3:18–19) and of those who sow discord in the church (Romans 16:17–18). Gluttony is not consistent with the Spirit-filled Christian life.

THE NEED FOR SELF-CONTROL IN ALL THINGS

But the fruit of the Spirit is love, joy, peace, longsuffering, gentleness, goodness, faith, meekness, temperance. (Galatians 5:22–23)

In contrast to gluttony, self-control is a fruit of the Spirit. It signifies moderation or self-restraint, especially curbing one's desires for the sake of something better. You will recall that Paul was willing to curb his own appetite in order to avoid offending a weaker brother. Every Christian should pursue self-control (2 Peter 1:5–8). It is to be a character quality of the elderly (Titus 2:3–4) and is one of the requirements for being a church leader (Titus 1:7–8). In other words, self-control is essential to a proper testimony and Christian ministry.

Why is it important that we exercise self-control in the area of eating just as in any other area? Because whatever passions we fail to control will eventually control us. We will become their slaves.

All things are lawful unto me, but all things are not expedient: all things are lawful for me, but I will not be brought under the power of any. Meats for the belly, and the belly for meats: but God shall destroy both it and them. (1 Corinthians 6:12–13; see also 2 Peter 2:19)

This indeed has been my personal experience. No matter what the area, if I fail to exercise self-control, that failure will become a foothold for the adversary to gain an advantage in my life (Ephesians 4:27). I have also found, as you may have, that consistently exercising self-control in the area of diet is one of the greatest battlegrounds between the flesh and the spirit (see Galatians 5:17 again). Solomon warned that one who is "given to appetite" should figuratively "put a knife" to his throat when eating in the presence of a leader (Proverbs 23:2).

And every man that striveth for the mastery is temperate in all things. Now they do it to obtain a corruptible crown; but we an incorruptible. I therefore so run, not as uncertainly; so fight I, not as one that beateth the air: But I keep under my body, and bring it into subjection: lest that by any means, when I have preached to others, I myself should be a castaway. (1 Corinthians 9:25–27)

Notice that Paul states that as we pursue an "incorruptible crown" we are to be temperate "in *all* things." This includes what we eat. In fact, Paul understood that his flesh was such a threat to his eternal goals that he said, "I buffet my body and make it my slave, lest possibly, after I have preached to others, I myself should be disqualified" (1 Corinthians 9:27 NASB).

The word "buffet" here is not pronounced buf-fay—meaning to treat oneself repeatedly to church potluck dinners. Instead, Paul was saying that he treated his body hardly, that he might "make it know its master" (NEB).

STEPS TO CONTROLLING YOUR APPETITE

Expect That You Will Be Tempted to Eat What Is Harmful to You

And when the woman saw that the tree was good for food, and that it was pleasant to the eyes, and a tree to be desired to make one wise, she took of the fruit thereof, and did eat, and gave also unto her husband with her; and he did eat. (Genesis 3:6)

Food was the means by which Satan first tempted Adam and Eve. Likewise, Jesus, the "Second Adam," was tempted by Satan to eat when He was hungry and alone in the wilderness. Therefore we should also expect to be tempted to eat that which we should not. The area of food can be just as much a battleground with the flesh as any other physical desire. As Neil Anderson, who has counseled many in spiritual bondage, says,

Temptation means being enticed to have genuine needs met through the world, the flesh, and the devil instead of through Christ. Every temptation is an invitation to do things our own way instead of God's way . . . . There was nothing wrong with Jesus eating bread at the end of His fast—except that it wasn't the Father's will for Him to do so yet. . . . When Satan tempts us through the channel of the lust of the flesh, he will invite us to meet our physical needs in ways that are outside the boundary of God's will. Eating is necessary and right, but eating too much, eating the wrong kinds of foods, and allowing food to rule our lives are wrong.[3]

As offspring of Adam, we were all born into Adam's failure in the Garden. Being his seed, we have inherited his fleshly nature. But as believers, we have been born again, this time into

Christ and into His victory over Satan in the wilderness and on the cross. As Jim Logan says in *Reclaiming Surrendered Ground,* the key to victory over temptation is to understand that we are in Christ.[4] Then, as we walk by faith, abiding in Christ, we are able to experience the reality of the victory that He has already accomplished over the lusts of the flesh.

And they that are Christ's have crucified the flesh with the affections and lusts. If we live in the Spirit, let us also walk in the Spirit. (Galatians 5:24–25)

Don't Walk Alone

As in any other area of battling the flesh, victory usually eludes those who try to do it alone. Not only must we abide in Christ, but we often need the assistance and support of others. If you are the only one in your home who desires to exercise self-control in the area of appetite, it will be a far greater challenge than if your spouse is willing to walk with you.

Chew Your Food Slowly

One should also eat slowly. In the words of a famous teacher: "He who lingers at the table prolongs his life." This may explain why conversation at the table is encouraged among Jewish people.[5]

An important mechanism for controlling our food intake involves the "metering" of food by receptors within our mouth and throat area. As food is tasted, chewed, and swallowed, signals are sent that inhibit the feeding center deep inside the brain's hypothalamus. This inhibition lasts for twenty to forty minutes and lends credibility to the ages-old recommendation to thoroughly chew your food. Take a bite, lay down your utensil, and place your hands in your lap while you thoroughly chew. By doing so, satiety will be reached earlier than if your food is ingested rapidly.[6]

Follow a Biblically Based Diet Plan

The dietary plan outlined in the next several chapters can help curb appetite and help you maintain your ideal weight in several ways.

It encourages water intake. Regular intake of water, especially if taken twenty or thirty minutes before a meal, is a common component of many weight-loss programs and will be part of the biblical diet plan.

It limits energy intake. When it comes to food intake and fat, there is a very basic law that operates within the human body:

$$\text{Energy intake} - \text{Energy expended} = \text{Energy stored}$$

In other words, if a person eats 2,000 calories worth of food in a day (energy intake) and uses only 1,500 calories during that twenty-four hour period (energy expended), 500 calories will be stored in the body for future needs.

Energy needs vary greatly depending upon a person's physical activity. Thus, the key to weight control is simply a combination of (1) reducing energy intake and (2) increasing energy expenditure, primarily through increased physical activity.

In light of the above principle, how easy is it to put on extra weight? Consider the example of the relatively sedentary individual who needs only 1,500 calories per day but who eats an extra half sandwich (with the trimmings) and a couple of extra cookies after each meal. That extra food eaten each day amounts to about 500 calories. In one week, the total extra intake would reach 3,500 calories, the equivalent of a pound of body fat. Thus, by simply eating a little extra each day, an additional fifty-two pounds could be gained each year!

It controls fat intake (dense calories). Fats contain more than twice the calories of an equivalent-sized portion of protein or carbohydrate. Though the biblical diet plan is not overly strict on fat calories, the *types* of fat that are allowed are not as readily associated with obesity and disease.

It controls "empty" calories. These are especially found in processed and refined foods. Stripped of their natural nutrients, these foods not only tend to promote weight gain, but they also rob the body of its vitamin and mineral reserves.

It increases dietary fiber. The biblical diet plan is rich in natural fiber, which is of great value in reducing weight and the occurrence of a variety of diseases.

It enhances the activity of brown fat. Unlike the white/yellow adipose tissue that stores extra calories, brown fat actually burns energy to increase body temperature and the metabolism rate. It is stimulated by eating, by cold, and by unsaturated oils, which are found in abundance in the biblical diet plan. By contrast, the typical Western diet is high in saturated animal fats, which have the lowest rates of metabolism.[7]

It improves insulin/blood sugar stability. There is a direct relationship between abdominal obesity and insulin: the larger the waistline, the higher the insulin level.[8] Insulin acts like a key in the lock of the body's cells, opening the "door" so that cells take glucose and fat out of the bloodstream.

But in order to limit further weight gain in an already obese person, the cells "change the locks" so that the cells no longer respond to insulin, thereby keeping them from taking up additional glucose or fat. This is called insulin resistance and results in high levels of glucose and fat (especially in the form of triglycerides) in the blood, even in the presence of high insulin levels. Elevated blood lipids (fats) have been associated with hardening of the arteries (atherosclerosis), heart attack, stroke, and other diseases.

In order to burn off extra calories, the high insulin levels stimulate the sympathetic nervous system (SANS). That in turn stimulates brown fat thermogenesis to increase energy expenditure. In addition to stimulating brown fat, the increased SANS activity can result in increased stimulation of the kidneys, blood vessels, and heart, resulting in hypertension and other diseases, as we will see in chapter 14.[9]

Identify and Eliminate Food Cravings ("Addictive" Foods)

Research has confirmed that many people eat sugar in order to get a "lift." For example, the increased appetite and weight gain following smoking cessation is due to an increased consumption of sugar. This is possibly due to an attempt to improve mood and thereby reduce withdrawal symptoms. Unfortunately, whenever sweets are eaten to elevate mood, the effect is only temporary. A worsening in symptoms soon follows.[10]

One possible reason for craving sweets is that eating sugar appears to increase the level of endogenous opioids. These are morphinelike substances that occur naturally in the human brain. They can reduce pain and produce an overall sense of well-being. The medial hypothalamus, which houses the satiety center, also contains the highest concentration of beta-endorphin (a natural opioid) in the brain. Thus it appears that opiates are involved in the control of eating.

In addition, there is growing evidence that cravings for other types of food may play a key role in the development and continuation of obesity. In fact, entire diets have been developed around this concept. Some have argued that such cravings are actually a form of food allergy ("addictive allergy") and therefore must be eliminated if weight loss is to be successful.[11] (This, along with fasting, will be examined further in chapter 13.)

Make a Plan for Vulnerable Situations

As I have endeavored to implement a lifestyle of self-control in eating, I have found that there are three situations in which I find it especially difficult to maintain self-discipline: desserts, snacks, and eating out. Most people will be unable to lose weight without addressing these three. Here are a few tips.

Desserts tend to be high in calories and low in food value. Therefore, set a limit for yourself, such as once a week and special occasions. If you have too many such occasions, then limit your portion size and include them only in the evening meal.

Snacks are often a source of great temptation (and tremendous guilt). But they don't have to be. The key is to plan ahead. Determine in advance upon what foods you will snack.

As you will read in later chapters, it is my personal belief that our Creator specifically designed snack foods that would tend to keep without refrigeration and require no preparation prior to serving. These include fresh fruit, nuts, cheeses, and even breads. Or combine several of these, such as sunflower seeds, raisins, dried papaya, coconut, and so on in the form of a trail mix.

In addition, don't shop when you're hungry. You'll tend to overspend and purchase unhealthy snack foods for immediate relief.

Dining out also can be a major challenge, particularly because so many restaurant selections are loaded with sugar, salt, fat, or all three. For those who are "given to appetite," it may be wise to get something healthy into your stomach *prior* to going out. When your cravings have subsided, you will be able to use better judgment. Once you're at the restaurant, look for the low fat or "heart healthy" options on the menu. If your spouse does not care for fish, use your dining out opportunities to get a regular intake of this excellent food. Consider also the salad options. Or consider making up a meal of combined side dishes of vegetables. Make sure that any meat selections are prepared in a manner to minimize fat (for example, broiled or steamed).

Get Proper Physical Exercise

This may come as a surprise, but regular exercise is an important part of appetite control. For one thing, exercise improves your sense of well-being. It also stabilizes blood sugar, increases cardiovascular fitness, and reduces the activity of the adrenal (stress) organs.

The evidence that regular strenuous activity is beneficial is so overwhelming that I have wondered why Scripture seems to say so little about it. A closer look at the Word, however, reveals that there is probably more there than we realize. Paul acknowledged that physical training is of some value (1 Timothy 4: 8), and many of the references addressing the flesh, particularly 1 Corinthians 9:25–27, could easily apply to exercise. In addition, numerous passages mention the strength and valor of men. These are attributes that do not just happen but require diligent physical training.

Finally, a strenuous, physically active lifestyle was a given in Bible days. The culture was agrarian, and most people walked to their destinations. But because of our modern means of transportation, urban lifestyles, and desk jobs, the average individual must set aside time each day specifically to challenge himself physically in order to make up for the lack of activity in his normal routine. For more information on exercise, see chapter 15.

Conclusion

Armed with a purpose in life that requires our optimum health, we are obligated by love and as temples that house the Holy Spirit to cherish and care for our human frames. Our ultimate goal—to bring glory to Christ—can only be accomplished as we remove anything that might hinder others or ourselves from accomplishing this great task. Like Paul, each believer needs to bring his or her body into subjection, making it a slave, rather than remaining a slave, to its carnal appetites.

Wherefore seeing we also are compassed about with so great a cloud of witnesses, let us lay aside every weight, and the sin which doth so easily beset us, and let us run with patience the race that is set before us, looking unto Jesus the author and finisher of our faith; who for the joy that was set before him endured the cross, despising the shame, and is set down at the right hand of the throne of God. (Hebrews 12:1–2)

6

DIETARY STRATEGY BASED UPON THE LAWS OF NATURE

The Creator has written certain laws into nature. They govern the physical world. They govern, for example, the circuits of the moon around the earth and the earth around the sun. They determine the seasons, the times of the high and low tides, and sunrise and sunset. They describe the cycle in which rain falls to the ground and is collected into streams, rivers, lakes, and oceans, evaporated into clouds, then condensed into rain once again. They rule photosynthesis—how plants take in carbon dioxide and metabolize it to release oxygen.

The laws of nature are unchanging and universal (they apply to everyone). Therefore, they continue to operate even if one is unaware of them or just plain doesn't believe in them. Let's say you don't believe in the law of gravity and step off the top of a three-story building. Despite the fact that you don't believe in it, the law of gravity is in effect and has already determined that you will fall toward the ground (gravity "pulls" you toward the center of the earth). Only divine intervention, in which the Creator would have to supersede His own physical law, would spare you the harm that would otherwise naturally befall you.

Similarly, our cells are designed to live on only pure oxygen, water, and glucose. It is a law of nature: the law of cellular respiration. It is always in operation, whether we believe in it or not. Our cells were not designed to live on gasoline, or arsenic, or strychnine, or mercury, or man-made chemicals. To put any of these into the human body certainly could mess up the cell machinery, even damage it permanently, and in some cases do so enough to cause death.

THEORIES, THEORIES—WHO CAN YOU TRUST?

With regard to diet, a tremendous number of theories are swirling about. One camp says man came from hunters and is genetically programmed to eat mostly animal products. Another says that man has been a farmer for thousands of years and is programmed to be vegetarian. Others say that we should avoid animal products because animals should be reverenced as equals with man. Some say you can eat anything—just don't eat certain foods at the same time. Still others tell us we are to eat according to our blood type, or body type, or personality, or the seasons (macrobiotics). Some tell us to have a programmed schedule of eating; others say to eat whenever you're hungry. Some say carbohydrates are good; others say that they are bad. Some say acidity causes cancer; others say the opposite. With all these varying opinions floating about, to whom should you listen? Whom should you trust?

WHY NOT THE CREATOR?

Amazingly, God is usually conspicuously absent from these verbal and written discussions. Yet, He is the one who designed us and designed food to nourish us. Therefore, with regard to each dietary question, we will first examine His Word to discover what He has said about it. Then we will look at scientific information that will show us that with diet, as with anything else, we can take the Creator at His word.

LOOKING INTO THE WORD FOR NATURAL LAW

Now that we have established that we are free to choose amongst the many varieties of foods, let us search the Word for principles that will help us in making wise choices. As always, let's start with Genesis, the book of beginnings. Bear with me, because on the one hand these strategies will seem ridiculously obvious. On the other hand, they are so obvious that most of us never think of them. Therefore, we don't live by them, and our health suffers.

Strategy #1: Eat Only What You Need

Solomon warned, "Hast thou found honey? eat so much as is sufficient for thee, lest thou be filled therewith, and vomit it" (Proverbs 25:16). As we have discussed, a proper dietary strategy begins with appetite control. To repeatedly take in more or less than your body needs violates natural law and will result in serious health consequences.

Strategy #2: Obtain Adequate Exercise

If you do not obtain adequate exercise through an active lifestyle, then you need to set aside time for it each day. The only exception to this would be the Lord's Day, during which we cease from regular activities in order to place emphasis on worship and rest.

Strategy #3: Eat "Real" Food

So God created man in his own image, in the image of God created he him; male and female created he them. . . . And God said, Behold, I have given you every herb bearing seed, which is upon the face of all the earth, and every tree, in the which is the fruit of a tree yielding seed; to you it shall be for meat [i.e., food]. (Genesis 1:27, 29)

"You can't improve upon God," Dr. Lorraine Day says in her video by that title. Since the Creator, who designed us as well as our food, is perfect and wise, man should assume that he cannot improve upon God's invention. And yet, particularly since the industrial revolution, man has repeatedly attempted to do so, and claimed to have done just that. But margarine is *not* superior to butter. Artificial sweeteners are *not* better than honey. Infant formula is *not* better than Creator-designed human milk.

This should be no surprise to someone operating with a biblical worldview. It would seem obvious, no matter what the current scientific claims, that what the Creator designed can't be beat. No one will ever improve upon God. We should show respect and honor for His perfect wisdom by handling carefully that which He gives to us. Many of the foods He has given us have been so changed that they can do more harm than good in their altered state. Rex Russell put it this way: "Eat what God gave us for food, and don't alter His design."[1]

Unfortunately, with the birth of the food industry there has been a drastic change in the way we eat and what we consider to be food. We have become so disoriented that it is now necessary to stop and define what we mean by *food.*

A complete meal today is often pictured as a hamburger, French fries, and a soda. After all, in addition to plenty of calories (energy) and the protein in the beef, one can get two "servings" of grains in the bun. And the slices of tomato, onion, pickle, and lettuce add up to four servings of vegetables, don't they? French fries have become the most popular vegetable in America, now accounting for fully one-third of all vegetables consumed by teenagers. Need a dairy product? Then a milk shake ought to do, or perhaps a sundae. Fruit? Well, how about a banana split? That combines fruit along with the dairy, does it not?

But this really isn't what I mean by "food." What is food anyway? Let's be simple about it. Real food grows on trees. Real food grows out of the ground. Real food swims in the water or walks on the land. In other words, real food occurs in nature without man's intervention other than to plant it, harvest it, or catch it. Eat real food—that which has been designed not by man but by our Creator. The Inventor's wisdom will never be matched by the feeble mind of man.

Shopping. In order to eat real food, we should eat those things that are found naturally in creation, things that you find growing on trees, or out of the ground, or that swim in the water or that walk on the ground. Boxes and cans are not found growing on trees or shrubs. Therefore, they should immediately be suspect.

Today, in nearly every grocery store, you can usually find the real food by shopping the following path. When you first enter the doors, get your cart and turn immediately right. Working your way along the four walls, pick up your fresh fruits and produce, then nuts and whole grains (skip the donuts). Turning the corner, get your dairy products, fish, and meat. Skip the ice cream. Pick up a fresh salad at the deli if you don't have time to fix one of the meals of the day and some flowers for your spouse. Then proceed to the checkout counter.

Having "shopped the walls," you have probably partaken of most of the "real" food in the store. The middle aisles don't usually meet the criteria. I can almost guarantee that if you shop, and eat, that way, your health will benefit and your bank account too.

And the next time you are shopping, consider the incredible variety our loving Creator has given to us. Think about that for a moment. He could have given us just beans and rice. But He didn't. He gave us so many different tastes and textures to enjoy. He could have made everything the same color, but He didn't. He gave us bright red apples and tomatoes, yellow bananas, orange carrots, green peas, pink grapefruit, and on and on. The next time you sit down at your plate, do as the psalmist did: thank God for the blessing of not only food but for the variety that He has given.

> *Who giveth food to all flesh: for his mercy endureth for ever. O give thanks unto the God of heaven: for his mercy endureth for ever.* (Psalm 136:25–26)

Organic food. One does not have to be in the health food environment very long before hearing about organic food. What is organic food? Basically, it is food that has been raised without the use of commercial fertilizers or pesticides. The advantages include an avoidance of exposure to potentially harmful chemicals (pesticides), and greater nutritional content with the use of natural fertilizers. One study demonstrated that foods raised organically averaged twice the nutrient concentration when compared on a fresh weight basis with commercially grown foods.[2]

This makes sense when you consider the fact that commercial fertilizers usually contain only three nutrients (nitrogen, phosphorus, and potassium). There are more than fifty-five vitamins and minerals in the soil. If we repeatedly remove those nutrients from the soil with crops but return only three, it stands to reason that the ground will eventually become depleted.

God commanded His people to give the land a rest every seventh year. But rather than follow the biblical guidelines and allow the fields to rest, we are double- and triple-cropping repeatedly. As a result, it is common practice for cattle farmers to feed their livestock supplements such as selenium, a trace mineral that has been lost from much of our farmland.

When encouraged to obtain organic foods, many people complain of the increased cost or difficulty in finding them. With regard to cost, it appears that at least in some cases it may be worth it, since the nutrient content may be much higher. Cost concerns can often be alleviated by purchasing larger amounts directly from farmers or from markets that make a special effort to provide the organic food option. The demand for organic products has escalated in recent years, leading an increasing number of farmers to employ these methods. That has resulted in lower costs for organic foods.

The cheapest way to get good quality vegetables is to grow your own. This does take time, but a relatively small garden can yield a sizeable harvest of vegetables. Remember that God told Adam that he would eat his bread by the sweat of his brow (Genesis 3:19).

Finally, keep in mind these suggestions concerning organic produce:

- For the best quality foods, grow your own, or obtain them from a local organic grower whom you trust.

- Wash all foods well. If they have pesticide residues, most will be removed with washing and peeling.
- If organic or home-raised foods are not available, use commercially grown produce. It is far better to get adequate amounts of fresh fruits and vegetables than to be concerned that they be "organic." As you will see in the next chapter, these foods contain natural compounds that help detoxify such residues. But, of course, if one can avoid a toxin, then that would be ideal.

Food preparation. Every food in nature comes packaged with all of the vitamins, minerals, and enzymes necessary for its use in the human body. Enzymes in the food go to work in the upper part of the stomach, breaking the food down and digesting it for us. Once digestion is complete, vitamins and minerals are needed to help in chemical reactions necessary to use the food properly.

Since enzymes are made of protein, they are especially sensitive to heat and will be destroyed if heated above around 110 degrees Fahrenheit. We should try to preserve the integrity of the Creator's design as much as possible, choosing preparation methods that would least alter the food.

Some foods are most nutritious if they are eaten raw. This especially applies to fruits, most vegetables, nuts, and even milk.

Other foods don't appear to be designed to be eaten in a raw state but rather to be cooked in some fashion. Following the age-old practice of grinding grain into flour and using the flour to make bread products is more desirable than eating them raw. Indeed, the proper kneading and baking of bread *increase* its nutritional value, since grains in their natural state contain *phytates* that keep nutrients bound and unavailable for our benefit.

If a food is going to be heated, particularly if it is a food that is edible in the raw state, then care should be taken to choose lower temperature heating methods. Steaming or boiling (referred to as "seething" in the King James Version), especially when not done to extreme temperatures, can preserve many of the nutrients inherent in the food. Another option is a low-temperature slow cooker. This method is especially attractive to individuals who do not have much time for food preparation. Very nutritious meals can be placed in a slow cooker and left on low heat overnight or throughout the workday. Baking can also be utilized. But again, lower temperatures for a longer time may preserve more of the nutritional content of the food.

With regard to frying, the first rule is: Do not deep-fry anything! Heating oils to high temperature damages them and can create toxic compounds. These soak into what is being fried and make for a potentially injurious food. If one is to fry, stir-frying is probably best, especially if it is done in water. If oil is desired, it should be sprinkled lightly on top of the food, rather than being placed in the hot pan before adding the food to be fried.

Microwaves heat up food by bombarding them with a beam of electrons. Some have expressed concern that radiating food in this way damages it. Although there has been some possible connection between cancer and exposure to microwave radiation (such as with the use of radar guns in law enforcement), there is little, if any, research to substantiate the concern that microwaving foods is seriously detrimental. However, if one thinks in terms of not altering God's design, it would seem prudent to use this mode of heating with caution. In particular, a microwave oven should not be relied upon to kill bacteria in food, since it does not heat food evenly and thoroughly.

Food spoilage and refining. If you were to take an apple and slice it in half, you would notice that discoloration of the fresh-cut surface rapidly takes place. This is an indication of oxidation, the process by which food spoils when it becomes exposed to light, heat, or oxygen.

Foods will not spoil as long as they are not removed from the vine (unless they become overripe) or until their protective "cover" is removed (as with grains). Removing the hull exposes the vulnerable nutrients (especially the fatty acid) to oxidation, leading to rancidity within seventy-two hours.

In order to improve shelf life and keep food from becoming rancid, the food industry has developed the process of refining. Not only can food be stored longer when it is refined, but it can also be shipped long distances and kept on the shelves of grocery stores for prolonged periods. Thus, refining has been essential to the development and profitability of the food industry.

The problem is that the only way you can improve the shelf life of a food once its protective cover has been removed is to destroy the live nutrients inside (which would otherwise go rancid). Refining, then, greatly reduces the nutritional value of the food and in some cases may make it even harmful.

Strategy #4: Make Plant Food the Foundation of Your Diet

As we read in Genesis 1:29, God gave man plants to eat—grains, fruits, vegetables, and nuts—at the time of Creation. This was his sole diet for more than 1,600 years, until the time of the Flood. On this diet, man lived an average of more than 900 years. Research has repeatedly confirmed that, except for those in extreme climates, an optimum diet is one in which plant sources make up the great percentage of our food intake. This is not to say that we are to be vegetarians; we have already addressed that issue.

In the next several chapters, you will see overwhelming scientific reasons for keeping your diet predominantly (but not exclusively) grains, fruits, vegetables, and nuts. You will also learn how to safely incorporate animal products into your diet.

Strategy #5: Drink Pure Water

Water preceded all other forms of matter and constitutes more than half our body weight. The need for water resulted in several disputes between Isaac and the inhabitants of Canaan (Genesis 26:18–22). Later, as Moses led Israel from Egypt through the wilderness, it did not take the Israelites long to recognize their need for water. Three days after crossing the Red Sea, they came to Marah (meaning "bitter"), where they were unable to drink the water because it was contaminated. God then showed Moses how to purify the water by throwing a certain tree into it (Exodus 15:22–25). Water is essential to life, but it must be pure. We shall look at this topic in detail in chapter 8 ("Beverages").

Strategy #6: Prefer "Clean" Animal Flesh

A major dietary change came after the Flood—animal flesh was introduced into man's diet (Genesis 9:3). Animal flesh had already been classified as "clean" or "unclean," and with regard to being food for man, clean animals have clear advantages over those that are unclean, and they should be preferred. Remember that this choice should be a *preference*. It should not bring division or discord.

Strategy #7: Don't Eat Blood or Improperly Prepared Meat

> *But flesh with the life thereof, which is the blood thereof, shall ye not eat.* (Genesis 9:4)

When God gave man flesh to eat, He expressly forbade the eating of blood. This commandment was repeated several times in the Law of Moses and again by the Jerusalem Council in their letter to the new Gentile converts (Acts 15:29). It is a commandment for us today as well.

I used to think that this command was quite irrelevant, since the practice of eating blood surely would be detestable to any civilized people. But, unfortunately, this is not the case. Blood sausage, also known as blood pudding or black pudding, is a favorite food of many Europeans. It is made by taking the blood and fat of a pig, cooking it, then stuffing it into a sausage case. To the Jew, there could be no greater dietary abomination than "blood sausage."

> *And whatsoever man there be . . . which hunteth and catcheth any beast or fowl that may be eaten; he shall even pour out the blood thereof, and cover it with dust. For it is the life of all flesh; the blood of it is for the life thereof: therefore I said unto the children of Israel, Ye shall eat the blood of no manner of flesh: for the life of all flesh is the blood thereof: whosoever eateth it shall be cut off.* (Leviticus 17:13–14)

Notice that the blood was to be poured out on the ground and buried. This would not only indicate respect for the life that had been taken from the beast but would also serve a sanitary purpose, preventing the spread of disease that might be present in the blood of the animal just killed.

Indeed, as part of the body's waste disposal system, blood is a major carrier of disease, including toxins and the deadliest of infectious diseases. Today we recognize these as the hepatitis viruses, cytomegalovirus (CMV), human immunodeficiency virus (HIV), which causes AIDS, and numerous other blood-borne infections. This is probably why God's people were also commanded not to eat animals that had been killed by strangulation or torn by beasts. Their blood could not be properly drained from them.

Strategy #8: Don't Eat the "Hard" Fat of Animals

> *It shall be a perpetual statute for your generations throughout all your dwellings, that ye eat neither fat nor blood.* (Leviticus 3:17)

In addition to prohibiting blood, God also forbade His people to eat fat. As we will learn, this was not all types of fat but only the "hard" fat of domesticated beasts. These "cover fats" are those that lie under the skin and envelop organs and muscles.

Ye shall eat no manner of fat, of ox, or of sheep, or of goat. (Leviticus 7:23)

I am convinced that the reason this fat was forbidden was because it was the only kind of fat in the Jewish diet that would be harmful if eaten. As we shall see in chapter 11, no other forms of fat have the detrimental effect that this fat clearly has. A prudent diet should always abstain from the hard animal fats. God stated repeatedly that "the fat is the Lord's." Like the Jews, we should leave this fat for Him—it cannot harm Him, but it can kill you.

Strategy #9: Culture Your Dairy Products

Long before meat was allowed into man's diet, dairy products were likely a staple food. However, in light of studies of people living in Bible lands, it is probable that adults usually consumed these in their cultured forms, such as yogurt and cheese (see chapter 9).

Strategy #10: Don't Let Diet Take Precedence over God or Others

These lifestyle strategies are all based upon the Word and have been thoroughly validated by scientific research. Furthermore, they are based upon laws that have been as firmly written into nature by our Creator as the law of gravity. For these reasons they should be followed with a high degree of diligence and commitment.

Nevertheless, this "program" should not displace your faith in God. He is the One who will protect you from disease, not a dietary plan. And following these strategies must not take precedence over relationships with others.

Conclusion

Throughout the next several chapters, we shall examine strategies 4 to 9 in more detail. During our discussion, keep in mind the key concept behind strategy 3: reverence for God's design. In each instance we shall see that God has provided health-promoting, life-giving food. We shall also see that man has often altered it to such an extent that the same food God intended to give life can be an agent of disease and death. Nowhere is this seen more clearly than in the example of grains.

THE WORD ON NUTRITION

Some Dietary Laws and customs undoubtedly came into being for reasons of health. In fact, the word "Kosher" means "fit to eat or clean."... Modern science bears this out by recognizing that some animals harbor parasites that are disease carriers.... It is known that during the Middle Ages, Jews enjoyed better health and longer life than their neighbors. Even today, Jews are immune or less susceptible to certain diseases. There is good reason to believe that the superior health and longevity of the Jews have been partly due to the Dietary Laws.

—Ben M. Edidin
(Jewish Customs and Ceremonies)

PLANT FOOD: FOUNDATION FOR A WORD-BASED DIET

He causeth the grass to grow for the cattle, and herb for the service of man: that he may bring forth food out of the earth; and wine that maketh glad the heart of man, and oil to make his face to shine, and bread which strengtheneth man's heart. (Psalm 104:14–15)

GRAINS

It has been estimated that in the Orient three quarters of the people live entirely upon eating bread or upon that which is made from wheat or barley flour. It is unquestionably the principal food of the [Middle] East.[1]

In general, it may be said that the Arabs in eating do not use knives, forks, spoons, plates, or napkins, which are considered so essential in the West. They say: "What does a man want of a spoon when God has given us so many fingers?" Sheets of bread, about as thick as heavy flannel, take the place of spoons or forks to some extent. A piece from this bread is broken off and shaped so as to put some of the food on it. They use this bread to scoop up any partially liquid dish, such as soups, sauces, or gravies. Each torn off piece of bread that best serves as a spoon is eaten along with the food it contains.[2]

God fed the people of Israel for forty years in the wilderness by giving them manna—"bread from heaven." Scripture says the Hebrews ground the manna into flour. They made bread from it (Exodus 16:4), and that bread from heaven sustained them.

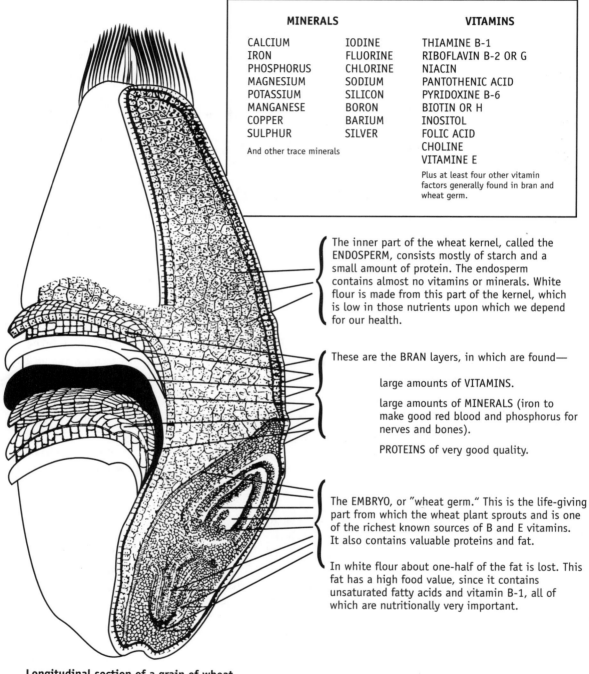

MINERALS

CALCIUM	IODINE	
IRON	FLUORINE	
PHOSPHORUS	CHLORINE	
MAGNESIUM	SODIUM	
POTASSIUM	SILICON	
MANGANESE	BORON	
COPPER	BARIUM	
SULPHUR	SILVER	

And other trace minerals

VITAMINS

THIAMINE B-1
RIBOFLAVIN B-2 OR G
NIACIN
PANTOTHENIC ACID
PYRIDOXINE B-6
BIOTIN OR H
INOSITOL
FOLIC ACID
CHOLINE
VITAMINE E

Plus at least four other vitamin factors generally found in bran and wheat germ.

The inner part of the wheat kernel, called the ENDOSPERM, consists mostly of starch and a small amount of protein. The endosperm contains almost no vitamins or minerals. White flour is made from this part of the kernel, which is low in those nutrients upon which we depend for our health.

These are the BRAN layers, in which are found—

large amounts of VITAMINS.

large amounts of MINERALS (iron to make good red blood and phosphorus for nerves and bones).

PROTEINS of very good quality.

The EMBRYO, or "wheat germ." This is the life-giving part from which the wheat plant sprouts and is one of the richest known sources of B and E vitamins. It also contains valuable proteins and fat.

In white flour about one-half of the fat is lost. This fat has a high food value, since it contains unsaturated fatty acids and vitamin B-1, all of which are nutritionally very important.

Longitudinal section of a grain of wheat

Figure 7.1
Whole Grain Wheat:
a Powerhouse of Nutrition

Whole grain bread is appropriately referred to as "the staff of life." You will recall that Jesus said, "I am the bread of life" (John 6:35). An outstanding, complete food, it forms an excellent cornerstone of a proper diet. In the Middle East, the principal grain of the poorer classes is barley, whereas a family that is able to have wheat bread is considered quite well off. To get a better understanding of this divinely designed food, let's use wheat as an example.

Containing a complete line of nutrients, a whole grain of wheat (known as the "berry") is a powerhouse of nutrition to give us strong, healthy bodies. The berry is made up of three basic parts. The hard, outer layer is the *bran,* or hull. It contains high-quality proteins, large amounts of vitamins and minerals, and fiber. Inside is the *endosperm,* or starch, from which we get flour. Finally, there is the *germ* (embryo), one of the richest known sources of B and E vitamins, as well as a good source of protein and oils. In addition to fiber, notice the long list of vitamins and minerals present in natural, whole grains (figure 7.1).

REFINING: HOW A GIFT FROM GOD IS DESTROYED

The first sound to greet the air in the early morning in many a Palestinian village will be the sound of the grinding of the grain. Today, as in the long ago, many . . . resort to the hand mill for this purpose. The women are the ones who engage in this task, and they begin it early in the morning, and it often requires half the day to complete. Bread was and is still today, often baked in a semi-public oven, or in the oven of a public baker.[3]

That is the grain as God provides it to us, but unfortunately, it is not the same as what most of His people are eating today.

The most popular way for grains to be utilized is in the form of flour, particularly for the making of bread. In order to obtain flour from grains, it must be milled. The problem is that as soon as the airtight protective outer hull is broken, the inner contents are at risk of spoiling and will turn rancid within seventy-two hours.

Therefore, prior to around 1900, grains were always milled locally, and only enough were milled for the particular day's needs. But with the development of advanced roller milling in the West in the late 1800s, the bran and wheat germ could be more completely and efficiently removed from the starch. The bran and wheat germ were then sold as supplements for cattle, leaving only the starch, which could be stored for prolonged periods of time without turning rancid. Long-distance shipping and storage were now possible, allowing for larger, centrally located mills to prosper. The smaller local mills went out of business. And here in the West, fresh whole grain flour became almost a thing of the past.

Refined white flour meant longer shelf life, easier storage, finer texture. But a better product than the original? Not on your life! The 1930s noted a rise in vitamin deficiency diseases (beriberi, from deficiency of thiamine; pellagra, from deficiency of niacin; and anemia, from deficiency of iron). Investigations were conducted, and the problem was traced to the increased consumption of refined white flour. Analysis of the new flour demonstrated that, compared to the whole grain flour from which it was derived, refined flour was drastically reduced in nutritional content.

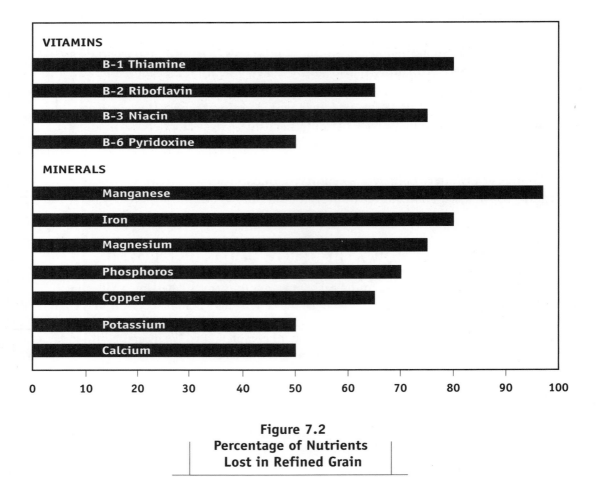

Figure 7.2
Percentage of Nutrients
Lost in Refined Grain

The federal government asked the food industry to return to the use of only fresh whole grain flour. But the industry was unwilling to give up its newfound profits. It simply took the refined, nutrient-stripped white flour, put thiamine, niacin, iron, and riboflavin back into it, and called it *enriched*.

The return of these four nutrients to the flour did help to ameliorate the most obvious (especially childhood) diseases associated with refined flour, but a number of additional deficiency diseases were eventually discovered to be directly related to the refining of grains. In particular, the loss of fiber has proved to be especially devastating.

Fiber

Dennis Burkitt served in Africa as a missionary surgeon for more than twenty years. During his tenure, he noticed that the African nationals rarely presented with certain types of surgical cases that were common back in England and among the British troops stationed in Africa. These included appendicitis, diverticulitis, and gallbladder disease, in addition to a variety of other ailments. The difference was so remarkable that surgical residents were

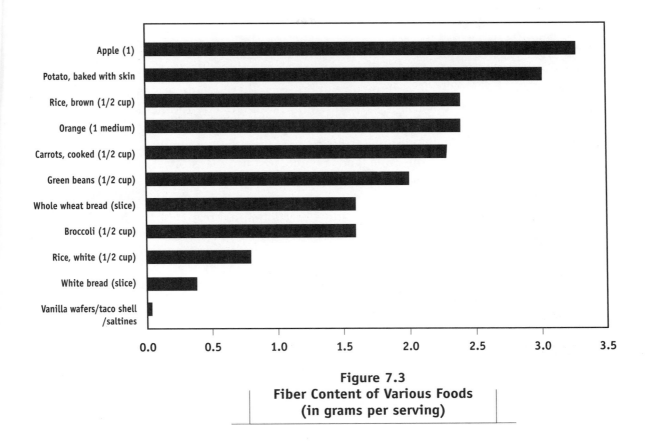

Figure 7.3
Fiber Content of Various Foods
(in grams per serving)

discouraged from diagnosing a national with appendicitis unless he had been associating with British troops and eating their diet.

In trying to understand why, Burkitt noticed that the daily weight and volume of stools in the native Africans was more than three times that of the British (don't ask me how he discovered this). Eventually, he determined that the difference in stool weight was due to the fact that the Africans consumed more than 30 grams of fiber each day, over three times that of their English counterparts.

Fiber is the part of plant food which, by design, is not digested or absorbed from the gut. It draws water from the colon, softening the stool and making it travel faster through the colon so that toxins within it are not in prolonged contact with the bowel wall. It also binds cholesterol, estrogen, and other steroids, reducing their levels in the blood.

Numerous diseases have now been directly linked to a lack of dietary fiber. These include constipation, hemorrhoids, diverticulosis, appendicitis, varicose veins, gallbladder disease, diabetes mellitus, coronary artery disease, and colon cancer.

What is the answer? If possible, use only whole grain flour that has been freshly milled (that is, within seventy-two hours or less). In Cincinnati, Big Sky Bakery grinds whole grain flour each morning and uses it to bake fresh bread and pastries each day. A number of bakeries around the country are going back to this ancient practice. It is more expensive and time consuming but worth it.

The least expensive method of obtaining whole grains is to buy them in bulk directly from farmers or distributors. They usually come in sacks of 25, 44, or 50 pounds. They are also available in buckets from certain suppliers. Since these whole grains are intact, they will keep indefinitely as long as they are stored in a cool, dry environment.

To mill these whole grains, you might consider purchasing an electric grain mill. Or, for those who prefer to do it manually, nonelectric hand-operated grain mills are also available. (If you really want to be like the Bible lands people, just use two stones!) Once the flour is ground, it is optimally used that same day. If you have some left over, it can be stored in the refrigerator or freezer for a few days in an airtight container. For those who are intimidated by the thought of going back to kneading bread dough, bread makers and some home mixers are now available with powerful enough motors to do the job.

CAUTION: GLUTEN SENSITIVITY

Though whole grains are generally a healthy and inexpensive food, some people's bodies may react to them. This is usually due to an allergy to gluten. In severe cases, a small amount of gluten can dramatically inflame the intestines, resulting in abdominal bloating, pain, or even bloody diarrhea. In milder cases, symptoms may be much less severe and perhaps not even associated by the patient with the eating of grain products. For more information on food sensitivities, see chapter 13.

To summarize, eat whole grains. Avoid refined substitutes that have been stripped of their God-given value. Eat several servings of grains each day. The U.S. Food Pyramid calls for six to ten servings daily.

Grains can be eaten as cereals, breads, muffins, pastas, and so on. Use whole grain breads instead of crackers in dips and soups. Use them in the place of silverware, as in the Middle East. This will greatly increase your whole-grain intake.

> **Hot Whole Grain Cereal**
> 2 cups whole grain of choice
> 4 cups water
> a pinch of salt
> a taste of vanilla

Just before bed, place in slow cooker on low heat setting. A very nutritious, tasty, inexpensive breakfast awaits you in the morning. Sweeten with raisins, fresh fruit, or honey as desired.

VEGETABLES, FRUIT, LEGUMES, AND NUTS

Although everyone is familiar with vegetables and fruits, not everyone knows exactly how to define them. From a scientific perspective, all seed bearing plants, including veg-

TABLE 7.1
CRUCIFEROUS AND ALLIUM VEGETABLES

Cruciferae (Mustard family)		Allium
Broccoli	Mustard	Garlic
Brussels Sprouts	Radish	Leeks
Cabbage	Rape	Onions
Cauliflower	Resurrection	
Collards	Rutabaga	
Cress	Stock	
Horseradish	Sweet Alyssum	
Kale	Turnip	
Kolrabi	Wallflower	

etables, produce "fruit." A grain of wheat, peas in a pod, a walnut, or an apple are all fruits. And, though crops such as tomatoes and melons are classed as vegetables, they are more properly called *vegetable fruits*.

For our purposes, though, *fruits* refer to those crops that usually grow on trees, shrubs, or vines that produce for a number of years. *Vegetables* refer to those foods that grow during only a single season. Tops on the list are the cruciferous (so named because of their cross-shaped leaves) and allium vegetables.

Legumes are those vegetables that belong to the pea family. There are more than 13,000 species of legumes. The most common ones in North America are alfalfa, bean, lentil, lima bean, pea, sweet pea, peanut, and soybean. Beans and lentils, both legumes, were the most common vegetables in biblical times. As we will see in chapter 12, legumes are an important part of a diet proven to dramatically reduce heart disease.

Nuts refer to the type of seed or fruit that grows inside a hard fibrous shell. In parts of Europe, nuts play a much larger role in the regular diet than in North America. They are particularly rich in protein, as well as valuable oils. They make an ideal snack food but should be eaten raw or dry roasted. When they are roasted in vegetable oils, the heat-damaged oils soak into the nuts, making them much higher in fat and a threat to our health.

A woman in West Palm Beach, Florida, died alone at the age of 71. The coroner's report was tragic. "Cause of death: *malnutrition*." The dear old lady wasted away to 50 pounds. . . . That woman had begged food at her neighbor's back doors and gotten what clothes she had from the Salvation Army. From all outward appearances she was a penniless recluse, a pitiful and forgotten widow. But such was not the case. Amid the jumble of her unclean, disheveled belongings, two keys were found which led the officials to safe-deposit boxes at two different local banks. What they found was absolutely unbelievable.

TABLE 7.2 LEGUME (PEA) FAMILY		
Acacia	Honey Locust	Lupine
Alfalfa	Horse Bean	Mesquite
Bean	Indigo	Paloverde
Bluebonnet	Kudzu	Pea
Brazilwood	Laburnum	Peanut
Broom	Lentil	Redbud
Carob	Licorice	Rosewood
Cassia	Lima Bean	Soybean
Clover	Locoweed	Sweet Pea
Cowpea	Locust	Trefoil
Furze	Logwood	Vetch
Guar	Lotus	Wisteria

The first contained over seven hundred AT&T stock certificates, plus hundreds of other valuable certificates, bonds, and solid financial securities, not to mention a stack of cash amounting to nearly $200,000. The second box had no certificates, only more currency—lots of it—$600,000 to be exact. Adding the net worth of both boxes, they found that the woman had in her possession well over A MILLION DOLLARS. Charles Osgood, reporting on CBS radio, announced that the estate would probably fall into the hands of a distant niece and nephew, neither of whom dreamed she had a thin dime to her name. She was, however, a millionaire who died a stark victim of starvation in a humble hovel many miles away.[4]

No one disputes the fact that fruits and vegetables are our most valuable foods. After all, "Eat your vegetables—they're good for you" are the first words that many of us can remember hearing (other than the word "No"). That millionaire woman, despite having at her fingertips the resources to abundantly provide for her health and well-being, perished needlessly of malnutrition. Likewise, all too often we spurn the true riches of life-giving, Creator-designed fruits and vegetables for empty substitutes. Fruits, vegetables, legumes, and nuts are no less valuable than the widow's stock certificates. They are an outstanding source of energizing vitamins, minerals, and enzymes. They are also devoid of high-risk saturated fat.

Recently we were given even more reasons to liberally consume these invaluable foods. Scientists have now discovered that they contain numerous *phytochemicals* (phyto means "plant") that have the capacity to protect us from cancer, perhaps the most dreaded of all diseases.[5]

- In a major 1992 review, 128 of 156 dietary studies showed a significant protective effect of fruit and vegetable intake. Those individuals with low fruit and vegetable intake doubled their risk for most types of cancers. Fruits were especially protective for cancers of the esophagus, mouth, and larynx.[6]

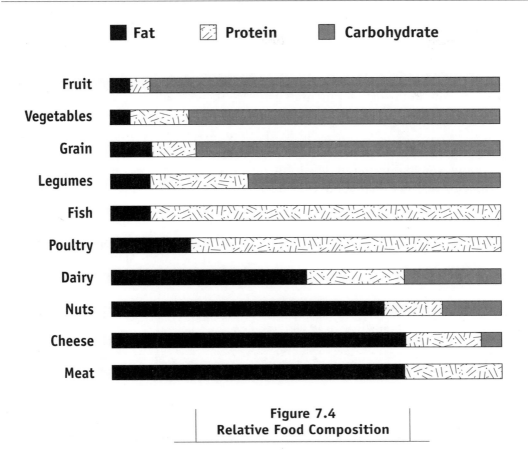

**Figure 7.4
Relative Food Composition**

- A 1996 study reported that lower intakes of vegetables and fruit are consistently present in those who subsequently develop cancer. This was especially true for raw and fresh vegetables, leafy green vegetables, and cruciferae.[7]

- Men who eat at least ten servings of tomato per week have up to 45 percent less likelihood of prostate cancer. Four to seven servings per week reduced the risk 20 percent. Of forty-six fruits and vegetables studied, tomatoes and strawberries were the only foods effective against prostate cancer.[8]

- In a review of the research, fruits and vegetables were found to protect from renal cancer in most controlled studies.[9]

- Increased vegetable intake showed strong protective effect against lung cancer. Milk consumption increased the risk.[10]

- In a study specifically looking at the effect of twenty-six types of vegetables and fruit, carrots and raw vegetables lowered breast cancer risk.[11]

- Finally, a 1996 review of 228 studies again confirmed that fruit and vegetable intake consistently protected from a multitude of different types of cancer. The most protective foods were, in order, raw vegetables, allium vegetables, carrots, green vegetables, cruciferous vegetables, and tomatoes.[12]

FACTORS ASSOCIATED WITH THE DEVELOPMENT OF CANCER

Despite the fact that we are living in the postindustrial revolution era with all of its production of chemicals and pollutants, these potential toxins actually seem to play a relatively insignificant role in the development of cancer. Likewise, although emphasis is often placed upon family history as putting someone at risk for diseases such as cancer, it too plays a relatively insignificant role. *The most important factor contributing to cancer is diet,* even exceeding smoking (see figure 7.5). Thus, if one were to eat a healthy diet and abstain from smoking, the likelihood of developing cancer would be drastically reduced.

The principal dietary factors that have been shown to be associated with cancer include:

High Fat/Calorie Intake

Just eating too many calories puts one at risk for cancer. In addition, high animal-saturated fat has been found to correlate especially with cancer of the colon, breast, prostate, and ovary. This will be dealt with more extensively in chapter 11.

High Temperature Cooking
(especially with vegetable oils; dealt with in chapter 11.)

Processed Foods

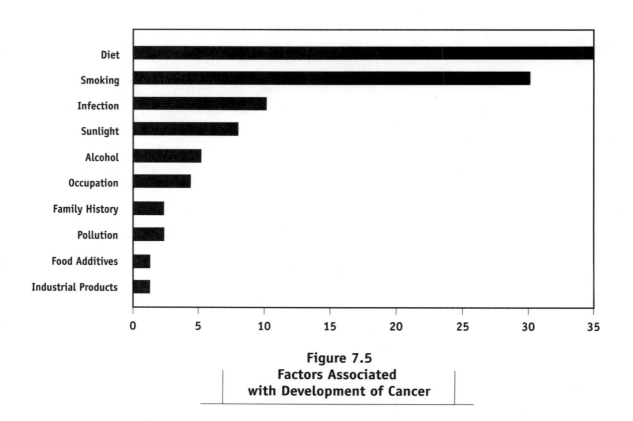

Figure 7.5
Factors Associated
with Development of Cancer

Nitrites

Nitrites (salts of nitrous acid, NO^2) are added to processed meats in order to keep their flesh pink and attractive. Nitrites are made from *nitrates* (i.e., salts of nitric acid, NO^3).

Nitrates

Nitrates are found in the soil as a result of commercial fertilization (usually a form of ammonia is sprayed). They get into our water and vegetable food chain. When food or water containing nitrates is ingested, certain gut bacteria (especially *Bacterioides* species, which tend to be more prominent in the intestinal tracts of those who have high red meat intakes) convert nitrates into nitrites.[13] Nitrites, when exposed to the amino acids from protein, can form *nitrosamines*, which are *potent* cancer-causing substances.

Molds *(aflatoxin)*

Aflatoxins are found in some contaminated peanut products. They damage the cell's DNA, which results in daughter cells with damaged DNA, thus potentially leading to cancer.

Smoked/Charbroiled Foods

Preparing foods in this way creates toxic compounds such as heterocyclic amines, which can also damage cell DNA.

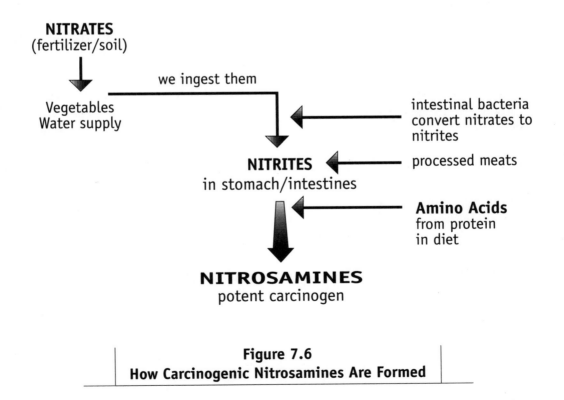

Figure 7.6
How Carcinogenic Nitrosamines Are Formed

PROTECTIVE SUBSTANCES FOUND
ESPECIALLY IN FRUITS AND VEGETABLES

How do plant foods protect us from cancer? There are several mechanisms.

First of all, fruits and vegetables contain compounds that activate "Phase II" enzymes, which detoxify carcinogens. For example, the indoles and sulphurophane are found in the cruciferous vegetables, and S-allyl-cysteine is especially present in the allium vegetables (garlic, onions, and leeks).

In addition, plant foods are the best sources for the *antioxidants,* which are involved in the neutralization of toxic substances called free radicals. A brief summary of the most important antioxidants follows:

Vitamin A protects against epithelial (surface cell) cancers, such as mouth, larynx, lung, bladder, and cervix. The best way to get Vitamin A is in the form of provitamin A, more commonly known as beta-carotene. Beta-carotene is water soluble and nontoxic. It is converted into vitamin A only as the body has need of it. It is what gives carrots their orange color. In fact, individuals who drink large amounts of carrot juice will find their skin taking on an orange, carrotlike hue. Other forms of vitamin A include alpha-carotene, lycopene (especially rich in tomatoes), and lutein.

Vitamin C is the major water-compartment antioxidant. It is a "nitrite scavenger" and blocks the conversion of nitrites into the deadly nitrosamines. This is a major reason why high intakes of fruits and vegetables protect us against cancer. The best sources of vitamin C are citrus fruits, strawberries, kiwi, potatoes, cabbage, and green pepper.

Vitamin E scavenges free radicals, especially in protecting the membranes of cells. It is found in the highest concentrations in the seed oils and in nuts. Once vitamin E scavenges a free radical, it can be recycled if adequate vitamin C is present. If vitamin C is deficient, vitamin E antioxidation is also paralyzed.

Selenium is necessary for the activation of superoxide dismutase, a critical antioxidant enzyme involved in the scavenging of hydrogen peroxide radicals. Therefore, a lack of dietary selenium should be a consideration in anyone suffering from allergy or asthma. I used to suffer terribly from hay fever, which required me to be on medications nearly every day of the year. After correcting my diet and adding antioxidants, especially selenium, my problem essentially resolved.

Selenium is found in meats, seafood, cereals, and grains. Much of the nation's soil is depleted of selenium, which is why it is a common supplement to cattle feed. Farmers have repeatedly told me of the dramatic reductions in illness that their cattle have experienced when their feed was supplemented with selenium.

Folate (folic acid) is involved in several chemical reactions that are critical to the integrity of DNA. When folate is deficient, DNA is not repaired properly. Folate is similar in name to "foliage," another name for plant food—which is the richest source of this valuable B vitamin (leafy green vegetables, citrus fruits, and dried beans).

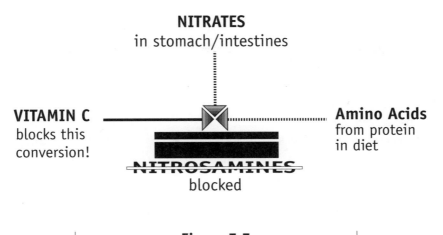

NITRATES
in stomach/intestines

VITAMIN C
blocks this
conversion!

Amino Acids
from protein
in diet

~~NITROSAMINES~~
blocked

**Figure 7.7
How Vitamin C Protects from Cancer**

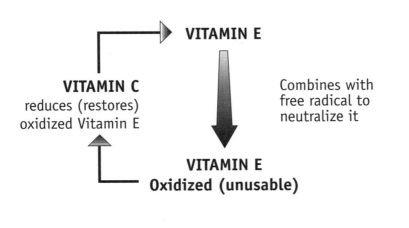

VITAMIN E

VITAMIN C
reduces (restores)
oxidized Vitamin E

Combines with
free radical to
neutralize it

**VITAMIN E
Oxidized (unusable)**

**Figure 7.8
Vitamin C Restores "Used" Vitamin E**

CONCLUSION

Plant food, the basis for man's diet since the Garden of Eden, is a gold mine of good, nontoxic nutrition. Loaded with vitamins, minerals, enzymes, and cancer-fighting phytochemicals, these foods must be the foundation for a healthy diet.

Fruits. A minimum of 2–3 fresh raw fruits should be consumed each day. These are ideally taken as snacks between meals.

Vegetables. A minimum of 4–6 servings of vegetables should be consumed daily, half of them fresh and raw (such as in a midday salad). Cruciferous vegetables are especially protective. A typical serving is one-half cup.

Legumes. One serving daily minimum from this highest plant source for protein.

Nuts. Rich in protein and oils, these are an excellent snack food, provided that they are eaten raw or dry roasted.

The following makes a delightful and healthful Middle Eastern dip:

Hummus
2 c. dry chickpeas (or 1 can)
salt
3/4 c. tahini (sesame paste)
4 cloves garlic
1/2 c. lemon juice
olive oil

Soak chickpeas overnight in warm water. Cook chickpeas in water to cover until tender. (If using canned chickpeas or garbanzo beans, there is no need to soak.) Blend hot chickpeas and water in blender, food processor, or meat grinder until smooth. Mix the tahini, lemon juice, mashed garlic, and salt in a large bowl. Add the blended chickpeas to the tahini mixture and mix well. Spread on a plate and pour a little olive oil on top. Garnish as desired with ground red pepper and parsley, tomato and onion wedges, and so on. Yield: about 3 cups.[14]

8

BEVERAGES

WATER

Even more than food, pure water is essential to life. According to Genesis 1:2, prior to the earth's ever coming into existence, water was present. Indeed, every living thing in creation is made up of mostly water. Corn, for example, is 70 percent water, a potato is 80 percent, and a tomato 95 percent. In addition, water makes up a major part of the body weight of both animals and humans. An elephant is about 70 percent water. And water makes up about 75 percent of the total body weight of a newborn infant. This ratio progressively decreases to an average of 57 percent of total body weight in the human adult. (Obesity may further decrease the percent total body water to as low as 45.)[1]

Water is necessary to nearly all of life's processes. It carries nutrients to all parts of the body. It provides a solution in which essentially all chemical reactions take place. In fact, many reactions, such as hydrolysis, specifically involve water as one of the reactants. Water is also necessary for the filtration process at the kidney, and to carry waste away through the bowels.

No one disputes the fact that water is important. However, despite all this, medicine actually puts very little emphasis on water. Yes, increased water intake is encouraged if someone comes down with a bladder infection or kidney stones. (Women with high intakes of fluids can reduce their risk of kidney stones by at least one-third.[2]) Still, there are some who say that water plays a far more important role in many of our diseases than is generally acknowledged.

TABLE 8.1
COMMON DISEASES CAUSED BY DEHYDRATION
ACCORDING TO F. BATMANGHELIDJ, M.D.

Abdominal pain	Stress
Ulcers	Depression
Colitis	High blood pressure *Chris*
Constipation	High blood cholesterol
Hiatal hernia	Overeating
Rheumatoid arthritis	Obesity
Low back pain	Asthma
Neck pain	Allergies
Headaches	Diabetes
Angina (heart) pain	Morning sickness
Pain on walking	

Preeminent among those sounding the alarm is Dr. Batmanghelidj, an Iranian-born physician who, while imprisoned during the Iranian Revolution, discovered that he was able to cure gastrointestinal ulcers through water alone. This, along with the fact that medications were very limited, led him to experiment with treating a number of diseases with water. After being released, he came to the United States and published his observations. In addition to ulcers (he states that he cured more than 3,000 cases with water alone), Dr. Batmanghelidj insists that a host of common ailments are essentially due to the body's being dehydrated.[3]

Whereas the medical profession looks at dry mouth and dry skin turgor, loss of tearing, and so on, as the only signs of dehydration, Dr. B. states that these are *late* signs and that there are many other thirst signals (including the diseases listed in his table). However, the body, according to Dr. B., loses its sensitivity to those signals when it becomes chronically dehydrated.

Unless there is a medical condition prohibiting it, he recommends drinking at least six to eight glasses of water each day. Beverages such as coffee, tea, juice, and soda do not count toward this water minimum. Many of these contain substances that cause the body to actually *lose* water (such as caffeine, which acts as a diuretic). The best times to drink water are one-half hour before eating and a couple of hours after meals. Extra water should be taken before the heaviest meal and before bed.

Now, everyone knows that we should drink six to eight eight-ounce glasses of water a day. Furthermore, everyone thinks it's a good idea. But few do it. While I have my doubts that all of these conditions would clear up merely by meeting these standards for water intake, it surely seems only prudent to take Dr. Batmanghelidj's advice. Some of his ideas make sense, and, if he's right, they are incredibly significant.

PROBLEM: IMPURITY

Doth a fountain send forth at the same place sweet water and bitter? (James 3:11)

Unfortunately, drinking water has its risks. Like other food items, these are not because of water's inherent, God-given properties but because of what man has done to it. Through the improper disposal of agricultural chemicals and industrial and human waste, water pollution has become a problem of mammoth proportions. In some nations, water quality is so suspect that it is not to be consumed from the tap. Several types of contaminants threaten our water supply.

TABLE 8.2
VARIOUS WATER CONTAMINANTS

Inorganics	**Infectious agents**
Arsenic	Bacteria (shigella,
Asbestos	salmonella, E. coli)
Mercury	Cryptosporidium
Lead	Parasites
Organic compounds	**Disinfection by-**
Atrazine	**products (DBPs)**
Benzene	Trichloroethylene
Nitrates	Trihalomethanes
Radioactive substance	
Radium	
Radon	

Source: Water Quality Association, Lisle, Illinois

A brief explanation of each of these types of contaminants is in order.

Inorganic Substances

Arsenic is a naturally occurring element in the earth's crust. A deadly poison, in the past it has been used in insecticides and commercial poisons. When a farm well that had a leaky casing became contaminated with an arsenic-containing waste pesticide, a family of nine developed arsenic poisoning; two died.[4] There is strong evidence that arsenic in drinking water contributes to cancers of the skin, liver, lung, bladder, and kidney.[5]

Currently, the Environmental Protection Agency (EPA) limits arsenic in drinking water to 50 micrograms per liter. However, at this level, it has been estimated that the lifetime risk of developing arsenic-induced cancer could be as high as 13 in 1000 (that is, greater than 1 in 100).[6] As a result, in March 1999, the National Academy of Sciences released a report calling for the EPA to establish a stricter standard for allowable levels of arsenic in the drinking water.[7] According to Joe Harrison, Technical Director of the Water Quality Association, the World Health Organization (WHO) recently set a new arsenic standard for drinking water at 10 micrograms per liter or less.[8]

Asbestos, the fibrous form of various minerals, is not a common water contaminant.

Lead, an element, was referred to by the Romans as *plumbum,* from which we get the word plumber. Until recently, lead was commonly used in pipe. It is still found in brass fixtures and pipes, as well as lead solders. Homes that are at least twenty or thirty years old may still have a substantial amount of pipes containing lead. However, while lead itself is not toxic, some substances (including those found in food or water) can react with it to form poisons. Therefore, lead is an important contaminant that must be kept out of drinking water.

Mercury. In the past, organic mercury has been used in fungicides on crops. Since mercury is very toxic, areas in which these products have been disposed may represent a greater water contamination threat.[9]

Fluorides are compounds containing the element fluorine, a highly reactive gas, in combination with other elements such as calcium. In the 1930s, it was discovered that children had up to two-thirds less dental caries in communities whose water had one part per million of naturally occurring fluoride. For this reason, in 1945 communities began fluoridating their water. Despite numerous studies, fluoride has not been shown to contribute to increased cancer risk. The point is probably moot today, since numerous products now contain fluoride, including toothpaste, as well as food products such as juices, which are made with fluoridated water.[10]

Organic Compounds

Next to bacteria, *nitrates* are the most prevalent and growing contamination threat to well water, especially in the Midwest farming areas in which 30 percent of the wells have nitrates in substantial amounts. They are a result of fertilizers and human waste.[11] In a 1996 study, nitrates in drinking water (but not those found in vegetables) were associated with an increased risk of non-Hodgkin's lymphoma.[12]

Radioactive Agents

Radium and *radon* are both naturally occurring by-products of the breakdown of uranium. In recent years, especially radon has received increasing attention for its potential for contributing to lung cancer. In addition to water sources, radon can penetrate the home environment through cracks in walls or foundations, construction joints, gaps around service pipes, and cavities in walls.

Microbial Agents

Infectious agents are by far the most significant threat from contaminated drinking water. For example, a well in an Idaho resort became contaminated with *Shigella* bacteria from a nearby subdivision's sewage system.[13] Sixteen residents of a north Georgia trailer park contracted hepatitis A from a contaminated private well.[14] Even somewhat more disturbing, in two separate outbreaks, fourteen pediatric surgical patients[15] and thirty-six neurosurgery patients became infected with resistant strains of *Pseudomonas* bacteria, each traced to contaminated tap water, and transmitted via the hands of nursing staff or nutrition solutions.[16]

Relatively new in the United States is the increasing threat of parasites in drinking water, particularly since some can survive chlorination and other standard public water treatments.[17] *Cryptosporidium*, an organism carried in cow manure, has caused repeated outbreaks of diarrhea illness.

- In 1987, an estimated 13,000 residents of west Georgia were infected through contaminated public water supply, despite water treatment that met federal standards.[18]
- Cryptosporidium struck 55 individuals who had contracted it through swimming in a contaminated public pool.[19]
- A large outbreak occurred in 1997 through a contaminated water sprinkler fountain at a Minnesota zoo.[20]
- Outbreaks also occurred in public water services in Nevada[21] and Washington State. In the latter, an irrigation system was using contaminated wastewater that had been presumed to be treated.[22]
- In 1993, Cryptosporidium passed through the filtration system of a Milwaukee water treatment plant, infecting an estimated 403,000 citizens.[23]

Disinfection By-Products

In 1912, in an effort to reduce the transmission of infections through drinking water, communities began to chlorinate their water. Although very effective at destroying most organisms, chlorination was discovered in 1974 to produce numerous by-products that may play a causal role in cancer, especially of the rectum and bladder, and leukemia.[24]

SOLUTION: WATER PURIFICATION

For the Lord thy God bringeth thee into a good land, a land of brooks of water, of fountains and depths that spring out of valleys and hills. (Deuteronomy 8:7)

Inorganic substances, organic and radioactive compounds, microorganisms, disinfection by-products—they sound ominous, and indeed they are cause for concern. How can you consume eight glasses of water a day without the other undesirables?

The answer is, don't put blind faith in any water source: make sure it is pure! For example, Milwaukee residents who drank only water that had been passed through point-of-use filters, such as at faucets, having pores less than one micron had dramatically reduced rates of infection during the Cryptosporidium outbreak.[25] Patients who have compromised immune systems (such as those on chemotherapy or with active hepatitis or HIV) are especially encouraged to take additional purification measures to ensure protection from Cryptosporidium.[26] Most people will need to choose from one of the following options.

Bottled Water

Bottled water companies are regulated by the Food and Drug Administration (FDA). And despite the fact that there are a few regulatory loopholes, bottled water manufacturers in general regulate their own. The International Bottled Water Association (IBWA) has its own internal regulations, and member companies submit to annual IBWA inspections. Thus, bottled water is quite reliable, particularly if the producer is an IBWA member.[27]

Home Water Purification System

Many, however, prefer the convenience of a home water purification system. This type of equipment is referred to as either point-of-entry, such as a whole-house sediment filter, or point-of-use, such as filters located at the faucet. Although no single water treatment technology is effective in treating every water contaminant, numerous systems combine components to effectively eliminate virtually all pollutants. Recommended water treatment technology for various contaminants according to the Water Quality Association, is seen in table 8.3 on page 99.

As you might conclude, reverse osmosis and distillation systems are the mainstay of point-of-use purification systems today. However, before deciding on a system for your home or office, I suggest you review your options with a reputable water systems distributor. There is a lot to learn about water purification systems, including their proper selection and maintenance. Make sure the water you put in your body not only meets the EPA's purity standards, but the Creator's as well.

COFFEE, TEA, AND CAFFEINE

Coffee

Coffee, the legend goes, was discovered in Ethiopia when goatherds noticed that their flocks stayed awake all night after feeding on coffee leaves and berries. Prior to becoming a beverage, coffee was used as food and medicine. In the 1200s, coffee came to Arabia—our name for it comes from the Arabic word *qahwah*. From Arabia, it passed to Turkey, then to Italy and on to the rest of Europe by the 1600s, at which time coffeehouses sprang up as a popular meeting place for serious discussions. Coffee came to America probably in the 1660s. Today, America ranks number one as the world's largest consumer of coffee. One-third of all coffee production is imported by the United States.

The ripe red coffee berries are picked by hand, washed, then sent through a pulping house where the red pulp is removed, exposing the beans (seeds) inside. Next, the beans are fermented and washed, then dried in the sun. Once cured, the beans are roasted at extremely high temperatures (900 degrees Fahrenheit, 482 degrees Celsius) for about fifteen minutes.

While remaining an appealing beverage to many, coffee has been the subject of considerable debate, particularly over its blood vessel narrowing and stimulant effects, which are

TABLE 8.3 RECOMMENDED WATER TREATMENT								
	ACF gran	ACF sb/p	AAF	Air	Anion	Cat	Disinf	Distil	RO
Arsenic			✔		✔			✔	✔
Asbestos		✔						✔	✔
Atrazine	✔	✔						•	✔
Benzene	✔	✔		✔				•	•
Fluoride			✔					✔	✔
Lead		✔				✔		✔	✔
Mercury	✔	✔			✔			✔	✔
Nitrate					✔			✔	✔
Trichloroethylene	✔	✔		✔				✔	•
Trihalomethanes	✔	✔		✔				✔	•
Radium						✔		✔	✔
Radon	✔			✔				•	•
Bacteria							✔	✔	#
Cryptosporidium		✔						✔	✔

ACF gran = Activated Carbon Filter (granular)

ACF sb/p = Activated Carbon Filter (solid block and precoat)

AAF = Activated Alumina Filter

Air = Aeration

Anion = Anion Exchange

Cat = Cation Exchange Softening

Disinf = Disinfection (chlorination, ultraviolet light)

Distil = Distillation

RO = Reverse Osmosis

• Carbon filters (usually part of these systems) treat these contaminants

Bacteria are several magnitude larger than RO pore size of ~.0005 micron

Adapted from *Water Contamination Solutions*, 1997. Water Quality Association: Lisle, Illinois.

usually attributed to caffeine (see table 8.4). In particular, the concerns have been in five areas: (1) cardiovascular disease (cholesterol, heart disease, high blood pressure, and stroke), (2) cancer, (3) reproductive effects (risk of miscarriage and birth defects), (4) osteoporosis (loss of calcium from the bones), and (5) addictive potential.

TABLE 8.4 CAFFEINE CONTENT OF VARIOUS BEVERAGES		
Beverage	**Size**	**Caffeine (mg)**
Chocolate, hot	6 oz	6
Chocolate milk	6 oz	4
Chocolate, candy		≤6mg/oz
Coffee, brewed	6 oz	103
Coffee, instant	6 oz	96
Coffee, decaf	6 oz	5
Tea, brewed	6 oz	36
Tea, instant	6 oz	32
Tea	1 leaf bag	30
Carbonated beverages		
Coca-Cola	12 oz	36
Mello Yello	12 oz	52
Mr. Pibb	12 oz	40
Mountain Dew	12 oz	54
Pepsi Cola	12 oz	38

Cardiovascular disease. In a meta-analysis of eleven controlled studies, S. H. Jee found that coffee did increase blood pressure.[28] Bong Sung also found that heart rate and blood pressure rose significantly higher during exercise if caffeine was given to borderline hypertensives just prior to beginning a workout.[29] Another study detected measurable EKG changes after intake of caffeine.[30] However, this does not appear to necessarily translate into increased risk of a heart attack.

For example, although in a major Kaiser Permanente analysis there was a slight increase in heart attack rate over eight years seen with coffee intake, another study concluded that there was no increased risk found for coffee consumption in more than 45,000 men who were followed for two years.[31] If these data seem confusing to you, take heart; they are to me too. However, based upon more detailed study, I think it is safe to conclude the following:

- Excessive intake of coffee (i.e., three or more cups daily) may raise blood pressure and may increase the risk of heart attack.[32]
- Coffee drinkers may have increased risk of cardiovascular disease at least in part due to the fact that they tend to have higher levels of other associated behaviors (such as smoking and lower levels of exercise).[33]

Cancer. We have noted that scientists have only recently begun to discover a myriad of cancer-fighting substances that occur naturally in our foods. Referred to as *phytochemicals,* these substances have also been found in components of coffee and tea plants. In 1996, cancerous mice who were offered an extract of coffee cherry to drink for ten days experienced a marked reduction in growth of their breast tumors.[34] Unfortunately, the coffee cherry is in the residue left behind in coffee processing, so coffee drinking does not appear to help us in the fight against cancer. But it does not appear to contribute to cancer, either. For example, 43,000 Norwegian men and women who were followed for ten years did not show any increased risk of cancer from coffee drinking.[35]

Reproductive effects. Increased caffeine consumption appears to cause a delay in conception.[36] In addition, heavy caffeine intake contributed to increased miscarriages,[37] low birth weight,[38] and sudden infant death syndrome (SIDS).[39] Another study indicated that heavy intake of *decaffeinated* coffee was more associated than regular coffee with miscarriage.[40]

Osteoporosis. Two separate studies reported that heavy caffeine intake was directly associated with increased bone loss.[41]

Addiction. Caffeine is an addictive substance. I recall a missionary's wife who suffered terribly of migraines. After some evaluation, we determined that she was allergic to caffeine (see food sensitivities in chapter 13) and that it was probably causing rebound headaches (headaches that occur as the blood levels of her medicine drop).

This woman had been drinking caffeinated beverages every day and also taking in a great deal of caffeine as a component in headache remedies. She quit the caffeine "cold turkey." Within hours, cravings developed, and, when she failed to give in to them, she began to hallucinate. This kind of symptom is typical of delirium tremens ("DTs"), which may occur when one is withdrawing from heavy, long-term alcohol intake. Nevertheless, in this case it was due to caffeine. In one study of ninety-nine coffee drinkers, sixteen were found to be caffeine-dependent. Of these, 94 percent experienced withdrawal symptoms, and most had great difficulty cutting back. They had become addicted.[42]

> *All things are lawful unto me, but all things are not expedient: all things are lawful for me, but I will not be brought under the power of any.* (1 Corinthians 6:12)

In summary, the research on coffee, while somewhat confusing, appears to indicate that drinking it in moderation (one or two cups daily) does not pose a significant health threat, but increased amounts may have a variety of adverse effects. On the other hand, if you are suffering from, or are at risk for, any of the five problem areas related to coffee, discuss its use with your doctor. You may want to consider subjecting coffee to the elimination and challenge test (see chapter 13).

Tea

The earliest known record of tea comes from Chinese literature dated A.D. 350. Tea drinking was confined to the Orient until the 1600s, when European merchants began importing it from the Far East and it quickly became the national drink of Great Britain. It came to the American colonies in the 1650s, and became famous here when the British government placed a tax on it, resulting in the Boston Tea Party. Iced tea and tea bags were both invented by Americans in 1904, as well as instant tea, first marketed in 1948.

To grow, the tea plant requires a tropical or subtropical climate. The three largest tea-producing nations are India, Sri Lanka, and China. Three kinds of tea are made from the tea plant: (1) black tea, in which the leaves are first air dried and cured before being oven roasted, (2) green tea, which is made by first steaming the leaves before oven drying, and (3) oolong tea, which is made by partially fermenting the leaves to a green-brown color.

Tea (and especially green tea) is known to contain polyphenols, which some believe have a protective effect against a variety of cancers.[43] However, the evidence is still quite weak. For example, green tea blocked cigarette-induced DNA mutations and appeared to reduce the risk of smoker-related lung cancer and possibly stomach cancer.[44] But in a study of more than 120,000 women, consumption of black tea did not protect against cancer. In some studies, the apparent protective effect of the tea was actually traced to increased fruit and vegetable consumption by tea drinkers.[45]

Herbal tea. While the tea plant, from which we get black and green tea, is not noted for its medicinal benefits, the same is not true for herbs and the teas that are made from them. "Herb" comes from a Latin word meaning "grass" or "blade" and refers to a large group of low-growing plants.

Throughout the ages, herbs have been used for a variety of purposes, including flavoring for foods (e.g., basil, horseradish, marjoram, parsley, peppermint, sage, spearmint, vanilla), as scents for perfumes, and as medicines. For example, the foxglove plant was used for congestive heart failure long before the drug digitalis was isolated from it. Licorice root, by virtue of its effect on beta-receptors, tends to raise blood pressure. Ginseng tends to inhibit the effects of cortisol. St. John's Wort is now a popular remedy used in the relief of depression. Some of our earliest chemotherapy drugs, vincristine and vinblastine, are derived from plants.

However, this druglike capacity may also be detrimental, particularly if consumed frequently and over a prolonged period. With a reverence for these potential effects, use herbal teas, as all herbs, under the advice of a health care professional knowledgeable about their properties.

In the midst of the street of it, and on either side of the river, was there the tree of life, which bare twelve manner of fruits, and yielded her fruit every month: and the leaves of the tree were for the healing of the nations. (Revelation 22:2)

Juice

The beverages of the Hebrews were principally water, milk, and the juice of the grape. Although the apostle Paul admonished believers not to be drunk with fermented wine (Ephesians 5:18), he encouraged Timothy to "use a little wine for thy stomach's sake and thine often infirmities" (1 Timothy 5:23). Even today, grape juice is known for its benefits to the digestive system. Grape seed extract is a popular natural remedy with significant antibiotic-like properties. Similarly, cranberry juice is commonly recommended for its ability to reduce bacteria in the urine.[46]

Since more than 90 percent of antioxidants can be found in the juice, alternative treatment centers commonly juice large amounts of vegetables in their regimens for cancer and other chronic diseases.[47] Usually, most residues from pesticides remain in the pulp. However, up to half of certain kinds may find their way into the juice as well. Washing and peeling of fruits and vegetables is recommended in order to reduce these potentially harmful chemicals.[48]

While fruit and vegetable juices have their merits, there are some cautions about their use. Due to the fact that they are high in natural sugar, they can cause significant swings in blood sugar (see chapter 13). For this reason, it is prudent to drink fruit juices in modest amounts, somewhat dilute, and generally not on an empty stomach. But most important, children should consume fruit juices sparingly for several reasons.

- Commercially prepared juices tend to contain substantial amounts of fluoride and therefore may pose a significant health risk if consumed too frequently by young children who are getting fluoride from other sources.[49]

- The high natural sugar content contributes to dental caries. Even carrot juice was seen to cause dental caries when given to nursing babies.[50]

- Children who drink excessive amounts of fruit juice may experience growth problems due to the displacement of more necessary foods.[51]

- Consumption of high amounts of fruit juices and malabsorption of fructose (fruit sugar) is often the cause of chronic diarrhea in one-to-three-year-olds.[52]

- Grapefruit juice, by virtue of its apparently unique ability to reduce the activity of a particular gut enzyme, significantly increases the blood levels of several types of medications, including antihistamines (allergies and colds), calcium-channel blockers (heart and high blood pressure), sedatives (anxiety or insomnia), and immune suppressants (rheumatoid arthritis, lupus, chemotherapy, etc.).[53]

Conclusion

Guidelines for beverage consumption:

• Drink water as your principal beverage: pure; eight glasses daily.

• Drink coffee and tea in modest amounts, perhaps on an occasional basis, and definitely not in amounts exceeding three cups daily.

• Consult a health care professional when utilizing medicinal herbs and teas, especially for a prolonged period.

• Do not give fruit juices to infants. Small children may consume them on an occasional basis.

• Avoid concentrated juices on an empty stomach.

• Avoid grapefruit juice when taking medications.

9

MILK PRODUCTS

My last tour of duty as an army major was serving the 101st Airborne Division at Fort Campbell, Kentucky. I recall a young soldier's pregnant wife who came into the clinic for her routine obstetrics check. Since she was nearing her due date, I went through the usual items that needed to be addressed prior to her delivery. When I asked her if she planned to breast-feed, a look of astonishment came over her face. With obvious discomfort at the suggestion, she replied, "That sounds so unnatural!" Despite my encouragement to consider the advantages of breast milk, she let me know in no uncertain terms that she fully intended to formula-feed her baby with a bottle.

Like so many others, that soldier's wife had bought into a lie. For a number of years, breast milk had been criticized as nutritionally inferior, whereas "scientific" infant formulas were said to be best suited for the growing baby. And so a generation of American women abandoned nursing. But as time has passed and the early claims have been put to the test, the facts have confirmed the Creator's wisdom: Human breast milk is unmatched as the perfect "designer" food for newborn babies. Consider its advantages:

- Human milk from a well-nourished mother contains everything that an infant needs, with no need for supplementation. (Some recommend supplementing with Vitamin D, although this is naturally produced when the skin is exposed to sunlight.)
- Human milk is higher than cow's milk in lactose, the milk sugar. Lactose promotes the growth of friendly bacteria in the intestines. A lack of lactose favors the growth of harmful bacteria. The friendly bacteria promoted by human breast milk are referred to as the "intestinal guardian" because they also keep out infection-causing bacteria.

- The higher levels of lactose also lower the pH, thereby improving the absorption of minerals such as calcium and magnesium. Much lower levels of calcium and magnesium are absorbed from cow's milk than human milk. Likewise, human milk has similar levels of iron to cow's milk, but more than 50 percent of iron is absorbed from human milk, compared to only 10 percent from cow's.

- Early exposure to cow's milk has been linked to an increased risk of insulin-dependent diabetes. Apparently this is because cow's milk carries bovine insulin, which is similar to but not exactly the same as human insulin. When exposed to it, children can make antibodies that may cross-react, attacking not only the bovine insulin but the child's own insulin-producing cells in the pancreas.

- Human milk contains antibodies that protect the newborn from infection. Some pediatricians claim that strep throat is unheard of in their patients who do not consume dairy products.

- Human milk causes far fewer allergic reactions. Thus, these children have a much lower rate of diarrhea, constipation, and colic, as well as less nasal congestion, asthma, and eczema. Pediatricians have noted that the earlier cow's milk is introduced into the diet, the greater the likelihood of allergy.

- Human milk is higher in total fat. However, it has much less saturated fat and much more of the invaluable essential fatty acids. That may be why infants who are breast-fed have dramatically lower incidence of sudden infant death syndrome (SIDS), or "crib death."

- Breast-feeding triggers the release of prolactin (*pro* meaning "in favor of" and *lactin* meaning "milk") from the pituitary gland. Prolactin has a pitocin-like effect on the uterus, causing the womb to clamp down after delivery and thus protecting the mother from excessive blood loss. In addition, prolactin blocks ovulation so that a woman who is breast-feeding regularly will not have a menstrual cycle. In other words, breast-feeding is a natural, Creator-designed and God-ordained form of contraception that puts natural spacing between children, allowing a mother to give her newborn the attention and care that he needs.[1]

In light of all of those advantages, it should come as no surprise that the mothers who chose not to breast-feed returned repeatedly to my office with their newborns, who were sick with a variety of the complaints listed above. Often, several changes in formula were made in attempts to alleviate the symptoms. The answer, of course, was human breast milk. But by then the decision had been made, and there was no turning back.

To today's young mothers I make this appeal: Do yourself and your little newborn a favor—don't deny him the life-giving food that God put within you. Human breast milk should be the principal food for infants at least through the first year of life. You will not find a better product.

But what about after the child is weaned? Should dairy (cow's milk) products then be consumed? There are those who believe that cow's milk, with its high content of protein, vitamins, and minerals, should never be removed from the foods best-seller list. Our encyclopedia claims that milk is the most nourishing of all foods, containing almost all the nutrients that a person needs for growth and good health.

That is what I was taught as I was growing up. Milk was considered one of the most desirable of all foods and was lauded by many for its medicinal value as well. But today, milk is not so highly esteemed.

Dr. Frank Oski is Physician in Chief of the Johns Hopkins Children's Center. In his little paperback *Don't Drink Your Milk: New Frightening Medical Facts About the World's Most Overrated Nutrient,* Dr. Oski lists the reasons he believes that milk was not designed as food for anyone but nursing infants. He refers to milk-drinking toddlers as "milkaholics" and like-minded adults as "milk freaks."[2] He cites evidence that a majority of the world's adult population are lactose intolerant, having lost the enzyme that is needed in order to properly digest the sugar in milk, lactose. (Only Caucasians from Scandinavia and western Europe tend to retain lactase production. Of the others, 50 percent of Indians, 60-80 percent of Jews, 70 percent of African-Americans, 78 percent of Arabs, 85 percent of Orientals and Greeks, and 90 percent of Filipinos lose their ability to digest milk sugar.)

And so the battle rages between the two camps. What are we supposed to think? Is milk harmful? Let's ask the Creator. Did He say anything about dairy products in Scripture? Actually, He did. The first mention of them in the Word occurs in Genesis 18. In this passage, angels on their way to judge Sodom and Gomorrah stopped to visit Abraham. When Abraham saw them, he hurried to get the best of his food to provide a meal for them: milk, butter, and beef.

And he took butter, and milk, and the calf which he had dressed, and set it before them; and he stood by them under the tree, and they did eat. (Genesis 18:8)

Neither Abraham nor the angels had a problem with drinking milk. Furthermore, in numerous instances we find the Lord referring to the Promised Land as a "land flowing with milk and honey." Proverbs 27:27 clearly indicates that goat's milk was a staple food item for the Hebrew people.

Milk was considered a food for all ages. The Hebrews used the milk of the cow, sheep, goat and camel (Genesis 32:15). A form of milk commonly used by today's Arab is "leben," which means "white." It is like our sour milk curds. In order to make it, they pour milk in a dish, put yeast in it and cover it over with a warm cloth. It is ready to serve after setting for about a day. Arabs are very fond of it and say, "It makes a sick man well." This is probably what Abraham gave to his guests and Jael gave to Sisera.[3]

Scripture indicates that dairy products were given to man for food. However, it appears that the milk of biblical days was actually more like our yogurt of today. We'll come back to that later. But first, let's take a closer look at the milk of our day. When we do so, several significant problems come to light.

First of all, dairy farming (like other forms of ranching and farming) is not conducted in the same way as it was in Bible times. Prior to the 1950s, most cattle were allowed to range freely. Today, in order to increase profit margins and ensure competitiveness in the market, dairy cows are often kept indoors for their entire production life.

Then, a variety of techniques are used to maximize milk productivity, including the use of steroid hormones, antibiotics, and commercial feeds. All of these substances can end up in the milk, calling into question its safety for long-term human consumption. In addition, these methods tend to dramatically increase the animal's body fat, which also leads to higher-fat milk.[4]

Some attribute both the accelerated maturation of our young people and the rise in degenerative disease in the old to the increased fat content in our diet and/or the unnatural substances in our animal products. For example, the average height in a male increased four inches from 1876 to 1977. Similarly, the average age at the onset of menarche [the onset of menses] has also progressively become earlier over the last 100 years.[5]

Homogenization

Once the milk is removed from the cow, it is further dramatically changed through homogenization and pasteurization.

Fresh whole milk, when allowed to stand, separates into two layers, creamy butterfat floating to the top and watery milk below. The cream can be skimmed off and used to make butter, whipping cream, sour cream, ice cream, or other products. The cream of fresh raw milk is rich in butterfat. According to Russell, these butterfat globules are very large, so large that they cannot be broken down by the bile and digested in the human intestines. Therefore, raw butterfat tends to just roll on through the intestines without being significantly absorbed into the bloodstream.

In homogenization, the creamy butterfat layer is broken up and thoroughly mixed into the milk portion so that it forms a uniform consistency. The benefits are a longer shelf life and milk that does not need to be stirred in order to serve it. Unfortunately, homogenization may have its drawbacks. Breaking up the large butterfat globules into smaller ones apparently allows them to be more readily digested by the intestines and absorbed into the bloodstream. This raises the blood levels of lipids (including cholesterol) in the blood.

Furthermore, homogenized milk may also contribute to heart disease through the release by digested butterfat of an enzyme (xanthine oxidase) that may cause ulceration of the inner lining of arteries. This claim was apparently first made by K. A. Oster in the early 1970s.[6] Since that time, a considerable controversy has raged in the medical literature over xanthine oxidase, homogenized milk, and the possible connection between milk consumption and heart disease.

- In 1976, Ho and Clifford reported that 59 percent of the xanthine oxidase in raw milk was actually destroyed in the homogenization process, and most of the rest was inactivated by acid below pH 3.5. They estimated that only 0.00008 percent actually would be absorbed into the bloodstream.[7]

- These and other studies have led several researchers to conclude that homogenized milk does not cause an increased amount of xanthine oxidase to get into the bloodstream and contribute to heart disease.[8]

- Despite this evidence, some still claim that the connection is there. In 1986, P. Rank stated that studies proved that milk caused heart disease. He believed this occurred through the transmission of bacteria.[9]

As Rex Russell states so well, whenever man takes what God has provided and alters it, we should be concerned about possible damaging effects. Homogenization is a man-made process that, unlike pasteurization, is really done only to improve milk's texture and usability—it has little health benefit. Therefore, despite the fact that there is conflict in the research, I still think we should be cautious as to its use.

Pasteurization

When it comes to milk safety, the potential for bacterial contamination has always been the greatest concern. Up until the mid-1800s, most American families obtained cow's milk from their own cow or from a neighbor's. However, as cities grew, local laws were enacted to prohibit the keeping of cows within city limits. Farmers outside the city began to increase the number in their herds and established dairy businesses. As the industry grew, it became more difficult to keep cows and provide fresh milk, so farmers began to add chemicals to milk as preservatives. When these were found to be harmful, laws were enacted and standards set in order to protect the public health.[10]

Bacteria tend to quickly multiply in raw milk that is not consumed fresh. In the 1890s, dairies began to implement pasteurization, a process invented by the French scientist Louis Pasteur. Pasteurization tends to destroy germs by heating the milk to a high temperature (180+ degrees F) for at least fifteen seconds. (There is also an approved longer, low temperature method.)

Unfortunately, these high temperatures can also dramatically change the structure and nutritional content of raw cow's milk. Pasteurized milk contains only 50 percent of the calcium and magnesium of raw milk—and only 10 percent of the enzymes that are needed for calcium and magnesium to be absorbed. In addition, fatty acids and two of the amino acids are damaged. Fifty to eighty percent of vitamins A, C, E, and B complex are also lost.[11] And the heating process destroys IgA and IgM milk antibodies, lactoferrin (the form of iron found in milk), and other important enzymes, including superoxide dismutase (an important antioxidant) and lipase, which is important for proper fat digestion.[12] Yogurt, which is known for its improved digestion of lactose, loses this beneficial effect when it is pasteurized.[13]

What then is the answer to this dilemma? Some recommend a return to natural, raw milk. The major concern with regard to raw milk is the increased risk of transmission of infectious disease, but proponents of raw milk believe that these concerns are adequately addressed simply by practicing good hygiene and not consuming milk from a cow that is demonstrating any sign of infection. They claim that one can safely drink raw milk if it is obtained through a certified raw milk dairy and that most milk-transmitted infections occur through *pasteurized* dairy milk. In their support:

- High amounts of many bacteria are common in any raw milk prior to pasteurization, even in dairies that receive high ratings for the quality of their milking procedures.[14]

- Knabel reported that *Listeria* (bacteria) can survive the low temperature pasteurization method.[15] In other words, pasteurization was not necessarily safer.
- A large interstate outbreak of *Yersinia* (bacteria that can cause sore throat or fever, abdominal pain, and diarrhea) was linked to a *pasteurized* milk dairy.[16]

However, there are a number of loud voices citing evidence to the contrary.

- In 1999 the Centers for Disease Control reported on the transmission of rabies to humans through raw milk. Eighty individuals received postexposure injections to protect them from rabies after it was discovered that they had ingested milk from rabid cows. The average cost of the injections was $2,376 per person. The CDC said that pasteurization normally inactivates the rabies virus.[17]
- In California, raw milk was responsible for 44 out of 1,133 cases of *Salmonella dublin* between 1971 and 1975. *S. dublin* infection was fatal in 22 of the patients.[18] It appears that individuals who had serious compromise of their immune system were at increased risk of death from this bacteria and were therefore encouraged to avoid raw milk.
- An outbreak of *Campylobacter* infection was traced to a local raw milk dairy in California in 1979 and in Atlanta in 1981. Twenty outbreaks were also linked to raw milk between 1981 and 1990.[19]
- E. coli, which has received much press for the deaths it caused a few years ago when transmitted through undercooked hamburger meat, has also been transmitted through raw milk.[20] Researchers have reported that E. coli can persist for more than a month in sour cream and buttermilk, and that raw milk testing standards do not provide adequate protection from this bacteria.[21]
- A total of forty-six raw-milk-associated outbreaks were reported to the Centers for Disease Control between 1973 and 1992.[22]
- Some experts have classified raw milk as "often unsafe" and recommend its avoidance.[23]

So what are we to think? Well, let's review the facts we have so far.

- God designed milk and, according to the Word, gave it to us for food.
- Raw milk, in its natural state, is nutritionally superior, but concerns over infection appear to be justified. Homogenization and pasteurization obviously damage raw milk but appear to be necessary if one is to reduce the risk of infection.

What a dilemma!

Once again, our problem appears to stem mostly from our desire to make a food (in this case, milk) convenient and accessible by preserving it beyond its natural, God-given shelf life. This preservation is done through culturing the milk into either yogurt or cheese. But if we are going to *drink* milk, we should try to get back to how the Creator originally provided it: fresh and raw from a clean, local source.

Now, that might be an insurmountable challenge. Perhaps you live in the center of Chicago, and the nearest dairy cow is at least an hour's drive and an expressway migraine away. Does your subdivision or apartment complex allow goats? (Just kidding.)

Actually, a substantial number of small farms maintain their own dairy cows and sell raw milk. We have been able to obtain raw milk without too much difficulty through friends or local farmers almost anywhere we have lived. If such an arrangement is available, you might consider it, provided that the source for the milk is reliably clean. Laws regarding the sale of raw milk vary from state to state.

Yogurt and Cheese

As I mentioned earlier, cultured milk products, particularly yogurt and cheese, are and have been the mainstay of how milk was taken in the Middle East. Not only do these forms of milk keep longer, but they have tremendous health advantages as well.

- Lactose intolerance, with symptoms that include abdominal pain, bloating, gas, diarrhea, bad breath, headaches, and fatigue, is a result of a person's inability to break down the predominant sugar of cow's milk. But bacteria in yogurt and cheese break down lactose, so that lactose intolerant individuals can often take cultured milk products without symptoms. Pasteurization destroys this benefit.[24]

- In Bible lands, cheese is commonly carried throughout the day and is used by workers as a snack food.[25]

- Being made from milk, cheese concentrates milk's nutrients. Eight ounces of cheese contain the same protein and calcium of six eight-ounce glasses of milk.

- Yogurt, because of its low pH, tends to be free of harmful bacterial contamination.

- Yogurt has been proven to be very helpful in correcting chronic diarrhea. The friendly bacteria in yogurt help to restore normal bacterial balance to the gastrointestinal tract (especially important after antibiotics).[26]

- Yogurt restores the health of the enzyme-rich brush border cells in the intestines.[27]

- Chronic candida vaginitis was cured over the course of six months in 85 percent of women who ate yogurt.[28]

- Consumption of fermented milk products has been shown to possibly protect against breast cancer.[29]

Two notes of caution: Cheese is high in fat (100 calories in one 1-inch cube). Therefore, eat it in moderation. Also, cow's milk is one of the most common food allergy producers known, affecting up to 30 percent of the population. Allergic individuals looking for another option might want to consider goat's milk, soy milk, rice milk, or even nut milks. For more on allergy, see chapter 13.

What About Combining Milk and Meat?

For thousands of years, the Jewish people have avoided the combination of milk and meat products in the same meal. This practice is based upon the following passages recorded by Moses.

Three times in the year all thy males shall appear before the Lord God. Thou shalt not offer the blood of my sacrifice with leavened bread; neither shall the fat of my sacrifice remain until the morning. The first of the firstfruits of thy land thou shalt bring into the house of the Lord thy God. Thou shalt not seethe a kid in his mother's milk. (Exodus 23:17–19)

Thrice in the year shall all your men-children appear before the Lord God, the God of Israel. . . . Thou shalt not offer the blood of my sacrifice with leaven; neither shall the sacrifice of the feast of the passover be left unto the morning. The first of the firstfruits of thy land thou shalt bring unto the house of the Lord thy God. Thou shalt not seethe a kid in his mother's milk. (Exodus 34:23–26)

For thou art an holy people unto the Lord thy God. Thou shalt not seethe a kid in his mother's milk. (Deuteronomy 14:21)

For this reason, Orthodox Jews do not mix dairy and meat products in the same meal—such as a hamburger with cheese, or cheese lasagna. Some Jews take this concept to such an extreme that they maintain two separate sets of kitchenware.

A distinguishing mark of Jewish homes and restaurants is the two sets of dishes, pots, and other kitchen utensils—one for meat and the other for dairy foods. Strict homes have also different stoves and sinks. The separation of meat and milk is an ancient custom observed very carefully all these centuries. In ancient times, the flesh of the kid could not be boiled in his mother's milk, for the Bible states several times: "Thou shalt not seethe the kid in its mother's milk." Later on this law was applied to every kind of meat and all dairy food. This also explains why observant Jews wait six hours after a meat meal before eating any dairy food.[30]

However, it is interesting to note that Abraham, the father of the Jewish people, did not follow this practice. When he served food to his honored guests, "he took butter, and milk, and the calf which he had dressed, and set it before them; and he stood by them under the tree, and they did eat" (Genesis 18:8).

Based upon this observation and the context of the verses, it seems to me that the intent of this commandment was not to prohibit dairy and meat products in the same meal but to show respect for the animal. Notice that in each case it refers to cooking a kid specifically in its own mother's milk. This seems to be confirmed by a similar command given with regard to an acceptable offering to the Lord:

And whether it be cow, or ewe, ye shall not kill it and her young both in one day. (Leviticus 22:28)

Conclusion

The best way to take milk is in its cultured form, as in yogurt or cheese. Yogurt can easily be made at home, and once you have a batch, you can keep perpetuating it. (Several years ago, Will Anderson, husband to Christian author Ann Kiemel Anderson, taught me how to make yogurt inexpensively and conveniently. See the recipe below.)

If you drink milk, consider the value of fresh, local raw milk. Most of the infectious outbreaks reported in the scientific literature appear to be related to raw *dairy* milk rather than what is obtained fresh and locally. However, caution is in order. Based on the Bible lands blueprint, noncultured milk at least should be limited. If you are drinking dairy milk, pasteurized skim milk seems to be safest, offering the advantages of being low in fat and un-homogenized, which should eliminate any concern over xanthine oxidase.

Will's Yogurt-While-You-Sleep Protocol

1/2 cup of low-fat plain yogurt
1 gallon of fresh skim milk
1 60- to 75-watt light bulb
1 trouble light with cord

- This recipe is intended to be prepared just before bedtime.
- Place milk into a large stainless steel pan. Heat the milk to almost boiling. Will says to heat it just to the point that you cannot stir your fingertip ten times in a small circle. This kills bacteria in the milk that we don't want multiplying.
- Let cool, either naturally or by placing this pan into a larger pan of cold water. Let cool to near room temperature.
- Add about one cup of this warmed milk to the yogurt for starter. Gently dissolve the yogurt.
- Add this milk-yogurt mixture to the pan of warmed milk and cover with a lid.
- Place in oven with oven heat turned off.
- Place in the oven the 60–75-watt trouble light with the shield removed (or use other similar light socket apparatus). Close the door and plug in the light.
- Your yogurt will be ready in the morning.
- For future batches of yogurt, always preserve at least 1/2 cup of fresh-made yogurt as a starter.

For a more nutritious yogurt, make a starter with friendly lactobacillus acidophilus bacteria. To do this, obtain a bottle of high quality bacteria in powder form from a health food store or pharmacy. *Before adding the other yogurt starter to the warmed milk,* remove 1 cup of warmed milk to a separate container. Add 2 tablespoons of acidophilus powder to this milk. Place it in the oven along with the other recipe. In the morning, you will have your new acidophilus yogurt starter. Every so often, make a fresh batch of starter from the original bacteria, which should be kept refrigerated.

MEAT AND EGGS

CLEAN ANIMALS

*I*n Leviticus 11:1–47 and Deuteronomy 14:2–21 God gave a specific list of animals that were to be used for food and referred to them as "clean." Land animals given for food were to be completely cloven and chew the cud. They had to have both characteristics in order to qualify. Therefore, clean land animals included:

- Deer
- Sheep
- Oxen/Cattle
- Goat

With regard to fowl, most were considered clean. These included:

- Chicken
- Turkey
- Duck
- Swan
- Quail
- Coot
- Pigeon

Fish were required to have both scales and fins. These included (but were not limited to):

- Salmon
- Trout
- Mackerel
- Tuna
- Bass
- Perch
- Herring

Fish that were unclean are typically classified today as seafood. These included:

- Crab
- Clam
- Oyster
- Octopus
- Lobster
- Shrimp
- Scallops
- Eel & Others

Kosher fish must have scales and fins, although those having scales and only rudimentary fins are allowed. Oysters, lobsters, and other shellfish are on the forbidden list because they are disease carriers, especially in hot climates.[1]

Certain insects were considered clean if they were winged, hopping, and had four primary legs. These included:

- Locust   • Beetle   • Grasshopper

Some of the animals deemed unclean are specifically mentioned in Leviticus 11. These included camel, coney, rabbit, and pig. Other unclean animals were squirrel, bear, horse, cat, and dog.

Why would God forbid the eating of certain animals? What appears to make the difference between "clean" and "unclean"? A modern-day Jewish source explains, "Practically all of the forbidden animals and birds are creatures of prey, or loathsome in appearance and mode of living."[2]

Rex Russell says that the differences "appear to be related to their primary food source and to their digestive systems. Scavengers that eat anything and everything are unclean. . . . Animals described as clean, and therefore good for food, primarily eat grasses and grains."[3]

After one reviews Scripture and examines the growing information available on the differences between the two classes, it is understandable why the Creator forbade unclean animals as food for humans: When we eat them we may be putting ourselves at increased risk of disease.

For example, shellfish are known for their ability to decontaminate cholera-infected water. Dr. Russell states, "Shrimp, oysters, crab, scallops and mussels . . . filter large volumes of water every day. Sewage laden with chemicals, toxins and harmful bacteria, parasites and viruses become concentrated in those shellfish."[4] Once shellfish have made contaminated water pure, the last thing you should do is eat the shellfish! This would expose you to significant concentrated sources of toxins and infectious agents.

It appears to me that when God created the earth, He prepared a perfect, balanced ecosystem, making it a suitable, clean home for His beloved mankind. Some of the animals are obviously designed to purify man's environment. In the case of shellfish, it is to give him pure water. In the case of vultures, it is to remove the carcasses of dead animals so that they do not spread disease. When man eats those foods that were designed for other purposes, he crosses the line of natural law and exposes himself and others to unnecessary illness.

In April 1997, *Science* published a discovery that the 1918 Spanish flu virus, which killed more than 20 million people worldwide, was caused by a virus contracted from pigs. The Armed Forces Institute of Pathology discovered this when they reanalyzed preserved lung tissue from an Army private who died in that epidemic. They stated:

The finding supports the theory that flu viruses from swine are the most virulent for humans. . . . Most experts think flu viruses reside harmlessly in birds where they are genetically stable. Occasionally, a virus from birds will infect pigs. The swine immune system attacks the virus, forcing it to change genetically to survive. The result is a new virus. When this new bug is spread to humans, devastating [results ensue].[5]

The article noted that, since 1918, two other flu viruses have spread all over the world: the Asian flu in 1957 and the Hong Kong flu in 1968. "Both mutated in pigs."

Consider the significance of this report, which stated that, prior to infecting pigs, many viruses are "genetically stable" and "harmless." But should a virus jump to swine and then infect humans, it becomes altered into a new, potentially lethal virus. Thus, when humans come in contact with infected pigs, they are exposing themselves to something against which they may have little resistance. Do you suppose the Creator knew this all along and therefore restricted pork from His beloved people for their own protection? I think so. The evidence continues to mount:

- At the very time this book was being written, a deadly swine virus was attacking Malaysia and had already taken the lives of five pig farmers. As a result, the Malaysian government announced that 1.3 million pigs would be destroyed. Officials believed that the deadly encephalitis virus is transmitted through direct contact with infected pigs, whether they are alive or dead. Soldiers, covered head-to-toe in spacesuits, entered pig-farming villages as part of a massive campaign to shoot the pigs.[6]

- Ingestion of pork has been associated with cervical cancer, as well as human papilloma virus [HPV], which is known to be a causative agent in many cases of this dreaded cancer of young females.[7]

- A rare allergy form of kidney failure (lipoid nephrosis) has been linked to the ingestion of pork and unclean seafood.[8]

- Nephrotic syndrome, a condition in which the kidneys spill large amounts of protein into the urine, has been successfully treated in some cases by eliminating pork and other animal products from the diet.[9]

- A thirty-two-year-old pregnant woman died after contracting viral pneumonia through exposure to pigs while exhibiting at a county fair. Studies on twenty-five pigs revealed that 75 percent of them were carrying the virus.[10]

- Pork is one of the foods most likely to aggravate arthritis in susceptible individuals.[11]

- Toxoplasmosis, a virus that silently attacks the retina, has been transmitted through uncooked pork.[12]

- Outbreaks of the parasite trichinosis have been linked to undercooked commercial pork sausage.[13]

- Nearly 20 percent of workers at a pork packing plant were found to be infected with brucellosis.[14]

- The pork tapeworm, if transmitted to humans, can cause neurocysticercosis, a potentially fatal condition in which cysts are formed in brain tissue.[15]

- Increased intakes of pork products, raw seafood, organ and rare meats have been linked to a disease in which the brain takes on spongiform characteristics (Creutzfeldt-Jakob disease).[16]

- Swine are also carriers of trichinosis, a parasite that causes muscle pain, headaches, fever, and swelling.[17]

If that doesn't make you want to quit pork, then why not sit down and watch the movie *Babe?* It is the hilarious story of a cute but confused piglet that thought he was a sheep dog. *Nutrition Week* reported that pork consumption in Thailand was dramatically reduced after the movie was shown there.[18]

In 1953, David Macht of Johns Hopkins University published a remarkable paper entitled "An Experimental Pharmacological Appreciation of Leviticus XI and Deuteronomy XIV." In that study, Dr. Macht exposed controlled growth cultures to various types of animal blood and flesh and measured the rate at which each slowed the growth culture. He noted two dramatic findings:

- In all cases, the blood of the animal slowed the growth culture to a greater extent than the flesh.

- Those animals that were listed as clean in the Old Testament slowed cultures to a dramatically lower extent than those that were unclean. The finding was 100 percent consistent across all types of animal flesh tested: Unclean meats demonstrated a toxic effect whereas clean meats did not.[19]

NOT ALL "CLEAN" FLESH IS

But it is possible to eat only meat that is classified as clean and still get into trouble with your health. One way to do this is to eat meat that has been changed substantially from the manner in which our Creator originally provided it to us. The primary means by which this takes place is the way these animals have been prepared for market.

In commercial operations, the goal is usually to get the animal to market as quickly as possible. In order to achieve this goal, specially designed commercial feeds are used as well as crowded living conditions, growth hormones, and antibiotics. All of these take their toll, particularly through dramatically increasing the fat content of the animals. Look at table 10.1.

TABLE 10.1 FAT CONTENT: FREE RANGING V. PEN RAISED		
	% Fat (wild/ranging)	% Fat (pen-fed)
Turkey	3–5	30–40
Deer/Venison	3–6	
Cattle	5–8	40

Notice the striking difference in fat content between free-ranging animals and those that are pen raised. Turkey contains 30–40 percent fat compared to wild turkeys, which have 3–5 percent fat. This is comparable to venison. By contrast, typical commercial methods of raising cattle result in beef with an average of 40 percent fat.

Likewise, commercial methods of raising chickens nowadays involve jamming thousands of birds into cramped quarters and feeding them processed feeds, hormones, and antibiotics. This produces poultry that no longer have a low-fat advantage over their red meat counterparts. It used to be that poultry fat was mostly located just under the skin. When the skin was removed and discarded, the meat that remained was relatively low fat. However, with the increased use of commercial methods, there is now an additional layer of fat that occurs *within* these meats.

Since the animals that God provides for food usually have body fat percentages in the single digits, it would appear that our modern methods of meat production result in a direct violation of the old prohibition against eating fat. And a look at the diseases that have been clearly associated with high intakes of long-chain saturated animal fat verify that we are reaping what we sow.

But avoiding the use of hormones doesn't necessarily guarantee a low-fat cut of beef. A brochure of a popular meat company that boasts of raising low-fat beef without using growth hormones and antibiotics indicates that many of the cuts of meat still had fat content that was above desirable levels.[20]

In other words, the best selections for lean beef from these particular cattle were from top round, strip steak, and tenderloin. The American Heart Association recommends dietary fat intakes of less than 30 percent. However, some studies indicate that total dietary fat needs to be possibly as low as 20 percent in order to truly prevent or improve existing coronary heart disease. An exception to this is the Mediterranean diet, which is high in vegetable fat but low in animal fat. This diet, which has been shown to cut heart attacks by 98 percent, will be discussed in chapter 12.[21]

TABLE 10.2 FAT PERCENT OF A "NATURAL" BEEF				
Uncooked 4oz (112 g)	94% Lean Ground Beef	Top Round	Ribeye Steak/ Eye of Round	Strip Steak/ Tenderloin
Calories	160	130	150	140
Fat (grams)	7.0	3.0	5.0	4.0
Fat % cal	39	21	30	26

KOSHER MEATS

Kosher meats are those that meet the standards of Jewish dietary law.

The meat a Jewish mother buys in a market is from kosher animals, prepared in accordance with the Laws of Shehitah, or slaughtering. Any other meat is considered Trefah. One important provision of the Laws of Shehitah is that only a certain individual, the Shohet, is allowed to slaughter animals for food. He must be a learned, pious man, specially trained and properly certified. The authority to grant a slaughtering certificate is vested in the Bet Din or in a rabbi, who must give the candidate a thorough examination before issuing the certificate.[22]

After the animal is slaughtered, its internal organs are examined for disease. If any is found, the animal is "declared to be Trefah." With regard to fowl, the housewife herself conducts the evaluation. All questions are directed to the rabbi. After this, the ligaments are removed. Any blood that may remain in the meat after proper butchering is removed through soaking the meat in water and then salt for a half hour each. Once a final rinsing is complete, the meat is ready for cooking.

Many United States government standards for meat handling have been based upon Jewish dietary laws. However, that may be changing. In the past, when fecal matter was visibly contaminating an animal carcass, it was declared unfit for human consumption. Some time ago, the United States Department of Agriculture (USDA) began to allow poultry processors to wash fecal matter away rather than condemning the meat. Then, in 1996, the USDA changed its policy for beef and pork as well. The problem is that some bacteria, such as salmonella, cannot be washed away from fecal-contaminated flesh, even with repeated efforts. Obviously, this puts consumers at greater risk for food poisoning from contaminated meats.[23]

ORGAN MEATS (EXODUS 29:13, 22)

What about eating organ meats? First, we see in the Old Testament that God commanded several abdominal organs to be burned along with the sacrifices rather than eaten. Scripture repeatedly mentions burning the liver, intestines, and kidneys along with their fat. This makes a great deal of sense, since these are the organs for detoxification and excretion of waste, and thus they carry the greatest risk for disease.

As to the other internal organs, there may be some debate. However, I have found no record of the Hebrews ever eating body organs. It appears to me that these were not intended for food.

FREQUENCY OF MEAT CONSUMPTION

Even though some meats are classified as clean, there is still the question as to the frequency with which we should eat them.

With fish, there are probably no limitations as long as the fish are clean and are taken from nature. (According to Russell, fish that are pond-raised lose their beneficial omega-3 fatty acids.[24]) Fish were eaten as a staple food on a frequent basis in Israel, and, generally speaking, researchers recommend fish be eaten at least once or twice a week.

One concern surrounding fish is their tendency to concentrate mercury and thus be a source of this damaging toxin. But several studies indicate that the greatest source of mercury in humans comes from dental amalgam, which contains about 50 percent mercury. And studies in the Seychelles, where the inhabitants average twelve fish meals per week, show no evidence of increased mercury toxicity over nonfish eaters. The benefits of eating fish far outweigh mercury concerns.

As to the frequency of consuming meats, we know that there was no artificial refrigeration available until this century. Thus, meat could not be stored for long periods unless it was preserved through other means.

Several years ago, I was in Jordan and visited the ancient cave city of Petra. On the way in, we stopped at the home of the man who was to be our guide. With his wife and children standing in the background, he asked if we desired chicken or lamb for our midday meal. Looking around at the small village, I saw no grocery store. The man lived in a very meager house with several animals ranging behind a fence. I realized that the only meat we would be eating was going to come out of his yard that day. So I requested chicken, and, sure enough, upon our return from the historic city we sat down in his home to a meal of freshly butchered and prepared chicken.

In Bible times, whenever common people wanted to eat meat, it generally required that they slaughter one of their own animals. This, along with the lack of refrigeration, drastically limited the meat consumption to occasions when there were special celebrations or honored guests. The exception to this would be in the case of the wealthy, particularly royalty. A look at the daily menu for Solomon's administration shows a phenomenal number of animals being slaughtered to provide meat for the king's table. As one might expect, it was the wealthy and royalty who suffered from many of the degenerative diseases that we have today.

> As a rule, Bible characters, like Orientals in modern times, have not eaten meat, except on special occasions. When a stranger or guest was entertained, or when a feast was made, then meat would be served. Kings and other wealthy men had meat often.[25]

Several years ago, I heard a radio broadcast discussing the alarming increase of degenerative diseases in a minority racial group in America. The rise had been traced back to the mid 1960s, when the welfare and food stamp programs were instituted. Prior to that time, poor people had been able to afford only the bare essentials. But once their incomes were increased through government assistance, they took the opportunity to eat like their "rich" neighbors. Soon they also began developing the diseases of their rich neighbors. The problem only accelerated when they became integrated into the working middle class.

In trying to get these "emancipated" minorities to go back to their old (healthy) way of eating, the health care professionals have had to combat (1) a mind-set that equates affluence with the standard American diet and (2) the sense that when one can afford it, he has "arrived." It reminds me of the man who said he spent all his life and energy climbing the ladder of success only to discover that it was leaning against the wrong wall!

EGGS

Very little is said about eggs in Scripture. The Old Testament makes only a few ambiguous references. However, "sometime between the days of Elijah and the time of Christ, the domestic fowl and the everyday use of eggs was introduced into Palestine."[26] Eggs became a common food in the Holy Land. This is confirmed by Jesus' reference in Luke 11:12, in which He states:

Or if he [a son] shall ask [of his father] an egg, will he offer him a scorpion? (Luke 11:12)

Today, largely due to the prevalence of heart disease in the West, eggs have been subjects of harsh criticism. The reason for this is that chicken eggs each contain more than five grams of fat and 250 milligrams of cholesterol.[27] Since Westerners already tend to have too much saturated fat in their diet, it makes sense that such a concentrated source of fat and cholesterol should be avoided. However, numerous studies measuring the effects of egg consumption on fat in the blood indicate that perhaps eggs should not be judged so harshly.

For example, Ginsberg found that women fed up to three eggs per day for eight weeks showed only mild changes in their cholesterol levels.[28] Others found that eating two boiled eggs per day for six weeks caused total cholesterol to rise only 4 percent and HDL (the good cholesterol) to rise 10 percent, actually *improving* cardiovascular risk.[29]

Vorster studied seventy young men for several weeks. He had them eat three eggs per week for two months, then had half the group increase their egg intake to either seven or fourteen eggs per week for five months. There was no significant change seen in the lipid levels of the young men who ate seven to fourteen eggs per week as compared to the controls, who continued to eat only three. Vorster recommended that lowering coronary heart disease risk should concentrate on lowering *fat,* not cholesterol.[30]

Indeed, it appears that eggs, while containing significant amounts of fat and cholesterol, apparently also contain other factors, such as lecithin, that may help process the fat and cholesterol so that they do not end up causing harm. Eggs are an outstanding source of high quality proteins and certain vitamins. In addition, eggs appear to stabilize blood sugar through slowing down stomach emptying and flattening the body's insulin response.[31] This can be very helpful particularly to individuals who suffer from either diabetes or hypoglycemia.

Scripture does indicate that eggs are food given to us by our Creator. Perhaps, however, while not completely avoiding them for their fat and cholesterol content, we should consider eating them in moderation. We have noted the adulteration of much of our meat sources, and we may expect the same kinds of practices with regard to chicken farming to yield changes that may be detrimental in our eggs. The data available to confirm this is only indirect, but it stands to reason that free ranging chickens that are not injected with steroids and other growth-enhancing drugs would tend to have lower levels of fat. Indeed, modifying the feeding of chickens is now being studied as a means of providing heart-healthy dietary factors through this popular staple food.

For example, laying hens fed with fish oil produced eggs that were enriched significantly with the beneficial omega-3 fatty acids. This was repeated in hens that were fed flaxseed.[32]

When these eggs were fed to twenty-eight male volunteers at a rate of four eggs per day for two weeks, no changes were noted in their cholesterol, but their blood levels of the beneficial omega-3 fatty acids, EPA and DHEA, rose substantially.[33] Furthermore, volunteers were unable to distinguish any taste between the eggs of hens fed fish oil and those given standard feed.[34]

In another attempt to improve the health of chickens and their eggs, beneficial friendly bacteria—lactobacillus acidophilus—were fed to laying hens for forty-eight weeks. Egg production increased nearly 10 percent, and egg cholesterol levels dropped nearly 20 percent. This was confirmed in other separate studies.[35]

One caution about eggs: They tend to be one of the more common causes of food allergy. In addition, as is true for other foods, nursing mothers who eat eggs can trigger allergy symptoms in susceptible breast-fed babies. For example, egg and pork from a mother's diet caused allergy symptoms of regurgitation, diarrhea, feeding difficulty, and malaise in one-month-old breast-fed males.[36]

CONCLUSION

In conclusion, consider the following suggestions with regard to meat and egg intake. Again, these are made not because certain meats or fat are forbidden any longer. Instead, they are based upon the wisdom that wrote the Laws of Nature into being and revealed them in the Old Testament dietary commandments.

- Eat only clean meats.
- Eat fish liberally, at least once a week.
- Eat meat as it occurs in nature, as God designed it, low in fat and without the use of man-made hormones, antibiotics, and commercial feeding procedures.
- When eating poultry, remove and discard the skin with the fat layer lying underneath.
- Limit red meat intake to special occasions, no more than once a week. Choose free-ranging or wild poultry over red meat.
- It would seem that a modest intake of eggs is appropriate—particularly those from free ranging hens and perhaps even supplemented with acidophilus and sources for omega-3 oils, such as flaxseed or fish oil. For those with coronary artery disease, keeping egg intake to a maximum of three per week may not be necessary. If you are such an individual and desire to maintain eggs in your diet, you may want to consider discussing a trial with your physician. You could have your blood lipid levels checked, then ingest the desired amount of eggs for a few weeks and retest to see if the eggs have had a significant impact.

DON'T CHEW
THE FAT

Numerous preachers have said that if God says something once, we should certainly listen. If He says it twice, it is unusually important. But if He says something repeatedly, what He is saying has highly significant bearing on our lives. Such a case is God's telling His people not to eat fat. He first stated this clearly through Moses:

It shall be a perpetual statute for your generations throughout all your dwellings, that ye eat neither fat nor blood. (Leviticus 3:17)

Moreover, in instructions concerning a variety of animal sacrifices, God repeatedly commanded that the fat covering the internal organs be burned along with the sacrifice. "All the fat is the Lord's" (Leviticus 3:16).

But there is significant evidence that this principle—that the fat was not for man but belonged to God—goes back to the beginning of time. In Genesis 4:4, we read that Abel brought an acceptable sacrifice (see also Hebrews 11:4). In that sacrifice, he *burned the fat* unto the Lord. This is exactly the procedure described more than two thousand years later in the Mosaic Law. Therefore it seems reasonable to assume that the guidelines for an acceptable sacrifice were known by mankind since the very beginning. Then, remember that Noah clearly understood the distinction between "clean" and "unclean" meats even before the Flood and hundreds of years before the giving of the Law. Since this is the case, man may have understood the prohibition concerning fat since *before* flesh was given to him for food.

The fat that was not to be eaten can easily be seen upon examination of an animal. It is the fat that appears as layers between the skin and muscle tissue and that envelops the internal organs. Why would God want to keep His people from eating the fat of clean animals? Was it because He wanted to deprive them of something that tasted good?

To the contrary, we now know that this "cover fat" is a repository for parasites, viruses, and other toxins. Therefore, eating this fat would unnecessarily expose the individual to damaging substances and potentially infectious disease. Furthermore, we also know that this type of fat is pure long-chain saturated fat, which is strongly linked to a number of serious diseases, including coronary heart disease and cancer. God's commandment prohibiting the eating of animal fat was His loving protection for His people and was at least one major reason for His declaring that those who ate it would be "cut off."

> *For whosoever eateth the fat of the beast, of which men offer an offering made by fire unto the Lord, even the soul that eateth it shall be cut off from his people.* (Leviticus 7:25)

On one occasion in Scripture this dietary commandment was not followed. As commanded by God, the priests would receive the offerings of the people. Then, after having burned unto the Lord the cover fat along with the internal organs, the priests would take of the designated and acceptable portions for their food. However, the sons of Eli did not follow God's specific commandment. Despite the fact that Eli was the high priest, his sons Hophni and Phinehas "did not know the Lord." They refused to burn the fat and even threatened to use force against any who would object.

> *Wherefore the sin of the young men was very great before the Lord: for men abhorred the offering of the Lord.* (1 Samuel 2:17)

God eventually confronted Eli with the sin of his household, accusing them of making themselves "fat with the chiefest of all the offerings of Israel" (v. 28). And indeed that is literally what they did. In Eli's later years, he became blind and obese. One day he heard the news that the ark of God was captured by the Philistines, and he fell backward from his seat, breaking his neck, "for he was an old man, and heavy" (1 Samuel 4:18).

ALL FATS ARE NOT CREATED EQUAL

In order to appreciate the significance and wisdom of God's commandment, we need a basic understanding of the chemistry of fats. This section will get a little technical, but hang in there, because once this is grasped, the pieces of the puzzle with regard to fats, their different types, and cholesterol will all fall into place for you.

Fats are referred to in biochemistry as lipids. They include not only *fats* (which are solid at room temperature) but also *oils* (which are liquid at room temperature). For years, many in the health care professions have told their patients that "fat is fat" and have warned them not to eat it, no matter what kind it is. "All fats are the same, and all of them are bad," they have claimed. A beef producer's brochure states, "Whether you eat it in chicken, fish, cooking oil, butter, milk or other products, *all fat calories are the same.*"[1]

But according to the Word, *all fats are not equal.* In fact, looking at Scripture, we find that there are five different kinds of fats:

- Fats that occur naturally in plant food, such as olives. These are always oils and are referred to in Scripture in a multitude of passages. This oil could be eaten freely.

- Butter. This was made from the butterfat of cattle, sheep, or goats. It was also eaten freely.

- Fish oils. This form of fat occurs naturally in fish and was allowed.

- Poultry fat. The poultry of biblical times was free ranging or wild, and it was lean. Fat that occurred naturally in such animals was permitted.

- Fat from domesticated red-meat animals (cow, sheep, and goat) was forbidden. God did not forbid eating the fat of venison, probably because deer were not domesticated and, therefore, were lean.

Speak unto the children of Israel, saying, Ye shall eat no manner of fat, of ox, or of sheep, or of goat. (Leviticus 7:23)

God forbade eating the hard cover fat of only these. He did not forbid the fat found in butter, fish, or poultry, or fat that occurred naturally in foods such as nuts and olives. The reason is that the original Ph.D. of Biochemistry understood the difference between these five sources of fat. But instead of explaining it to His people (who would have had no idea what He was talking about three thousand years ago), He simply commanded them to stay away from those foods that would be high in the damaging, long-chain saturated fatty acids. Man would eventually understand why, but until he did, he would need to take God at His word.

Today, we still need to take Him at His word. But now we are able to understand at least part of what the Creator has known all along: different fatty acids make up these five kinds of fats.

Fatty acids are the building blocks for all lipids. As you probably know, they are classified as either saturated, monounsaturated, or polyunsaturated. To understand the difference, we need to look at the chemical structure of a fatty acid.

All fatty acids are made up of only three elements: carbon, hydrogen, and oxygen. The carbons are linked in a chain to one another. The hydrogen attaches itself to the carbon atoms at the available locations. You may recall from a general chemistry class that carbon is assigned the number 6 in the periodic table of the elements. Carbon does not want to exist by itself. It needs to form four bonds with other elements in order to be stable (this is very important). A simple fatty acid is shown below.

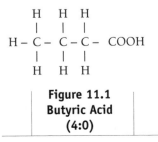

Figure 11.1
Butyric Acid
(4:0)

This is butyric acid, the predominant fatty acid found in butter. Notice that each carbon atom has four bonds. If it is a carbon in the middle of the chain, two of the bonds are with other carbon atoms, and two are with hydrogen. If it is on the end of the chain, it will be attached to only one carbon atom, leaving three positions available for hydrogen. (All fatty acids have a *carboxylic acid* end, which is represented by the COOH on the right. For simplicity's sake, we will ignore the acid end during this discussion.)

Now, let's look at another fatty acid. Stearic acid is commonly found in red meat.

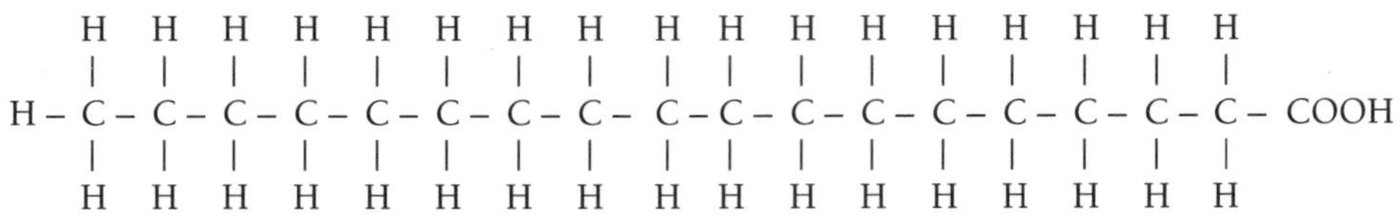

```
      H   H   H   H   H   H   H   H   H   H   H   H   H   H   H   H   H
      |   |   |   |   |   |   |   |   |   |   |   |   |   |   |   |   |
  H – C – C – C – C – C – C – C – C – C – C – C – C – C – C – C – C – C – COOH
      |   |   |   |   |   |   |   |   |   |   |   |   |   |   |   |   |
      H   H   H   H   H   H   H   H   H   H   H   H   H   H   H   H
```

Figure 11.2
Stearic Acid
(18:0)

Notice that it has eighteen carbons, making it much longer than the four-carbon butyric acid. The longer the chain of fat, the "harder" it is and the higher the temperature it takes to melt it. Consider the difference between butter, which is quite soft at room temperature, and the gristle of a fatty steak, which is hard and rubbery. The gristle from meat is very high in longer-chain fatty acids, such as stearic.

Both butyric acid and stearic acid are referred to as *saturated* fats. This leads us to Fat Principle #1.

Fat Principle #1: The Longer the Chain, the Harder the Fat

Furthermore, the longer the chain, the harder it is to melt and the harder for the body to digest and use. All fats are *not* created equal. Butter, despite the fact that it is a saturated fat, is *not* harmful to your health. To my knowledge, no published study has ever implicated butter as a direct health hazard. On the other hand, long-chain saturated fatty acids have been clearly identified as having detrimental effects on our health, including links with:

- Cancer of the colon, breast, and prostate
- Coronary heart disease
- Elevation of blood cholesterol
- Stroke
- Obesity
- Diabetes mellitus
- Gallstones

God did not discourage the use of butter, which is short-chain saturated fat, but He did forbid His people to eat foods high in the disease-causing long-chain saturated fats.

Now, what do we mean by "saturated"? Remember that carbon needs to form four bonds in order to be stable. In some fatty acids, carbon forms *two* bonds with a carbon next to it in the chain: this is called a *double bond.* Fatty acids that have no double bonds are called "saturated" because the fatty acid is *saturated* with hydrogen—all possible carbon bonds are dedicated to a hydrogen. Those that have any carbon-to-carbon double bonds are called *unsaturated.*

Unsaturated fatty acids are further classified by how *many* carbon-carbon double bonds they have. If they have only one, they are referred to as *monounsaturated* fatty acids; if they have two or more, they are called *polyunsaturated.* Let's look first at the most common monounsaturated fatty acid, oleic acid.

```
    H   H   H   H   H   H   H   H           H   H   H   H   H   H   H
    |   |   |   |   |   |   |   |           |   |   |   |   |   |   |
H - C - C - C - C - C - C - C - C - C = C - C - C - C - C - C - C - C - COOH
    |   |   |   |   |   |   |   |   |   |   |   |   |   |   |   |   |
    H   H   H   H   H   H   H   H   H   H   H   H   H   H   H   H
```

Figure 11.3
Oleic Acid
(18:1n–9)

Oleic acid has eighteen carbons and one double bond. It is commonly found in olive oil. Notice that, because there is a double bond between two carbons, each has one less bond to make with a hydrogen. Therefore, the fatty acid is *mono* (that is, one-time) unsaturated. Double bonds make a fatty acid "softer" and more likely to behave like an oil rather than as fat, which is solid at room temperature. This effect is so significant that even an eighteen-carbon fatty acid such as oleic is more liquid at room temperature than the much shorter, albeit saturated, four-carbon butyric acid of butter. This leads us to Fat Principle #2.

Fat Principle #2: Even Long-Chain Fats Are Liquid If They Are Unsaturated

This principle takes precedence over Principle #1.

Now let's look at a couple more fatty acids. These are *poly*unsaturated fatty acids because they have *many* (two or more) double bonds. The first is linoleic acid.

```
    H   H   H   H   H               H           H   H   H   H   H   H   H
    |   |   |   |   |               |           |   |   |   |   |   |   |
H - C - C - C - C - C - C = C - C - C = C - C - C - C - C - C - C - C - COOH
    |   |   |   |   |   |   |   |   |   |   |   |   |   |   |   |   |
    H   H   H   H   H   H   H   H   H   H   H   H   H   H   H   H
```

Figure 11.4
Linoleic Acid
(18:2n–6)

Because the first double bond occurs at the sixth carbon, it is also referred to as an *omega-6* fatty acid. The best sources of omega-6 oils are the seed oils of safflower, sunflower, evening primrose, borage, and black currant seed.

Next, we see that linolenic acid has three double bonds, the first occurring at the third carbon, therefore making it an *omega-3* fatty acid.

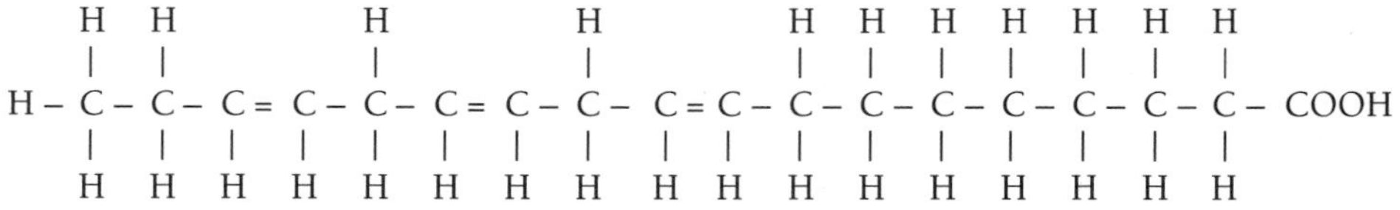

```
      H   H           H           H           H   H   H   H   H   H   H
      |   |           |           |           |   |   |   |   |   |   |
H  –  C – C = C – C – C = C – C – C = C – C – C – C – C – C – C – C  – COOH
      |   |   |   |   |   |   |   |   |   |   |   |   |   |   |   |   |
      H   H   H   H   H   H   H   H   H   H   H   H   H   H   H   H
```

Figure 11.5
Linolenic Acid
(18:3n–3)

The richest sources of omega-3 fatty acids in nature are flaxseed, cold-water fish, and canola (rapeseed) oil.

In contrast to long-chain saturated fatty acids, the mono- and polyunsaturated fatty acids have been associated with protection from disease. A number of studies have shown that fish oils, which are related to the omega-3 oils (linolenic acid), have multiple beneficial effects, including:

- prevention of heart dysrhythmias, especially ventricular fibrillation (the cause of death in approximately one-third of those who die from heart disease)
- opposition of clotting, reducing the risk of heart attack
- slowing down the growth of plaque in the arteries
- promotion of the manufacture of natural nitroglycerin to keep the heart vessels open
- lowering of plasma triglyceride fat levels
- slowing down the production of "bad" cholesterol
- lowering blood pressure
- protection against colon cancer

DAMAGED GOODS: TRANS FATTY ACIDS

Do you like butter but avoid it because you have heard that it is bad for you? Chances are you do. What do you use instead? You probably use margarine. Some restaurants, trying to be "heart health conscious," don't serve butter any longer, completely replacing it with its "healthy alternative," margarine.

Butter has been given a bad name. Particularly since the famous Framingham Heart Study, which showed a direct link between coronary heart disease and blood cholesterol levels, butter has been condemned as unhealthy. In its place, vegetable-oil-based margarine has been offered as a "healthy alternative."

Several months ago, a front-page article reported a new scientific study that finally "proved" that spanking was harmful to children. After taking a brief glance at it, I filed the article in the trash. Why? Because I had read other studies that proved spanking was good for children? No. I knew that this particular study's conclusion was false because it conflicted with the revealed Word of our Creator.

Likewise, when I was going through residency, routine newborn circumcisions were being condemned by the American Pediatric Association (APA) and other groups as "medically unnecessary" and potentially harmful to the emotional state of the baby. Did I discourage parents from having their boys circumcised? No. Why? Because God doesn't appear to believe that circumcisions are emotionally damaging to newborn boys, since He is the one who required the procedure of Abraham and his offspring.

And sure enough, after a number of years of fewer circumcisions, there was noted a substantial rise in infections seeded by bacteria under the foreskin (including sepsis, a life-threatening blood-borne infection) and penile cancer. And so the medical profession reversed its position and decided that circumcision was not so bad after all. (As of this writing, I understand that the APA is waffling again on the procedure.)

You may not have a medical background or the training to review scientific research. But you do have the Word, and you now have understanding of solid dietary principles. So let's think about butter from the perspective of the Word's "corrective lenses."

The first mention of butter in the Bible is that Abraham gave it to the angels who visited him.

> *And he took butter, and milk, and the calf which he had dressed, and set it before them; and he stood by them under the tree, and they did eat.* (Genesis 18:8)

Obviously, if Abraham fed butter to his special guests, it was something that he ate himself. In addition, several other Bible references refer to butter as a part of the diet of God's people (e.g., Judges 5:25; Proverbs 30:33). Isaiah prophesied that even the Messiah would eat butter.

> *Therefore the Lord himself shall give you a sign; Behold, a virgin shall conceive, and bear a son, and shall call his name Immanuel. Butter and honey shall he eat, that he may know to refuse the evil, and choose the good.* (Isaiah 7:14–15)

Did God give butter to man for food? Yes. Is the butter that we have today reasonably similar to the butter He gave to us originally? Again, I believe the answer is yes. Are we eating more butter than we need? Probably, though that is most likely related to the fact that we just eat too many calories. There are eleven grams of fat in one tablespoon of butter. But the problem is really not in butter itself, and substituting margarine is not the answer.

Prior to 1920, despite the fact that the typical American diet was quite rich in cholesterol and animal fat, including butter, death from heart attack was so rare that it had no name or medical recognition. Later in the 1920s, after the introduction of refined vegetable oils and margarine, coronary heart disease began to appear. Is this coincidental? I think not.[2]

Margarine is made from vegetable oils: usually safflower, sunflower, or corn oil. Obviously, we can't just take these oils and spread them on our bread, because the oils are in a liquid state. The reason they are liquid is that they are all high in polyunsaturated fatty acids, particularly linoleic acid (omega-6). On the other hand, butter, as you will recall, is all saturated fat. Therefore, in order to "harden" a vegetable oil to make it more like butter, it must be made more saturated with hydrogen. This process is referred to as *hydrogenation*.

Once again, here is a diagram of linoleic acid. Recall that it has two double bonds.

```
      H   H   H   H   H           H           H   H   H   H   H   H   H
      |   |   |   |   |           |           |   |   |   |   |   |   |
  H – C – C – C – C – C = C – C – C – C = C – C – C – C – C – C – C – C – COOH
      |   |   |   |   |   |   |   |   |   |   |   |   |   |   |   |   |
      H   H   H   H   H   H   H   H   H   H   H   H   H   H   H   H   H
```

Figure 11.6
Linolenic Acid
(18:2n–6)

To add hydrogen to linoleic acid, the oil is subjected to extremely high temperature and pressure in the presence of hydrogen. This breaks some of the double bonds and causes hydrogen to be added to the created vacancies around the carbon atoms.[3] Thus we end up with a fatty acid that looks like this:

```
      H   H   H   H   H   H   H   H   H   H   H   H   H   H   H
      |   |   |   |   |   |   |   |   |   |   |   |   |   |   |
  H – C – C – C – C – C – C – C – C – C = C – C – C – C – C – C – C – COOH
      |   |   |   |   |   |   |   |   |   |   |   |   |   |   |
      H   H   H   H   H   H   H   H   H   H   H   H   H   H   H
```

Figure 11.7
Trans-oleic acid

Source: Udo Erasmus, Fats and Oils (Burnaby, B.C.: *Alive Books*, 1986).

It looks quite like oleic acid. And we know that oleic acid is good for us, so this must be OK. Actually, it's not OK.

Take a closer look at figure 11.7. Now, compare this to the oleic acid in figure 11.3. Do you see any difference? Look at the hydrogens around the carbon- carbon double bond. You will notice that the hydrogen atoms in oleic acid are on the *same* side of the double bond. This is known as the *cis* ("same side") configuration. In the hydrogenated, man-made oleic acid, the hydrogens are on *opposite* sides of the double bond, making it a *trans* ("across") fatty acid.

What is the significance of this? When God designed fatty acids, He made only *cis* fatty acids. *Trans* fatty acids are not found in nature to any significant extent. The human body is not designed to utilize them.

This is very serious, because *cis* fatty acids are critical to our health. Among other functions, they are part of the wall of every cell in the human body. *Trans* fatty acids are bent the wrong way; they don't "fit" in correctly to where their *cis* counterparts are designed to be. Thus, *trans* fatty acids pose a significant health threat to us. For example, increased levels of *trans* fatty acids have been found in the fat stores of women with breast cancer.[4] In laboratory rats, margarine was found to enhance the growth of breast tumors, whereas butter did not.[5]

Note: *Anything* with hydrogenated or partially hydrogenated oils will contain *trans* fatty acids.

When it comes to heart disease, research now shows that *trans* fatty acids behave quite like saturated fats. They raise LDL (the "bad" cholesterol) and lower HDL (the "good" cholesterol).[6] In light of such changes, one study of males predicted a 27 percent increase in risk of heart attack by those consuming *trans* fatty acids.[7] And indeed, a Boston study involving 621 patients found that the risk of a first myocardial infarction was directly proportional to the intake of *trans* fatty acids and margarine.[8]

In another study, Italian women who had a medium to high intake of margarine had a 50 percent increase in risk of heart attack.[9] And, in the famous Nurse's Health Study, which involved more than 85,000 women, the "intake of *trans* fatty acids was directly related" to the risk of coronary heart disease. This correlation was also noted between each major food source for *trans* fatty acids, including margarine, biscuits, cake, and white bread.[10]

Isn't it ironic that the public is being told that butter substitutes such as margarine ought to be eaten in order to reduce one's cholesterol and risk of heart disease? The opposite is true. The bottom line is this: God knows, and He has told us butter is OK.

COOKING WITH FATS

Earlier, I sang the praises of the polyunsaturated fatty acids (PUFAs) for their ability to protect us from heart disease, cancer, and several other diseases. But there is one thing that PUFAs are *not* good for, and that is cooking.

Due to their love for oxygen and electrons, polyunsaturated fatty acids are extremely unstable and need to be protected. That is why the Creator carefully packaged them inside seeds. Their multiple double bonds make them extremely vulnerable to oxidation, the process by which foods become rancid. Cooking, especially frying, exposes these PUFA-rich oils not only to oxygen but also to light and intense heat.

Recall the hydrogenation process and the damage that it does to these oils. Similarly, when you put these omega-3- or omega-6-rich vegetable oils into the frypan and heat them, you are also damaging them considerably. For example, vegetable oils rich in PUFAs, when heated in a wok, produce a variety of toxic substances, including benzene, acrolein, and formaldehyde.[11] That is why deep-fat frying in vegetable oils is absolutely abominable from a nutrition perspective. Donuts, French fries, chicken fingers—mention these, and nutritionists in the know start covering their ears and gasping for air.

Figure 11.8 shows graphically the fatty acid content of various fats. From bottom to top are increasing levels of PUFAs. Therefore, cooking fats are listed in approximate order of preference from the top down. Those at the top are lowest in PUFAs and thus are most stable in heat.

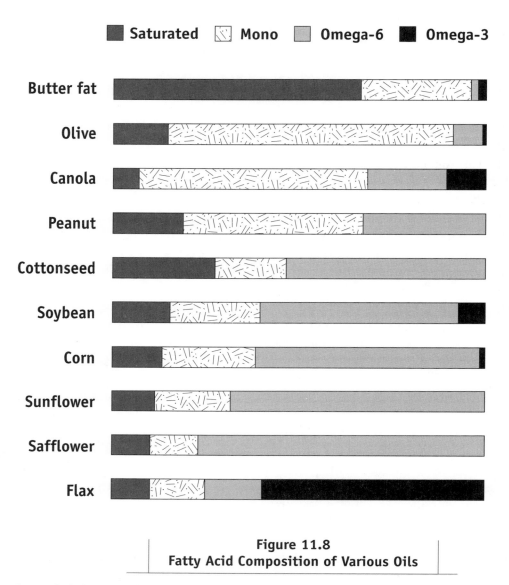

Figure 11.8
Fatty Acid Composition of Various Oils

Source: J. B. Reeves and J. L. Weihrauch, *Composition of Foods, Agriculture Handbook* No. 8–4 (Washington, D.C.: United States Department of Agriculture, 1979)

Don't damage sensitive PUFA-rich vegetable oils by using them in cooking. Instead, use butter or olive oil. These, because of their greater saturation, are much more stable in heat. In the Middle East, olive oil commonly takes the place of butter and is largely used in cooking meals. Canola oil is the third choice for cooking, although it is not as appealing because of its increased amounts of PUFAs and because it is difficult to find canola oil that is not refined.

The process of refining vegetable oils, which is generally done to make them crystal clear and free of any strong taste, subjects them to intense heat and chemical processes that *seriously* damage them. Vegetable oils, once removed from their natural food source, should be stored in a cool environment such as a refrigerator and in a dark bottle that is impenetrable to light. This is exactly opposite to how you will find most brands on the grocery store shelves. (An outstanding review of fats and oils is *Fats That Kill, Fats That Heal,* by Udo Erasmus.)

THE CHOLESTEROL CONTROVERSY

Numerous studies have linked cholesterol levels in the blood with coronary heart disease. One can reduce the risk of coronary artery disease approximately 1 percent for every point that cholesterol is reduced. Reducing cholesterol levels improves blood flow through coronary arteries that contain plaque. Also, reducing cholesterol tends to keep the artery from going into spasm and stabilizes the plaque, making it less likely to rupture.[12]

Therefore, strong and consistent recommendations have been forthcoming from the medical community, warning patients about the dangers of cholesterol. The food industry has chimed in, advertising foods as being "low in cholesterol." As a result, many individuals have worked diligently to greatly reduce their dietary cholesterol intake.

The problem is that just reducing the cholesterol in food tends not to have much effect on the levels of cholesterol in the blood. This is because most of the cholesterol in blood is manufactured in the liver. It is not made from food cholesterol but from long-chain saturated animal fat.[13]

Therefore, if there is too much long-chain saturated animal fat in the diet, cholesterol levels will naturally go up. These are the same fats that God commanded to be trimmed away prior to eating the flesh of "clean" land animals. Once again, we see the benefits of following our Creator's wisdom by avoiding the hard fat in animals. Therefore, don't worry about the cholesterol controversy. Instead, eliminate the intake of long-chain saturated fat, that is, animal fat. In doing so, you will be following the guidelines given in the Word.[14]

CONCLUSION

Here are some strategies to follow with regard to fats:

- Make plant food the foundation of your diet. Their naturally occurring oils are perfectly acceptable, even desirable, for optimum health. Adding whole or freshly ground flaxseed to your food whenever possible will provide a rich source of the priceless omega-3 oils.
- Eat fish liberally, again for their valuable omega-3 oils. The best fish are those that are "clean" and fresh caught or fresh frozen at sea.
- Eat only clean red meat that is low in fat and in moderation.
- Abstain from hydrogenated or refined oils.
- Have salad dressing "on the side," then dip your fork into it before each bite. You will get the full taste of the dressing but dramatically reduce your intake of it. Better yet, use olive oil and fresh lemon juice for salad dressing.

COOKING

- If a recipe calls for fat, you can often substitute applesauce or pureed fruit. Or use olive oil.
- If you must use a fat source, use olive oil or butter. Canola is third choice.
- Eat no deep-fried foods.

THE BIBLICAL
DIET PYRAMID

The ordinary food of the average Hebrew of Bible times was bread, olives, oil, buttermilk and cheese from their flock; fruits and vegetables from their orchards and gardens; and meat on rare occasions.[1]

Throughout the last six chapters we have established the scriptural and scientific basis for a dietary plan. Here are the conclusions that we have arrived at so far:

- Drink plenty of pure water—six to ten glasses per day.
- Make plant food the foundation of your diet.
- Eat food that is minimally processed, seasonally fresh, and locally grown.
- Eat only fresh-milled whole grains. Consume them liberally.
- Consume vegetables and fresh fruit liberally.
- Legumes (beans and peas) and nuts are high sources of natural protein. Eat at least one serving each day.
- Use olive oil as the principal fat as much as possible. Butter is also acceptable; margarine is not.
- Milk is best taken in the form of cultured products such as yogurt and cheese. Consume daily in moderation.
- Eat fish a minimum of once or twice per week. Poultry slightly more.
- Eat eggs in moderation (limit four per week if necessary).

- Limit sweets containing refined sugars or honey to just a few per week. Instead, eat fresh raw fruit as desserts or snacks.

- Reserve red meat for special occasions and guests. The goal is less than once weekly.

By following a diet based on the Word, you would naturally hope to reduce your risk of disease, especially those that are the greatest threats—heart disease and cancer. Indeed, the evidence is very strong in your favor. Some outstanding research has proven that this dietary plan drastically cuts the risk of these "diseases of the Egyptians."

PIVOTAL RESEARCH
THE SEVEN COUNTRIES STUDY AND LYON HEART DIET STUDY

It is common to hear people say that heart disease "runs in their family." As a result, they believe they are at high risk for the same. To a certain degree that is true, but it is a huge mistake to blame heart disease on genetic inheritance.

You will recall an earlier chapter in which I mentioned that prior to 1920, myocardial infarction (heart attack) was so rare that it did not have a name or recognition in the medical literature. Today, coronary heart disease (CHD) is the number one cause of death in most industrialized nations. In the United States alone, one out of every two Americans will die of heart disease. How can genetics account for this, since just three or four generations ago, *hardly anyone* had heart disease? There must be another cause, and naturally, people want to know what it is.

In order to find the answer, a study was conducted in the 1950s and 1960s in which death rates were followed in selected people-groups of seven different countries. Published in 1970 and now known as the Seven Countries Study, this landmark effort opened the eyes of the Western medical community to the powerful connection between diet, lifestyle, and heart disease. It also confirmed the extraordinary benefits of following a diet consistent with the Word. In this study, in which several thousand individuals were followed for five to fifteen years, the country with the highest death rate due to heart disease was the USA, while the lowest mortality rate was found in Crete. A partial listing of the countries is given in table 12.1.

Although there was only a modest difference in the average blood cholesterol level, the mortality rates of those in the USA and those in Crete were drastically different. Out of the US group, 1,153 subjects died during the period of observation. During the same time, there were only 514 deaths in the Crete group. But even more astounding, 574 Americans died of *heart disease* during that time frame while only 9 Cretans died of that cause. What could account for this 98 percent difference in deaths due to heart disease? Obviously, whatever the Cretans were doing was working.

First of all, the Cretan lifestyle was one of significant activity. There were not many desk jobs—most were farmers. Mealtimes were a pleasant, relaxed time to gather family and friends. Lunches were followed by an afternoon nap, which would tend to optimize digestion. Certainly, exercise and a more restful lifestyle when away from work were important components of the Cretan way of life. However, as we will see in the Lyon Study, the most important factor was probably diet.

TABLE 12.1 SEVEN COUNTRIES STUDY: CHOLESTEROL LEVELS & MORTALITY RATES

After 5–15 yr	Crete	Mediterranean	Netherlands	USA
Cholesterol	5.3	5.0	6.0	6.1
Deaths				
Total	514	1090	1091	1153
Coronary Heart Disease	9	184	420	574

TABLE 12.2 SEVEN COUNTRIES STUDY: DIET COMPARISONS
(1 ounce = 28.35 grams)

Grams/day	Crete	Mediterranean	Netherlands	USA
Alcohol	15	45	3	6
Edible fat	95	60	79	33
Fish	18	34	12	3
Meat	35	40	138	**273**
Bread	**380**	416	252	97
Fruit	**464**	130	82	233
Legume	**30**	18	2	1

Compared to the USA (see table 12.2), Cretans ate three times as much edible fat (olive oil), six times as much fish, four times as much bread, twice as much fruit, and thirty times the amount of legumes (peas and beans). Since the climate allows for planting several times a year, every main meal was furnished with an abundance of leafy green vegetables.

Conversely, Americans ate eight times as much meat as the Cretans.[2] Dr. Ancel Keys, who supervised this impressive study, noted that heart disease was almost totally absent from the Cretans in the 1950s, except for a small class of rich people who ate meat every day instead of every week or two.[3]

Once researchers understood what the Cretans ate, the big question was whether or not patients in Western countries would experience similar results if the Crete diet were adopted. Second, would it prove to be more effective than the standard "prudent" heart diet, similar to what was recommended by the American Heart Association? Finally, and perhaps most important, would Westerners be *willing* to follow such a dietary program?

In the early 1990s, a study was implemented in Lyon, France, to answer these questions.[4] In this study, 605 patients who had just had a heart attack were randomly divided into two groups. Those in the first group (controls) were placed on a standard, "prudent" low-fat diet that was designed to substantially reduce their risk of having another heart attack. Those in the other group (experimental) were placed on a diet based upon what Cretans ate during the 1960s while the Seven Countries Study was being conducted. (Many Cretans have since made a shift toward a more Western diet, despite its ominous consequences.)

In the Lyon Diet Heart Study, the Cretan diet was implemented in the experimental group through six dietary "commandments":

- More bread
- More vegetables and legumes
- More fish
- Less meat (especially beef, lamb, pork), replaced with poultry
- No day without fruit
- No butter and cream

Cretans in 1960 used very little butter and virtually no margarine. Instead, they used *liberal* amounts of olive oil. However, many Westerners are unaccustomed to the strong taste that olive oil adds to many foods and therefore avoid its use. Because of this, the Lyon study utilized a special erucic acid-free canola oil margarine that was high in omega-3 linolenic acid and low in *trans* fatty acids. That is, it specifically tried to eliminate the concerns we addressed in chapter 11.

Researchers followed the two groups for up to four years, averaging twenty-seven months each. In examining what the people actually ate, it was noted that the "prudent" heart diet group consumed similar amounts of fish as the experimental group ("Crete diet") but 63 percent more meat and deli products. Thus, the control group, despite being on a supposedly heart-healthy diet, had much higher intakes of long-chain saturated fats. Furthermore, the Crete diet group ate much greater amounts of olive oil and the omega-3 fatty acids.

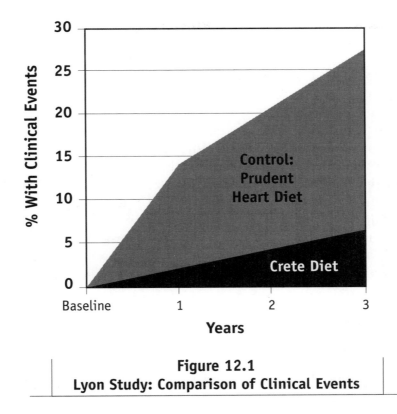

Figure 12.1
Lyon Study: Comparison of Clinical Events

In looking at the clinical events (another heart attack, stroke, sudden cardiac death, major blood clot), a substantial difference between the two groups was noted. This difference could already be seen by the second month of the study. By the end of the first year, only 2 percent of the experimental group had died or had another heart attack or stroke, compared to 14 percent of the control group. By two years, the experimental group was at only 4 percent, while the control group had risen to 19 percent. By three years, 27 percent (that is more than one in four) of the control group had had another serious cardiovascular event, compared to less than 6 percent of the experimental group.

The researchers concluded that the Southern Mediterranean diet, particularly rich in fruits, vegetables, grains, legumes, olive oil, and omega-3 oils, was markedly better than the standard low-fat prudent heart diet. The findings were so dramatic that the study was terminated early because of the need to inform the control group of the drastic advantages of the experimental program.

Two years later, the researchers went back to follow up these same patients in order to determine if the protective effects of the diet had been maintained. They confirmed that those patients following the Southern Mediterranean (Crete) diet continued to enjoy 68 percent less rates of recurrent heart attack and/or death due to heart disease.[5] Also, a second look at the data revealed that the experimental group patients had the benefit of a 56 percent lower risk of cancer as well.[6]

THE BIBLICAL DIET PYRAMID

Throughout this book, I have purposely focused on principles and tried to avoid unnecessary detail. However, it is time now to get down to specifics, so that you can know how to apply these principles to your life.

In 1992, the United States Department of Agriculture published the food pyramid as a guide to American dietary choices. This pyramid gave a visual image of the relative quantities one should consume from various food groups. Two years later, using information from the Seven Countries Study and other research, Oldways Preservation and Exchange Trust published the Mediterranean diet pyramid. This latter pyramid most closely represents a dietary lifestyle found from a study of the Old and New Testaments. I have taken this latter pyramid and modified it to comply with the concepts developed in this book.[7]

As you look at figure 12.2, consider the following important characteristics:

- Pure water, six to ten glasses per day, is a key aspect to proper diet.
- Ideally, food is minimally processed, seasonally fresh, and locally grown.
- Grains should be fresh milled, whole, and consumed liberally.
- Vegetable servings are one-half cup each and, like grains, are of fundamental importance.
- Fresh fruit is the typical daily dessert or snack between meals.
- Legumes (beans and peas) and nuts: At least one serving of these best plant sources for protein should be consumed daily.
- Olive oil is the principle fat. Butter may be used in moderation, particularly when high heat is needed. No margarine or other products made from hydrogenated or damaged oils are allowed whatsoever. This would include any foods fried in vegetable oil (chips, fries, etc). Once again, the only fat used in frying should be butter or olive oil.
- Cultured milk products such as yogurt and cheese are consumed daily. Milk is avoided unless it can be obtained raw from a safe source or as pasteurized skim milk. These should be used conservatively.
- Eggs are consumed in moderation (limit four per week if necessary).
- Fish is eaten a minimum of once or twice per week. Poultry slightly more.
- Sweets containing sugars or honey are limited to a few per week. Remember to avoid candies with hydrogenated oils.
- Red meat for special occasions and guests. Goal: less than once weekly.

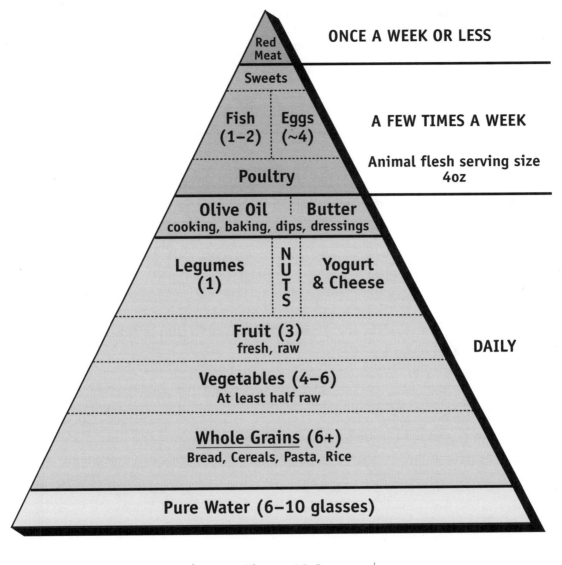

**Figure 12.2
Biblical Diet Pyramid**

MAKING IT WORK

How does this work out in a typical menu? Just follow these basic guidelines:

- Have yogurt or eggs at breakfast. These are outstanding protein sources that will balance out the starch from your breakfast grains.
- Have a large raw salad at lunch. This will provide at least your desired minimum of two servings of raw vegetables for the day. Use olive oil for dressing.

- Eat at least two more servings of vegetables at the evening meal. This will complete your minimum requirement of vegetables for the day—a top priority.
- Obtain your serving of legumes (beans or peas) at lunch or dinner.
- Eat fresh fruit for dessert and/or snacks between meals.
- Eat grains with each meal.
- Drink water throughout the day.
- At least one day a week, include a serving of fish with the main meal.

SAMPLE MENU

Here is a sample menu with a few explanatory comments:

On arising

- First thing on arising, drink two glasses of pure water.

Breakfast

- One-half cup of fresh, plain yogurt, flavored with fresh fruit or raisins, honey, etc.
- A bowl of hot whole grain cereal
- A glass of pure water

Midmorning snack

- Fresh fruit (e.g., apple, orange, banana)
- A glass of pure water

Lunch

- A large green salad, including one cup of romaine lettuce, garnished with numerous condiments, including sliced cucumber, grated carrots, pineapple, sunflower seeds, raisins, sprouts, grated cheese, etc.
- Perhaps more protein, such as lean chicken, nuts, or beans, to balance your blood sugar if you choose to include bread, such as a whole grain roll
- A glass of pure water

Afternoon snack

- Fresh raw fruit or nuts
- A glass of pure water

	Monday	Tuesday	Wednesday	Thursday	Friday	Saturday	Sunday
TABLE 12.3 **BDP WEEKLY WORK SHEET**							
Water	1 2 3 4 5 6	1 2 3 4 5 6	1 2 3 4 5 6	1 2 3 4 5 6	1 2 3 4 5 6	1 2 3 4 5 6	1 2 3 4 5 6
Grains	1 2 3 4 5 6	1 2 3 4 5 6	1 2 3 4 5 6	1 2 3 4 5 6	1 2 3 4 5 6	1 2 3 4 5 6	1 2 3 4 5 6
Veggies	1 2 3 4	1 2 3 4	1 2 3 4	1 2 3 4	1 2 3 4	1 2 3 4	1 2 3 4
Fruit	1 2	1 2	1 2	1 2	1 2	1 2	1 2
Legume	1	1	1	1	1	1	1
Yogurt	1	1	1	1	1	1	1
Cheese	1	1	1	1	1	1	1
Nuts	1	1	1	1	1	1	1
Poultry		1		2		3	4
Fish				2			
Eggs		1		2		3	4
Sweets				3			
Red Meat				≤ 1			

Dinner

- At least two vegetable servings—for example, yams and broccoli
- A Greek salad, with romaine lettuce, avocado, tomato, Feta cheese, olives, and olive oil
- Lean poultry or fish, four ounces
- Bread—two servings of whole grain

The weekly work sheet on the previous page is provided to help you in making sure that you achieve your daily minimums of each food group. You may copy it for your own personal use. As you take servings from the various choices, cross out the corresponding number. When all numbers are crossed out, you have met your objectives for that specific food group for the day (or week).

Conclusion

Certainly the most famous pyramids were those of ancient Egypt. Built as burial places for kings, these magnificent structures were also symbols of idolatry and an errant view of immortality. Don't make the same mistake. The Biblical Diet Pyramid is simply a commonly used method of graphically illustrating the dietary principles you have learned. Although I am convinced that, if diligently followed, it will optimize health, don't make it your god. It won't make you immortal any more than the Great Pyramid did King Khufu.

13

WHEN GOOD FOOD ISN'T SO GOOD

Sarah thought she was doing things right, but her body seemed to be telling her differently. Over the last several years, she had come to learn the hazards of eating refined flour. She had spent several hundred dollars on an electric grain mill and a heavy-duty mixer that had the capacity to knead several loaves of dough at a time. She bulk-purchased fifty-pound bags of high-grade wheat berries and began feeding her family nutritious whole grain wheat bread.

But before long it seemed that every time she ate this good whole food she felt tired and bloated and ached in her muscles and joints. Eventually, she inquired as to why and discovered that she was probably allergic to gluten, a common protein found in whole grains.

The purpose of this chapter is to address two situations in which the Biblical Diet Pyramid may not be best for some people.

- Food allergy. Although the food may be a "good" food, such as Sarah's wheat, an individual may be allergic, or sensitive, to the food.

- Blood sugar problems. Like the US Food Pyramid and the Mediterranean Diet Pyramid, the Biblical Diet Pyramid places heavy emphasis on plant food, whole grains, vegetables, and fruits. Except for legumes, all of these foods are high in complex carbohydrates and are somewhat low in protein. For diabetics or hypoglycemics who tend to struggle with controlling their blood sugar, this emphasis on carbohydrates may be poorly tolerated. Such an individual may need to balance his blood sugar with a larger share of foods that are rich in protein: legumes and animal products. Under the Glycemic Index section of this chapter, you will learn just how.

SOLVING THE PUZZLE OF FOOD ALLERGY

The term *food allergy* refers to a condition in which the individual reacts to an ingested food as though it were a toxin. Once the immune system has identified a food as "toxic" (i.e., an allergen), it manufactures antibodies against it. Then, whenever the allergic food is eaten, it reacts with these antibodies, resulting in a variety of possible symptoms.

A great deal of disagreement and confusion has surrounded the topic of food allergies. Some people tend to blame every possible symptom on them. Food allergies have been implicated in chronic fatigue, asthma, hay fever, migraine, chronic abdominal pain or diarrhea, learning disability, and even childhood behavioral disorders, seizures, and schizophrenia.

At the other end of the spectrum are those who would deny the existence of food allergies altogether. It seems that the answer lies somewhere between these two extremes. Perhaps one reason for the conflict has been the fact that there is more than one type of food allergy, and the more common kind is the one that is most difficult to understand and diagnose.[1]

I truly awakened to the problem of food allergy back in 1991, not during medical school or residency but when a patient brought me a book to read written by Dr. Marshall Mandell.[2] Since I had been suffering from severe allergies myself, and since I had been working with this patient and she had been able to resolve some chronic symptoms through the knowledge she had gained, I decided to take her up on her offer. As a result, I not only learned concepts that would eventually be of assistance to other patients, but I also discovered that much of my own hay fever problem was triggered by food sensitivity.

More Than One Type of Food Allergy?

As I continued to study, my understanding of allergy in general gradually changed. I used to think of all allergies as permanent and immediate. If someone was allergic to something, I thought that person would react every time he was exposed to it. But it appears that there are at least two types of food allergies. Sometimes they are referred to by how soon a reaction occurs after food ingestion and are thus divided into those that are immediate and those that are delayed.

The first type of food allergy appears to be frequently related to IgE antibodies. Typically, an individual who has this form of allergy will consistently develop symptoms within minutes of food ingestion. Therefore, some doctors refer to this type of allergy as "immediate" or "fixed." Fixed allergies include the more obvious and classic hives reactions that some people get whenever they come in contact with offending foods, such as shrimp. This kind of allergy seems to be very consistent: even though only a small amount of the allergic food is eaten, the reaction still tends to occur and occur quickly.

The second kind of allergy is much less obvious and has been related by some doctors to IgG antibodies. Symptoms from this allergy may not become manifest for a couple hours or even days following ingestion. It also may be dependent upon other factors, such as whether or not another illness is present, or how much of the food has been eaten, or how frequently it has been present in the diet. In other words, there appears to be a threshold of tolerance here, under which symptoms are often unnoticed. Therefore, even though you may eat a food every day, it is possible that you are allergic to it but see no correlation between food and symptoms.

That was the case with my hay fever. I used to take medication every day for my allergies, but now that I have made some corrections in diet and lifestyle, the hay fever rarely bothers me anymore. However, if I stray from a reasonably prudent diet or fail to get proper rest—and particularly if those factors are combined with exposure to various pollens—I can have a big flare-up of hay fever symptoms. Usually the attack comes after a meal.

COMMON ALLERGY-RELATED FOODS

Generally speaking, the foods that have a reputation for being most commonly implicated as allergenic are animal products (especially milk, eggs, and seafood), grains (especially gluten-containing grains), and nuts. This is not to say that you cannot be allergic to fruits or vegetables. Any food, no matter how healthy it may be for the general population, can be allergenic and therefore "toxic" to a particular individual.

I recall a patient who had been struggling for months to get into her diet a powder made from young barley plants. Since so many of her family and friends were claiming great benefit from the product, she felt that she had to be on it as well. However, every time she ate it, her heart would race and she would get jittery. She called an organization that espoused the product, and they tried to walk her through a desensitization procedure whereby she began with one-eighth teaspoon servings at a time. However, it was to no avail; no matter how small the dose, she still reacted. Her health was finally restored once she eliminated the product from her diet and went through an adrenal rehabilitation program similar to that described later in this book.

TABLE 13.1
FOODS STATUS ACCORDING TO
GLIADIN (GLUTEN) CONTENT

Potentially Toxic	Nontoxic
Amaranth	Arrowroot
Barley	Barley grass
Couscous	Barley malt
Kamut	Buckwheat
Oats	Corn
Quinoa	Millet
Rye	Rice
Soy (variable)	Rice, wild
Spelt	Tapioca
Teff	Taro
Wheat	Wheat grass

TABLE 13.2
GLIADIN CONTENT OF VARIOUS MEDICATIONS

Brand Name	Generic Name	Form	Gliadin
Actifed Plus	acetaminophen, pseudoephedrine HCl, tripolidine HCL	Caplets	+
Advil	Ibuprofhen	Tablets	+
	Amoxicillin	Capsule	–
	Aspirin	Tablets	+
Augmentin	Amoxicillin, clavulinate	Tablets	Trace
Bayer Plus	Aspirin	Tablets	+
Benadryl	Diphenhydramine HCl	Kapseals	+
Centrum	Multivitamin	Tablets	+
Excedrin IB	Ibuprofen	Tablets	+
Gas-X	Simethicone	Tablets	+
Lopressor	Metoprolol	Tablets	Trace
Naproxen	Naprosyn	Tablets	+
One-A-Day	Multivitamin	Tablets	+
Pepcid	Famotidine	Tablets	+
Premarin	Conjugated estrogens, USP	Tablets	+
	Prednisone	Tablets	+
Proventil	Albuterol	Tablets	–
Provera	Medroxyprogesterone	Tablets	–
Seldane	Terfenadine	Tablets	Trace
Source of Life	Multivitamin	Tablets	–
Synthroid	Levothyroxine	Tablets	–
Tagamet	Cimetidine	Tablets	+
Theo-Dur	Tablets	Tablets	–
Tylenol	Acetaminophen	Tablets	+
TUMS	Antacid	Tablets	–
Xanax	Alprazolam	Tablets	–
Zantac	Ranitidine HCl	Tablets	–

Source: "Introducing the Expanded ASI" (Kent, Wash.: Diagnos-Techs, 1995). Brochure.

Sarah, whose case introduced this chapter, is allergic to gluten (more accurately referred to as *gliadin*), a protein found in many grains and a host of processed foods and medicines. In some individuals, just a small amount of gluten can provoke an intense inflammatory response in the intestinal tract. This can result in significant damage to the intestinal wall. Gluten actually acts more like a direct toxin to the bowel wall than like an allergen. Such individuals will tend to have a problem with digesting and absorbing fats, as well as vitamin B12 and folic acid.[3]

A CLOSER LOOK: HOW ARE FOOD ALLERGIES DIAGNOSED?

Allergies to food can be diagnosed by three basic methods. Before doing any testing, though, I strongly recommend you keep a diet and symptom log for at least one week. This should help you identify some suspicious foods, allowing you perhaps to be more specific in your allergy testing.

To keep a diet log, record what you eat at each meal (use abbreviations liberally, in order to avoid taking too much time). In addition, record any symptoms you may have and their severity. Rate the symptoms on a scale: 0 = none, 1 = mild, 2 = moderate, 3 = severe. Your log should look something like the following:

Date/Time	Food	Symptoms since last meal	Severity of symptoms
3/25 8:00 a.m.	Oatmeal Egg, fried Honey	None	0
Noon	Romaine salad w/carrots, cucumbers, feta cheese, olive oil/vinegar	fatigue intestinal gas	2
6:00 p.m.	Yams, green beans, trout, Greek salad (as at lunch)	None	0

**Figure 13.1
Sample Diet Log**

According to the above day's log, you will notice that symptoms occurred only in the morning, between breakfast and lunch. That should alert you to the need to look closer at the foods you ate for breakfast, especially if similar symptoms recur after eating the same foods.

Elimination and Challenge Test

The elimination and challenge test can be conducted in a doctor's office or even at home. In this form of testing, suspicious foods are eliminated *completely* from the diet for at least four days. Then they are reintroduced one at a time (i.e., "challenged"). The reason that the food needs to be completely eliminated for at least four days is so that the immune system will be resensitized to the food and show a more immediate and obvious reaction when exposed to it again.

In the doctor's office, the patient is often challenge tested with a food extract placed under the tongue. The patient is observed for any reaction, and the results recorded. Often neither doctor nor patient is told which items are actually being tested until later ("double-blind challenge").

At home, it is usually recommended that the challenge test be carried out as a single-item meal. Let's say that you want to know if corn might be causing your headaches. So you eliminate all forms of corn from your diet for at least four days. Then you sit down for a meal and have a plate of *only* corn. If you get symptoms after challenging with this "new" food, you may have confirmed allergy as a contributing factor.

Warning: It is generally not recommended that patients who have severe illnesses—especially illnesses that are potentially life threatening—do home testing without the direct supervision of a physician.

Blood Testing

Several types of blood tests are now available for measuring antibodies to food in the serum. Most test for only IgE antibodies. Only a relatively small number of laboratories appear to offer comprehensive blood serum testing for both IgE and IgG antibodies. The problem with this form of testing is that it is still controversial as to its accuracy and effectiveness, particularly when it comes to IgG. Therefore, insurance companies often deny coverage. However, in my experience, food allergy testing with measurement of both serum IgG and IgE antibodies has been clinically very helpful.

Skin Testing

Skin testing is a commonly utilized method for testing food allergies. Some have strongly criticized this method, saying that it is inaccurate. However, there are different methods for skin testing (such as scratch testing, intradermal, etc.). Some may be more accurate than others for identifying food allergies.

When carefully performed and interpreted (using positive and negative controls, allowing enough time for delayed reactions, and so on), this method can be quite helpful. I have successfully uncovered food allergens using the MultiTest device (Lincoln Diagnostics), which is my personal preference for food sensitivity testing.

GENERAL TREATMENT GUIDELINES FOR FOOD ALLERGIES

Fasting

The mainstay of food allergy treatment is avoidance of the offending foods. This is especially true for food reactions that are moderate to severe. When given a rest from offending foods, the antibodies to such foods seem to die off. Offending foods should be discontinued for a minimum of six weeks. After that time, these foods may be able to be reintroduced into the diet without adverse reactions. Reintroduction is best done as a single-item meal, as described above for elimination and challenge testing.

If you experience a recurrence of symptoms, or if your symptoms that have been related to food allergy are made worse by reintroduction of the food, then you should eliminate it again from the diet for at least an additional six weeks. A few foods may always cause a reaction and thus may need to be avoided on a permanent basis. However, most food allergies will resolve with adequate avoidance, so that the food can eventually be returned to the diet.

Digestive Enzymes

Patients who have food allergy often have inadequate breakdown (digestion) of the food while in the stomach and intestines. A lack of stomach acid and/or inadequate release of digestive enzymes from the pancreas can cause this. In order to improve digestion, consider trying digestive enzyme supplements such as Pancrease® (available by prescription) or a supplement through health food stores, taken along with meals, especially when a potentially offending food is eaten.

A typical enzyme regimen is: snacks—1 capsule; typical meal—2 capsules; heavy meals or meals that contain offending foods—3 capsules.

Food Rotation

In order to avoid a redevelopment of the food allergy, it is often recommended that such foods be returned to the diet on a rotation basis—for example, every three or four days. In other words, avoid eating the same food every day.

BLOOD SUGAR PROBLEMS AND THE GLYCEMIC INDEX

Over the last several decades, those with blood sugar disorders (diabetes and hypoglycemia) have typically been counseled to eat a diet that is high in complex carbohydrates—starches such as breads, rice, potatoes, pasta, etc.—and to avoid sugar and fat. But recently this conventional wisdom has been called into question as a new concept in blood sugar control has emerged: the Glycemic Index (GI).

What Is the Glycemic Index?

Every time a food is eaten, digested, and absorbed into the bloodstream, a corresponding rise is seen in the blood sugar (glucose) level. This rise in blood glucose will vary depending upon the kind of food and how it has been prepared. The Glycemic Index is a measurement of how much the blood glucose rises after a food is eaten. Foods are measured against a standard (glucose or white bread), which is arbitrarily given a GI of 100. The more the food raises the blood sugar, the higher the GI.

Blood Sugar Control Systems

The body is designed to function best when things are in balance. Blood sugar control is no exception, particularly since most of the body's cells, including those of the brain and muscles, use glucose as their principal fuel.

The pancreas plays the most crucial role in keeping the blood glucose level (BGL) within a normal range. In response to a rise in blood sugar, the pancreas secretes insulin. Functioning like the key that unlocks a door to the body's cells, insulin causes the cells to open their "doors" and allow glucose to come in from the blood. That drops the blood sugar level back to the normal fasting level. However, if too much insulin is secreted, the BGL drops too fast or too low (i.e., hypoglycemia), and the body has to secrete hormones in order to boost the BGL back up. These counter-regulatory hormones include glucagon from the pancreas and cortisol from the adrenals. These swings in blood sugar are taxing on these two organs (particularly the adrenals) and can, according to some researchers, "exhaust" them.

KING FAILS TO MANAGE BLOOD SUGAR, LOSES LIFE

And Jael went out to meet Sisera, and said unto him, Turn in, my lord, turn in to me; fear not. And when he had turned in unto her into the tent, she covered him with a mantle. And he said unto her, Give me, I pray thee, a little water to drink; for I am thirsty. And [knowing the glycemic index for milk?] she opened a bottle of milk, and gave him drink, and covered him. . . . Then Jael Heber's wife took a nail of the tent, and took an hammer in her hand, and went softly unto him, and smote the nail into his temples, and fastened it into the ground: for he was fast asleep and weary. So he died. (Judges 4:18–19, 21)

Two factors that cause these hypoglycemic swings in blood sugar (and the related stress on the pancreas and adrenals) are (1) genetics and (2) diet. Researchers estimate that up to 20 percent of the population are genetically predisposed to secreting too much insulin, particularly in response to a high-carbohydrate meal. In other words, such individuals have their insulin secretors always half-cocked to "hit" carbohydrates.

This leads us to the second factor: diet. As explained above, when a rising blood sugar is seen, the pancreas responds by secreting insulin in order to bring the BGL back into the normal fasting range. Of the three basic macronutrients (protein, fat, and carbohydrate), carbohydrates cause the most rapid rise in blood sugar. So in order to control the rise in blood sugar (and thus the insulin response), any significant amount of carbohydrate in a meal needs to be balanced adequately with protein.

A Simple Way to Balance Protein and Carbohydrate

Divide your plate into fourths. Place a protein source (e.g., beans, soy, fish, lean poultry, or beef) in one quarter of the plate. Fill the rest of the plate with vegetables. A chicken Caesar salad is a good example of a balanced GI meal.

More Complex: How to Apply the Glycemic Index

Log. If you monitor your own blood glucose level (e.g., diabetics), keep a careful log of the foods you eat and your BGL in order to see which foods cause the greatest rise in your blood sugar. If you do not monitor blood glucose, keep a symptom log. Low blood sugar tends to result in fatigue, especially after the noon meal. In addition, if adrenal hormones are released to boost the blood sugar, you may also experience headache, jitteriness, nausea, rapid heart or breathing rates, cold clammy hands, or a sense of panic.

Keep the carbohydrate: protein ratio to about 2:1 (in grams). Most people eat far more carbohydrates than they do protein. By limiting the carbohydrate intake to only twice as many grams as protein, the BGL rises more slowly and the pancreas secretes a limited amount of insulin, properly balanced with glucagon. This is especially beneficial in those with obesity or diabetes, because it limits insulin demand.

Eat foods that have a low Glycemic Index (between 50 and 80). Consider picking up a pocket-size book with charts showing nutritive values in foods. Generally speaking, the following factors affect the index of a food:

- Starch content. Eat foods that are low in starch. Minimize grains (breads, pastas, rice). Nonstarchy vegetables such as broccoli, raw carrots, peppers, and so on can be eaten freely and do not need to be calculated into the Glycemic Index because they do not generally alter the blood sugar level and insulin-glucagon balance.

- Food preparation. Because the preparation of a food affects how quickly it can be digested, the same food can make big differences in its GI, depending upon whether it is eaten raw, boiled, dried, canned, or fried. For example, dried green lentils have a GI of 36, whereas canned green lentils have a GI twice that high at 74. Likewise, raw apples have a lower GI compared to applesauce.

- Meal size and frequency. Eating smaller meals more frequently (for example, four to six small feedings daily versus three larger meals) slows the rate of digestion and may thus improve blood sugar control.

- Although it is expensive, consider fructose when sugar is needed. The GI for honey is 138, for sucrose (table sugar) 83, and fructose 26.

CONCLUSION

Eating good, God-given food will go a long way toward achieving optimum health. However, certain individuals with food allergy or blood sugar problems may have trouble with certain foods. In such cases, adjustment from the Biblical Diet Pyramid may be necessary.

THE SPIRITUAL SIDE OF ILLNESS

Come unto me, all ye that labour and are heavy laden, and I will give you rest. Take my yoke upon you, and learn of me; for I am meek and lowly in heart: and ye shall find rest unto your souls. For my yoke is easy, and my burden is light.

—Jesus Christ
(Matthew 11:28–30)

14

STRESS:
THE TROJAN HORSE

Sometime around 1100 B.C., Greece was at war with the city of Troy. After ten years of conflict, with things not going well for the Greeks, one final assault was attempted against the well-fortified city. Once again, Troy successfully repelled the attack, and the Greeks dejectedly returned to their ships and sailed away. Left behind was a mammoth wooden horse and a city rejoicing in its long-awaited triumph.

Considering the horse a prize of war, the Trojans brought it within their gates and held a huge victory celebration. But that night as the city lay fast asleep, Greek warriors exited the hollow belly of the wooden horse and opened the city gates for their comrades, who had quietly returned in their ships. Taken completely by surprise and now exposed to internal attack, Troy suffered overwhelming defeat.

In many respects, our conflict with disease and death resembles that Trojan War. We fortify ourselves against disease by erecting the massive walls of sound nutrition. We regularly drill and train to keep our bodies in top physical condition. Then we wait to see if disease will be able to breach our well-fortified wall. But like the Trojan horse, it may be that our adversary has entered through the gate of our souls. And out of its belly has come the warrior Stress, who, having breached our defenses, has launched a devastating attack on our health.

CASE HISTORIES

Andy: Stress-Induced Heart Attack

District Attorney Andy Patterson knew this was going to be a big day. The forty-two-year-old prosecutor looked forward to the hearing that he was sure to win, a major child abuse case. Meanwhile, his wife, Carol, planned to spend the day at a local hospital where our heart study was hosting an author and physician who was speaking on diet and the prevention and treatment of heart disease. The two went their separate ways. At the hospital, Carol was thoroughly enjoying the fascinating presentation. But across town, things were not going so well for Andy. Unexpectedly, the judge ruled against the prosecution team, a decision that infuriated the normally mild-mannered attorney. Andy left the courthouse in a fit of rage and stormed home.

To work off some steam, he quickly changed into sweats and went for his daily run. Once that was complete, Andy began his twenty-minute routine on a stationary bike. But instead of feeling better, he became progressively worse. Overwhelming pressure and pain replaced the anger that had been in his heart.

Something was terribly wrong, and Andy was having a hard time believing it. *This can't be happening to me,* he thought. *My cholesterol is below 200, I exercise regularly, and try to eat right.* But when his chest pain continued, he drove himself to the emergency room, where his fears were confirmed. He was told that he was having a heart attack. After a clot-busting drug was promptly given, Andy's chest pain quickly resolved, and he spent a quiet night in the hospital.

The next day, when Andy underwent a coronary angiogram—a test in which dye is injected into the coronary arteries to check for blockage—it was the cardiologist's turn to disbelieve. Despite a confirmed heart attack, the angiogram revealed that Andy had almost no disease in his coronary arteries. Only one small plaque obstructed less than 20 percent of the right coronary artery. (Plaque is not normally considered to be a significant cause of symptoms unless it is obstructing at least 70 percent of a blood vessel.)

But that was all it took. His outburst of anger had apparently ruptured the plaque and caused a large clot to form, completely cutting off blood flow to that portion of the heart.

Beth: Stress-Induced Stroke

Beth was the sixty-nine-year-old woman you learned about in chapter 3. She had spent much time and effort over the last twenty-five years practicing a prudent lifestyle that was touted by many as guarantee against today's killer diseases. A practicing vegetarian, she with her husband had a thriving home business involved in promoting nutrition. But, despite all her efforts, Beth had a serious weakness that was a far greater threat to her health than a poor diet: she handled emotional stress poorly.

Some months earlier, business associates had pressured her husband into an arrangement that had cost them thousands of dollars. Finally, he decided to confront his associates and arranged for a meeting in his home.

As things got under way, Beth busied herself in the kitchen, trying unsuccessfully to maintain the internal calm she so desperately needed. Ironically, while forcing carrots through a juice machine, her arm suddenly went numb. Two days later the warning sign became a reality as she suffered a massive stroke that almost completely destroyed her ability to see, speak, swallow, and write.

Someone has said, "Strokes are cruel." Beth would agree. All of her dietary efforts to avoid premature disease evaporated in a split second in the face of the overwhelming power of stress.

The Disease-Causing Effects of Stress

> Stress begins in the mind but ends in the body . . . there is no such thing as stress only being in the mind.[1]

Whether the situation is heart attack, stroke, high blood pressure, fibromyalgia, irritable bowel syndrome, insomnia, anxiety disorder, or a host of other problems, stress is becoming increasingly recognized for its significant role in health and illness.[2] Some have estimated that stress accounts for as much as 75 percent of all visits to a physician.[3] But how could stress be central to such a wide variety of seemingly unrelated health problems?

In 1970, Holmes and Rahe of the University of Washington published a "Stress Scale" in which various stressors of life are ranked according to the toll they take on the individual. On a scale of 1 to 100, death of a spouse ranks first, with a ranking of 100 points. It is followed by divorce (93 points), jail term or death of a family member (63), personal illness or injury (53), marriage (50), being fired from a job (47), reconciliation of marriage and retirement (45), among others. The authors stated that the accumulation of 300 or more points in any one-year period puts an individual at great risk for disease.

Notice that stress does not have to be "bad" in order to contribute to disease. Obviously, marriage or the reconciliation of marriage, as well as retirement, are all considered good things. The essence of stress is not necessarily in its character but simply because *any* change causes stress, whether good or bad.[4]

This understanding of the disease-causing effects of stress is very new. In fact, it was not until the scientific discoveries of the twentieth century that many in medicine began to realize it.

THE HISTORY OF STRESS RESEARCH

In 1842, British physician Thomas B. Curling first described acute gastrointestinal ulcers in patients with extensive skin burns. In 1867, Viennese surgeon Albert C. T. Billroth reported similar findings after major surgery was complicated by infection.[5] Today, largely due to the extensive research of Hans Selye, we refer to these as "stress ulcers" and routinely treat burn patients and those in intensive care with medication to protect their stomachs from ulcers.

Selye: Initial Discovery of Alarm Triad

Hans Selye's initial stress discovery, like so many in the history of science, was quite unexpected. While unsuccessfully attempting to isolate a "new" hormone at McGill University in 1935, Dr. Selye noticed that laboratory rats injected with a noxious chemical consistently demonstrated three responses:

Gastric ulcers. Just like Curling and Billroth, he observed the development of stomach ulcers.

Adrenal gland hypertrophy (swelling). The triangular-shaped adrenal glands rest on top of each kidney and are extremely important in the production of numerous key hormones.

Some of these include adrenaline and noradrenaline, both neurotransmitters (hormone-like substances that trigger nerve receptors). In addition, the adrenals, through the production of aldosterone and antidiuretic hormone, play an important role in the regulation of blood pressure and salt and water balance. Estrogen, progesterone, and testosterone are all produced in the adrenal glands, especially in males and postmenopausal females. Last, but not least, the adrenals produce the all-important "stress hormone" cortisol and DHEA (dehyrdoepiandrostenedione).

Thymus and lymph node atrophy. The thymus and lymph nodes are part of the body's immune system, which is primarily involved in fighting infection and inflammation. When subjected to stress, the lymph nodes and thymus shrink, indicating suppression of the immune system.

With further experiments, Selye discovered that it did not matter what the stress was. The triad of response was always the same.[6]

Selye: Pinpointing the ACTH-Cortisol Connection

But Selye didn't know why or how the changes were produced. To get his answer, he removed the thymus glands of laboratory rats and then repeated the experiment. But the adrenals still became enlarged. Therefore he knew that the pathway was not from thymus to adrenal.

Next, he removed the adrenal glands prior to exposing the rats to stress. This time, he found that the thymus (and stomach) no longer showed the characteristic stress-related changes. It became obvious that the pathway went from adrenal to thymus and not the reverse. Multiple further experiments were conducted in order to find out what caused the adrenal changes. Eventually, Selye discovered that the adrenal hyperactivity was caused by ACTH, a hormone released from the pituitary in response to stress.[7]

TWO PATHWAYS FOR THE EFFECTS OF STRESS ON THE BODY

Since Selye's pioneering work, additional research has given us an even clearer picture of the effects of stress on the human frame. External stressors (such as temperature extremes, exercise, and difficulties) or internal stressors (such as disease, pain, or emotional distress) are perceived by the brain and trigger the stress response, which we now know follows two pathways.

As discussed above, the first pathway travels through the pituitary gland, which responds by releasing ACTH. This hormone travels through the bloodstream to the adrenals, where it stimulates the outer "cover," known as the adrenal cortex, to release cortisol. Cortisol fights inflammation, increases muscle tension, frees up fatty acids, and increases blood sugar for energy availability.

The other pathway stressors take is to activate the sympathetic nervous system. The sympathetic nervous system is part of the autonomic (i.e., "automatic") nervous system. It controls functions that need to be performed without conscious thought. It stimulates the heart to beat, lungs to breathe, intestines to move along food, and so on. (Imagine if you had to consciously remember to breathe. Thank our Creator that He designed us with an autonomic nervous system!)

The activity of the sympathetic nervous system is dramatically increased during an emergency in what is popularly known as the "fight or flight system." Selye called it the "alarm reaction." In this pathway, nerve impulses are triggered from the brain stem and spinal cord that stimulate the *inner core* of the adrenal glands to release adrenaline and noradrenaline, which are neurotransmitters for the sympathetic nervous system.

These greatly increase the performance of several organs that are critical in an emergency. For example, when the sympathetic nervous system is stimulated, blood sugar is raised to make it readily available for fuel.[8] In addition, the heart beats faster, the lungs breathe more rapidly, the eyes dilate, and blood is shunted to organs such as the brain and muscles that are essential for fight or flight.

On the other hand, organs that are not needed in such an emergency are essentially shut down. These would include the liver, spleen, and digestive organs. That is why "fast food" is somewhat of a contradiction in terms. When you are in a hurry and under stress, the last thing you should do is eat a high-calorie meal of fried food. Under stress, food is not digested, so it just sits in the gut. The Hebrews had it right when they "lay at table," relaxing and enjoying fellowship along with their meal and thereby greatly enhancing the digestion of their food.

Better is a dinner of herbs where love is, than a stalled ox and hatred therewith. (Proverbs 15:17)

Although an increase in sympathetic nervous system activity is beneficial, even perhaps lifesaving in an emergency, if its stimulation is prolonged, it can have a host of detrimental effects on numerous organ systems.

GENERAL ADAPTATION SYNDROME

How will stress affect you? That largely depends upon your constitutional makeup.

In the body, as in a chain, the weakest link breaks down under stress although all parts are equally exposed to it. [9]

Despite the fact that there is a great deal of individual variation, everyone under prolonged stress will tend to follow the same general pattern—what Selye referred to as the General Adaptation Syndrome. This syndrome describes the overall health and resistance to disease of the individual under stress as he goes through three classic phases.[10]

Alarm (Triad) Reaction

In this first phase when the individual is challenged by stress, he is temporarily weakened so that his resistance to disease is lowered.

Stage of Resistance

As the stress continues, however, adaptation develops, and resistance to disease and other stress is actually increased above baseline.

Stage of Exhaustion

But eventually this acquired resistance is lost, as the body's resources are exhausted and the individual's health fails. In this stage of exhaustion, even mild degrees of stress result in exaggerated increases in cortisol that stay elevated for much longer than normal periods of time. In other words, to an individual in this stage it seems to take hardly anything to trigger an aggravation of symptoms. The person just can't "handle it" anymore.[11]

Of course, every disease causes a certain amount of stress, since it imposes demands for adaptation upon the organism. In turn, stress plays some role in the development of every disease; its effects—for better or worse—are added to the specific changes characteristic of the disease in question.[12]

Now let us look in more detail at the physical consequences of stress. First, we will examine the pathway of stress-induced adrenaline excess.

DETRIMENTAL EFFECTS OF EXCESSIVE ADRENALINE

Gastric Ulcers

As Curling, Billroth, and Selye all noted, stress induces increased secretion of stomach acid, leading to an increased risk of ulcers.[13] In a recent example, the occurrence of gastric ulcers was noted to increase dramatically in Japanese residents who survived the devastating Hanshin-Awaji earthquake.[14] The presence of another significant disease further increases the likelihood that stress will cause gastric ulcers.[15]

Skin Disorders

Stress may also play a role in some skin diseases. For example, vitiligo is a disease in which cells lose their pigmentation, causing white blotches to form on the skin. A. Morrone and colleagues demonstrated that the onset and progression of vitiligo correlates with increased levels of adrenaline.[16]

High Blood Pressure

A growing body of evidence seems to support the potential connection between stress and high blood pressure. In one study, patients who had borderline hypertension or a family history of high blood pressure were more likely to have stress-related behavior patterns.[17] And in a long-term study involving nearly 3,000 patients, those who had high anxiety or high depression were nearly twice as likely to develop high blood pressure over time.[18]

Heart and Circulatory System Damage

According to the doctors who discovered the link between personality type and heart disease, "The most serious effect of elevated adrenaline, when persistent and unrelenting, is its damage to the heart and arteries."[19] Adrenaline's detrimental effects include the following:

Constriction of blood vessels. This can result in spasm of the coronary arteries, reducing blood flow to the heart.

Increased cholesterol production (especially LDL, the "bad" cholesterol) and *decreased cholesterol clearance.* This results in increased formation of plaque on artery walls.[20]

The evidence that stress raises cholesterol levels is abundant. Accountants' cholesterol levels have been found to be highest at tax time; medical students registered 10 percent higher during examination time; employees fired from their jobs showed a 10 percent drop in cholesterol when they finally secured new work.[21]

But cholesterol may not be so deserving of all of the bad press it has been receiving. Archibald Hart cites evidence that elevated cholesterol does not increase the risk of heart disease unless it is combined with stress.

Simply put, if blood cholesterol levels are high, stress will much more likely contribute to heart disease. On the other hand, if stress levels are kept low, even a high cholesterol will probably not result in heart disease.[22]

Plaque disruption. As was true in Andy's case history, the development of plaque was only a part of his problem. His outburst of anger apparently caused his small plaque to rupture and a large clot to form upon it, resulting in the obstruction that caused his heart attack. His case is not unique. Two-thirds of all acute coronary events tend to occur when there is only mild to moderate obstructive plaque. The culprit does not appear to be the plaque itself but the adrenaline surge that precipitates the crisis.[23]

Arterial spasm and increased clotting. Stress depletes magnesium, which results in increased arterial spasm and an increased clotting of platelets.[24]

Heart dysrhythmias. Adrenaline stimulates the heart to beat faster and more erratically. For example, when given intravenously in amounts to match stressful situations, adrenaline induced episodes of PSVT—a condition in which the heart spontaneously beats extremely rapidly—in patients that were being medicated for this condition.[25] Healthy physicians, when paged while on call in the hospital, showed derangement in their EKG similar to those seen preceding fatal dysrhythmias.[26] Likewise, when rats and dogs were subjected to acute stress, there was a corresponding destabilization in their ventricular rhythm as the heart showed signs of increasing injury.[27]

Sudden death. Most episodes of stress-related sudden death appear to be due to the direct effect of stress upon the heart. For example, thirty-eight out of forty-three cases of stress-related sudden death were determined to be due to heart problems. This was despite the fact that 90 percent who died from an underlying heart condition during this stress episode had no known prior history of heart disease. Two died of stroke. All of these episodes of stress-related sudden death were witnessed. Fear and anger were the stressful triggers in forty out of forty-three cases, and death occurred without warning in any.[28] This is exactly what happened to Nabal when he heard from his wife that David had come to take his life.

But it came to pass in the morning, when the wine was gone out of Nabal, and his wife had told him these things, that his heart died within him, and he became as a stone. (1 Samuel 25:37)

Mitral valve prolapse. MVP is a relatively common diagnosis given to patients who have chest pain that is not due to coronary artery disease. Such patients are more than twice as likely to suffer from panic disorder or major depression than are patients who have chest pain due to coronary artery disease.[29] Similarly, another study demonstrated that 40 percent of patients with noncardiac chest pain met the diagnostic criteria for panic disorder, compared to none of the patients with typical angina.[30]

Panic Disorder

This stress-related disorder is especially common in middle-aged women and is characterized by rapid heart rate, pressure or burning sensation in the chest, neck, or head, shortness of breath, and a sense of impending doom. Patients with panic disorder are usually able initially to identify the triggers for such episodes. But as time progresses, it is common for there to be no obvious connection between stressors and anxiety attacks. This is not to say that these attacks are no longer caused by stress but that the individual's adrenals have reached such a stage of exhaustion that they are clinically bordering on a "nervous breakdown." Their stress system needs genuine rest.

Since panic attacks, ulcers, skin problems, high blood pressure, heart disease, and even sudden death all are linked to stress, one might be ready to hear what he can do to prevent all of this. But the list is only half complete. Several other problems are associated with the second pathway for stress: elevated cortisol. Before we look at treatment, we need to at least be aware of the detrimental effects of prolonged increases in cortisol levels.

DETRIMENTAL EFFECTS OF EXCESSIVE CORTISOL

The adrenal cortex produces two of the most critical stress hormones, cortisol and DHEA. Cortisol is a steroid hormone, with effects very similar to those of the medication prednisone. It powerfully blocks inflammation, and it suppresses the immune system. On the other hand, DHEA serves to balance out the effects of cortisol. It is believed to have anti-aging effects, to be an immune system booster, and to have important effects on the sex hormones and, therefore, fertility.

Normally, the adrenal cortex increases production of cortisol by about 50 percent within the first few days of the onset of stress. At the same time, DHEA levels fall off. Once the stress is removed, cortisol and DHEA levels will typically return to the normal range.

However, with prolonged stress, these changes become even more exaggerated. Cortisol rises to nearly 240 percent of normal, and DHEA production drops to near zero. The elevated cortisol, with its prednisone-like effects, along with virtually no DHEA to counteract it, eventually wreaks havoc on a variety of the body's organ systems.[31]

Note that the adrenal glands always produce cortisol, even at the expense of other hormones. This is because cortisol is essential to life. The emphasis here, however, is placed on the negative effects of excess cortisol in response to stress. Its other important functions are beyond the scope of this discussion.

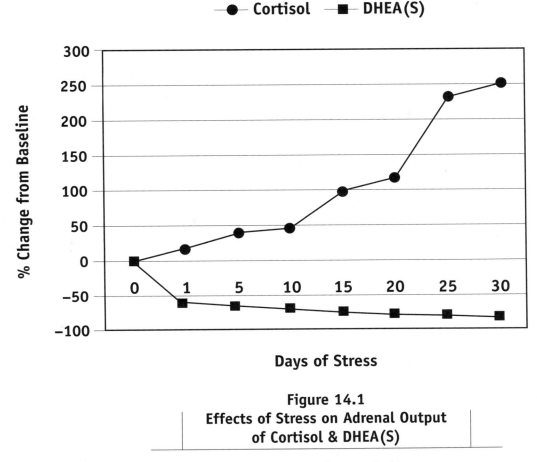

Figure 14.1
Effects of Stress on Adrenal Output
of Cortisol & DHEA(S)

Source: Diagnos-Techs, Kent, Washington

Effects on Hormones

First of all, cortisol stimulates the conversion of noradrenaline to adrenaline, resulting in increased levels of adrenaline in the blood. This puts the individual at increased risk for all of the problems related to adrenaline excess noted above. Cortisol also blocks the conversion of the T4 thyroid hormone to the more active T3 form, so that individuals under stress may develop symptoms of hypothyroidism (even though the thyroid function tests may appear normal).

Infection

Cortisol suppresses antibody production and T-cell (a type of white blood cell) activity. This puts the stressed individual at much greater risk for infections.[32] For example, risk of the common cold has been found to correlate directly with the level of stress one is experiencing.[33] Selye said:

If a microbe is in or around us all of the time, and yet it causes no disease until we are exposed to stress, what is the "cause" of our illness, the microbe or the stress? I think both are—and equally so.[34]

Increased risk of infection is of particular concern with surgical patients, since in addition to the exposure of the inner sanctum to germs, surgery itself has been demonstrated to be a potent stressor, depressing the immune system through dramatically stimulating increased cortisol.[35]

Louis Pasteur, the first great microbiologist, was constantly challenged by Claude Bernard, who insisted on the body's own homeostasis being more important than the microbe. Upon his deathbed, Pasteur said, "Bernard was right. The microbe is nothing, the soil is everything."[36]

Protein Breakdown Increase

Under the influence of cortisol, protein breakdown increases 38 percent while the manufacturing of protein drops 28 percent. Together, this translates into a 66 percent drop in protein production. Thus, lean muscle is converted to fat, so that individuals with chronically elevated cortisol may develop a "buffalo hump" between their shoulders.[37] A lack of protein also leads to poor wound healing.

Arthritis

Selye claimed that gout is related to stress.[38] In addition, researchers have indicated that rheumatoid arthritis activity correlates with the degree of emotional stress.[39]

Heavy Metal Chelation

Today, especially in alternative medicine, there is a growing interest in the treatment of heavy metal toxicity with chelation. "Chelation" comes from the Greek root word *chele*, meaning "claw," and refers to the manner in which protein molecules or other substances grab and bind heavy metals in the body. The human body is already designed with an inherent, powerful chelation system for binding and removing toxic heavy metals. But stress, through elevated levels of cortisol, blocks this process, rendering the stressed individual more vulnerable to heavy-metal-toxicity–related illness.[40]

Cancer

Elevated cortisol also suppresses killer cells, which are critical in the destruction of tumor cells.[41] Giving cortisol to rats with cancer caused their cancer to spread in direct proportion to the amount of cortisol administered.[42] Incidentally, stress also triggers a release of endogenous opiates (morphinelike compounds that are found naturally in the body). Studies show that these appear to block immune responses and interfere with the body's ability to reject tumor cells.[43]

The association of stress with cancer has led investigators to identify the personality or behavioral profile of the typical individual who is at increased risk for cancer. Now referred to as "Type C," such an individual is characterized by denial and suppression of emotions (especially anger), "pathological niceness," avoidance of conflicts, exaggerated social desirability, harmonizing behavior, overcompliance, overpatience, high rationality, and a rigid control of emotional expression. Christians understand that love, joy, patience, kindness, and self-control are fruit of the Holy Spirit (Galatians 5:22). The point here is that these characteristics must not be "put on" but come from a sincere, pure heart.

This pattern, usually concealed behind a facade of pleasantness, appears to be effective as long as environmental and psychological homeostasis is maintained, but collapses in the course of time under the impact of accumulated strains and stressors, especially those evoking feelings of depression and reactions of helplessness and hopelessness. As a prominent feature of this particular coping style, excessive denial, avoidance, suppression and repression of emotions and own basic needs appears to weaken the organism's natural resistance to carcinogenic influences.[44]

These and other findings have led researchers to recommend that "more attention should be paid to the manipulation of the psyche in the prevention and management of cancer."[45]

Diabetes

Laboratory animals that are genetically susceptible to insulin-dependent diabetes mellitus develop this dreaded disease more commonly when they are subjected to stress.[46] And, since cortisol blocks insulin, patients who already have diabetes have a more difficult time controlling their blood sugars when they are under stress.[47]

George, the leader of a large Christian ministry, has struggled for several years with adult-onset diabetes. Although he has had some degree of success controlling his blood sugar with proper diet, it has become clear over the last year or so that the level of his blood sugar is more related to stress than to anything else. He can get up in the morning, have normal blood sugar and eat a healthy breakfast with no sugar or starches. But if he has a stressful morning at work, his blood sugar can easily shoot up 100 points or more. On the other hand, when he is out of a stressful environment, he tends to have little difficulty keeping his blood sugar under control.

Adverse Effect on Sex Hormones: Infertility, Miscarriage

Cortisol stimulates the conversion of DHEA to estrogen in fat cells (especially abdominal fat). Therefore, a woman who is obese and under stress can have blood estrogen levels equivalent to that of a woman in her thirties. This estrogen-dominance picture is consistent with an increased risk of estrogen-related disorders such as cancer, especially of the breast and uterus.[48]

Years ago, Selye reported that stress had a definite negative effect on the reproductive system. "During stress, the sex glands shrink and become less active," and nursing mothers stop producing milk. In addition, monthly cycles become irregular or may even stop altogether. Likewise, in men who are under stress, sperm cell formation is reduced.[49]

In addition, stress increases miscarriages by blocking protective mechanisms and promoting an increased release of the natural inflammatory chemicals that can cause miscarriage.[50]

Memory Loss

In order for us to recall stored information, our brains must be able to make connections at nerve endings called "dendrites." Cortisol "fries" the delicate dendrites in the brain that are necessary for the transfer of information. Therefore, stress can lead to learning disabilities and memory loss problems similar to what Alzheimer's disease patients experience.[51]

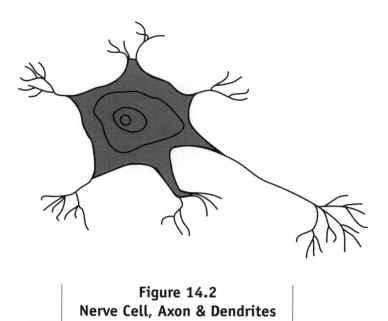

Figure 14.2
Nerve Cell, Axon & Dendrites

Emotional and Mental Illness

Selye noted that certain breakdown products of adrenaline can cause hallucination, and he proposed that it might therefore play a role in some mental illness.[52] Certainly, stress has been implicated as a cause of depression.[53] And no wonder. I'd be depressed, too, if I were suffering from infections, protein loss, arthritis, cancer, diabetes, infertility, miscarriages, mental illness, and—what was that other one?—oh yes, memory loss!

CONCLUSION

In light of increasing awareness of the relationship between diet and disease, many health-conscious individuals are making important lifestyle changes to reduce their risk. The ability of stress to trigger excess adrenaline and cortisol can produce a host of different diseases—so many that some experts believe stress to be the leading cause of disease today. Therefore, prudent lifestyle changes must include effective stress management.

EVALUATION AND TREATMENT OF STRESS-RELATED ILLNESS

By now you are probably overwhelmed with the stress of knowing how many different ways stress can kill you. But take heart! Don't surrender yet. You already have available to you the resources to conquer this intimidating foe. The first step is to get an accurate assessment of your stress picture. Once this is complete, we can look at steps to treat (or to prevent) stress-related illness.

EVALUATION

Step #1: Consider Your Personality/Behavioral Type

Does your pattern of thinking and/or responding emotionally to different situations put you at risk for stress-related illness? Your personality/behavioral type reflects a perspective of life that has developed as a result of experiences, whether good or bad. As such, they become deeply ingrained into an individual and difficult, although not impossible, to change. (Important keys to changing behavioral patterns will be discussed in the next two chapters.)

Type C behavior pattern is possibly associated with increased risk of cancer. It involves excessive denial and suppression of one's emotions, a practice that eventually compromises the immune system.

Type A behavior is at increased risk for heart disease. Such an individual is characterized by the following:

- Intensely competitive
- Impatient

- Achievement oriented
- Aggressive and driven
- Distorted sense of time urgency
- Constantly moving[1]

Selye wrote that someone with this behavior type can become addicted to his own stress hormones.

> It is instructive to know that stress stimulates our glands to make hormones that can induce a kind of drunkenness. Without knowing this, no one would ever think of checking his conduct as carefully during stress as he does at a cocktail party. Yet he should. The fact is that a man can be intoxicated with his own stress hormones. . . . In all our actions throughout the day, we must constantly look for signs of being keyed up too much—and we must learn to stop in time.[2]

As in other forms of addiction, one of the easiest ways to determine if there is a problem is to note if there are withdrawal symptoms when the individual abstains from the addictive "substance." Signs of adrenaline withdrawal include:

- A strong compulsion to be "doing something" while at home or on vacation
- An obsession of thoughts about what was left undone
- A feeling of vague guilt while resting
- Fidgetiness, restlessness, pacing, leg kicking, or fast gum chewing
- Inability to concentrate for very long on any relaxing activity
- Feelings of irritability and aggravation
- A vague or sometimes profound feeling of depression whenever you stop an activity[3]

Step #2: Review Stress-Related Symptoms and Illnesses

Ask yourself if you suffer from stress-related symptoms in addition to the above. Review the list of symptoms that are often related to stress.

TABLE 15.1 SYMPTOMS POSSIBLY RELATED TO STRESS	
abdominal: pain, cramps, bloating, diarrhea	depression
	infections
skin rashes	irregular menses
chest pain	memory problems
palpitations	fatigue
shortness of breath	confusion
muscle/joint pain, stiffness	tingling/numbness

Now review the list of illnesses that are known to have a possible relationship to stress. Are you currently suffering from any of these?

TABLE 15.2 **STRESS-RELATED ILLNESSES**	
Gastrointestinal ulcers	Poor blood sugar control
Skin disorders, e.g. vitiligo	Endometriosis
High blood pressure	Irregular or absent menses
Elevated cholesterol	Reduced lactation (milk)
Coronary artery disease	Infertility
Heart dysrhythmias	Miscarriage
Mitral valve prolapse (MVP)	Memory loss
Panic or anxiety attacks	Learning disability
Frequent infections	Mental illness
Loss of lean muscle mass	Depression
"Buffalo" torso or "hump"	Heavy metal toxicity
Arthritis	Hypoglycemia
Cancer	Fibromyalgia
Diabetes	Insomnia

Remember that just because you have one or more of these illnesses does not mean that it is caused by stress. In each case, factors other than stress may be at the root. However, if you are suffering from any of these illnesses, stress should not be dismissed without serious consideration of its role in either causing the disease, contributing to flare-ups, or both.

Step #3: Monitor Adrenaline Activity

You have reviewed the list of possible stress-related symptoms and illnesses, as well as the personality/behavioral types that put one at risk for them. The next step is to check your stress system for signs of activation by (1) monitoring the cardiovascular system for adrenaline stimulation and (2) keeping a stress diary. This will not only help you confirm whether or not your illness or symptoms are stress related but is also an important tool in learning how to better respond to stress.

Heart rate and blood pressure. Regularly check and record your pulse and/or blood pressure, especially before getting out of bed in the morning. This gives you a baseline. Depending on your particular lifestyle and needs, it may also be beneficial to check regularly at one or two other times during the day, such as right after work and before bedtime or in conjunction with any stress-related symptoms you may have.[4]

Temperature dots. Popularized by psychologists several years ago, these dots are placed on the back of the hand in the web of skin between the thumb and forefinger. Since adrenaline causes blood to be shunted away from the extremities and toward the vital organs, someone under stress will typically experience a lower skin temperature in the hands, causing the dot to turn a lighter color. That is also why a stressed individual will notice that his hands feel cold when applied to his cheeks.[5]

Stress diary. Psychologist Andrew Goliszek recommends keeping a "Stress Diary" in which a record is kept of signs and symptoms that may be stress related. In each entry, the individual records the time the symptoms occurred, the stress symptom, the current activity, and the previous activity (since symptoms may not show up immediately).[6] Keeping such a symptom diary is helpful in a variety of illnesses.

Completing a stress diary will help you to see more clearly the cause of your stress symptoms and, therefore, what you can do about them. In our earlier example, the cause of symptoms in each case was the anxiety (fear or worry) associated with paying bills.

Just a quick note about possible solutions to that particular stress problem: First of all, you may be the wrong person to be handling the bill paying. Is that your God-given responsibility, or does it belong to someone else? Worry has been wisely defined by someone as "carrying responsibility for burden(s) that are not my own." Second, the financial pressure associated with paying the bills may reveal poor money management habits. Perhaps wise financial counseling would be a solution. Or the pressure may reflect a materialistic lifestyle, particularly one in which things are constantly purchased to fill a void in one's life. Finally, it may simply reflect a lack of faith—the inability to trust God that He will indeed provide for all of your needs.

STRESS DIARY FOR _____ (date)			
Time	**Symptom**	**Activity**	**Previous**
10:00 a.m.	Fast heart beat, breath	Got mail, saw bills	Housecleaning
10:30 a.m.	Burning in chest, constant foot tap	Paying bills feeling: worry	Got and read mail
11:30 a.m.	Headache	Preparing lunch feeling: worry	Paying bills

Figure 15.1
Stress Diary

Source: Reprinted from: *Breaking the Stress Habit,* by Andrew Goliszek.

Step #4: Evaluate Adrenal Function

The next step is to determine the condition of your stress organs, the adrenal glands. The adrenals (along with the heart) are extremely sensitive and responsive to stress, whatever the cause. The symptoms listed in table 15.1 may be warning signs of mild adrenal fatigue. Warnings of a more severe adrenal exhaustion problem include the following:

- Intense depression of short duration (say, three days to one week) that occurs every few months
- Unusual difficulty in getting energy going in the morning
- Being overcome by great tiredness whenever energy is let down
- Strange body sensations (tingling up and down the arms or across the chest) or strange aches in the joints and muscles
- Exhaustion that occurs very easily or frequently
- Feelings of panic triggered by activity or exercise[7]

CLINICAL ADRENAL TESTING

Once again, keep in mind that having some of the above signs does not necessarily mean that stress is the cause. But if adrenal involvement is suspected, then clinical tests may need to be ordered.

The most common method of assessing adrenal function is to check blood cortisol levels in the morning and afternoon. However, I have found that adrenal assessment is far more accurate and helpful when it is accomplished through a test called an Adrenal Stress Index (ASI), available through Diagnos-Techs Lab in Seattle. This test must be ordered by a health care professional. The test kit is then given to the patient, who takes four samples of saliva at specific times throughout the day. In my experience, the ASI has been more helpful clinically than the standard blood cortisol measurements.

The ASI measures levels for cortisol, DHEA, and two other functions. Depending upon the results of your lab test, a specific treatment program can be tailored to your needs to get you back on track. In general, most individuals will benefit from the regimen that follows. An adrenal program is usually maintained for approximately six months, although it may take a year or two to restore the adrenals to normal. A follow-up ASI is often recommended in order to assess response to treatment. For more technical information on understanding the Adrenal Stress Index, see appendix B.[8]

TREATMENT OF STRESS-RELATED ILLNESS

Regardless of what your laboratory studies show, certain general recommendations are part of a typical regimen to rehabilitate the adrenal glands. The principle underlying all such treatment is to eliminate or minimize unnecessary triggers of adrenal stress. Numerous medications also are used to manage stress, including tranquilizers and sleep aids, but

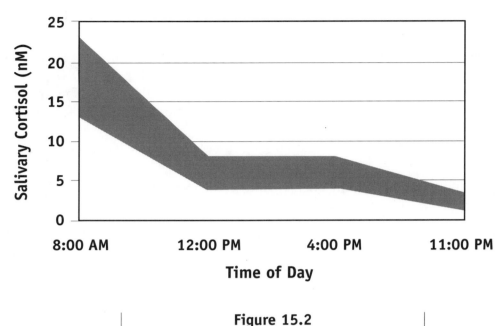

Figure 15.2
Normal Cortisol Output for 24-Hour Period

Source: Diagnos-Techs, Kent, Washington

I will not discuss these here. Instead, I will focus on steps to take that address stress-related illness at a more basic, yet often overlooked, level.

Step #1: Control Pain and Inflammation

Pain and inflammation are major stressors on the adrenal glands. Thus, these must be properly treated and controlled if the adrenals are to be restored. Having an osteopathic background and a practice treating chronic pain, I have found that most chronic pain problems can be classified as structural, metabolic, or both.

Chronic structural pain is generally due to prior injury, whether that injury was a major singular event (such as from an auto accident) or an accumulation of small injuries (such as from poor posture). Often, postural problems and poor body mechanics weaken the individual over time and set up one for a more major injury, such as an acute back strain while lifting at work.

Chronic pain due to structural injury is usually confined to a limited area—one or two joints—and most often involves the ligaments, tendons, and joint capsules. This kind of pain is usually best treated with osteopathic or chiropractic manipulation and aggressive physical therapy. If pain still persists two months after the injury, a little-known injection treatment (prolotherapy) will often relieve the pain permanently through restoring strength and stability to the damaged connective tissue.

Chronic metabolic pain problems are usually associated with the presence of excess inflammatory compounds. Since these can travel anywhere in the body, this type of pain is usually present in multiple areas or joints of the body ("I hurt all over"). Selye reported that dental infections such as abscessed teeth can contribute to systemic inflammation and symptoms by acting as a stressor on the adrenal glands.[9]

Another possible source of systemic inflammation is food sensitivity. We have discussed gluten, a component of a variety of grains. Gluten can have such an inflammatory effect on the intestinal tracts of susceptible individuals that disturbance in their adrenal function can result.

Metabolic (inflammatory) pain is best treated with dietary change, supplements, and, if necessary, medication. For example, rheumatoid arthritis patients placed on a vegetarian diet experienced a reduction in painful joints.[10] Likewise, following dietary principles similar to those contained in the Biblical Diet Pyramid has been repeatedly demonstrated to reduce inflammation.

Step #2: Control Blood Sugar

In addition to pain and inflammation, hypoglycemia (low blood sugar) can place a significant strain on the adrenal glands. This is because the adrenals are a backup organ to the pancreas in keeping blood sugar under control. Therefore, meals high in carbohydrates—through their tendency to cause dramatic swings in blood sugar—can place significant stress on the adrenal glands and should be avoided. See chapter 13 for how to control blood sugar.

Step #3: Get Proper Rest

Getting proper physical rest is an important part of our response to stress. As Selye said, no organism can live continuously in a state of alarm. Every person, after stress, must go through a period of recovery, or rest.

We tend to experience the adverse consequences once the pressure is off: headaches, pain, bowel symptoms, depression, and so on. Migraines often strike on the weekend, after the pressure of the week has let up. Likewise, depression typically follows an episode of stress. Selye stated that "it is necessary to be keyed up for peak accomplishments, but it is equally important to be keyed down by the secondary phase of depression, which prevents us from carrying too long at top speed."[11] In other words, depression is a natural, perhaps even necessary, part of a healthy response to stress.

> Depression is one of these healing emotions. It serves to remove us temporarily from involvement in our environment so that our bodies and minds can be restored.[12]

Therefore, when we know we are facing something that will challenge us (an examination, a project at work, hospitalization of a family member, a business trip), we should anticipate that we will need a period of rest immediately following. Plan for it. Make it as high a priority as the challenge itself. God did so at the end of six days of Creation—though clearly He did not need "rest"—and He mandated that His people follow His example.

Sleep. If you were to examine references to sleep in Scripture, you might come to the conclusion that sleep is bad for you, since several verses warn against sleeping too much. But these are referring to slothfulness, not to getting proper rest. The Word also says:

Thou shalt lie down, and thy sleep shall be sweet. (Proverbs 3:24)

The sleep of a labouring man is sweet. (Ecclesiastes 5:12)

In a study conducted a number of years ago, hospitalized patients who slept the most were observed to have the shortest life expectancy. Therefore, the researchers concluded that getting too much sleep could shorten your life. But this study was distorted by the fact that these were sick, hospitalized patients. They weren't dying because they were sleeping too much; they were sleeping because they were dying![13]

Through medical research in recent years we have learned a great deal more about the value of proper sleep, as well as what happens when we sleep. When we lie down, we don't just drop into a state of unconsciousness and remain there for eight hours until we wake up. Instead, we go through several phases of sleep, and we repeat those phases several times during the night.

Normally, after a brief light, semiconscious state, we move into deep sleep, where we stay for some time. After about ninety minutes, we enter what is called REM sleep. During this phase, muscle tone throughout the body is exceedingly depressed, except for a few ir-regular movements such as "rapid eye movements," from which this phase of sleep gets its name. The heart rate and breathing become irregular, and the individual actively dreams.

In fact, brain activity dramatically increases during this time, and this is critical to the storage of memory, not only of the dreams themselves but also of information received throughout the day.

REM cycles tend to occur approximately every ninety minutes in normal sleep. However, the more exhausted a person is, the less REM sleep he will get. In fact, in extreme fatigue such as from sleep deprivation, there may be no REM sleep at all. Without REM sleep, memory storage becomes almost impossible, thus interfering with learning.[14]

Not only does exhaustion contribute to poor sleep quality, but stress—through the stimulation of adrenaline and cortisol at night—can disrupt an individual's normal sleep cycle and prevent proper rest. Essentially, surges of adrenaline and cortisol throughout the night are destroying his sleep. Such a person may be unconscious, but, because he fails to obtain adequate REM sleep, his sleep is not restful, and he awakens unrefreshed.

General rules for getting better quality sleep include:

- Go to bed and arise at the same time every day, including weekends, holidays, and vacations.

- Avoid stimulation just before bedtime. This would include work, television, caffeine, soda, sugar, vigorous exercise, and even bright lighting.

- Find a quiet place to sleep.

- Do not *try* to go to sleep; wait for it to come.

- Go to bed praying and meditating on Scripture.[15]   *Hart "Adrenalin + stress" p. 160 - 161*

My soul shall be satisfied as with marrow and fatness; and my mouth shall praise thee with joyful lips: When I remember thee upon my bed, and meditate on thee in the night watches. (Psalm 63:5–6)

Blessed is the man that walketh not in the counsel of the ungodly, nor standeth in the way of sinners, nor sitteth in the seat of the scornful. But his delight is in the law of the Lord; and in his law doth he meditate day and night. (Psalm 1:1–2)

- If you awaken during the night, don't get up, unless you must.

Exercise. Although this may surprise you, regular aerobic exercise is an important aspect of getting proper physical rest. Adrenaline is increased during a workout, but regular aerobic exercise actually results in an overall reduction in adrenaline and "fight or flight" system activity. This reduces adrenal stress.

This form of exercise needs to moderately challenge your cardiovascular system. In other words, you need to exercise for at least thirty minutes a day, five or six days a week, at your aerobic heart rate. To calculate your aerobic heart rate, follow these steps:

1. Subtract your age from 220.
2. Multiply the result by 60 to 80 percent. This is the approximate rate at which your heart should beat during the aerobic exercise period. For example, if you are forty years old: 220-40=180 X 0.70 = 126.

Once you have determined your aerobic heart rate, make sure that you are exercising at a level that will keep your heart beating close to that rate. This can be done by briefly pausing after several minutes of exercise and checking the pulse rate at the wrist. Once this is determined, the exercise can be adjusted accordingly. Note: If you are on certain medications, such as beta-blockers, you may not be able to achieve your aerobic heart rate. It is generally recommended that you consult your physician prior to instituting any exercise program.

CONCLUSION

The key to treating stress-related physical problems is to give the adrenal glands the rest they need. We have looked at three steps to accomplishing this: control pain and inflammation, keep blood sugar stable, and get proper physical rest. But the fourth and final step to restoring taxed adrenals is the most important: Reduce "fight or flight" system responses. In other words, find rest for the soul.

16

REST FOR
THE SOUL

illy Graham once quoted a stressed-out secretary as saying, "When this rush is over, I'm going to have a nervous breakdown. I earned it, I deserve it, and nobody's going to take it from me."

Why do we have stress? For the answer to this question, we will follow the advice of Herb Titus, former dean of Regent University's College of Law and Government. Dean Titus often challenged his students to look first in the first eleven chapters of Genesis for the answer to any question they had. He proposed that by doing so one can identify underlying principles that give clear direction to practically any conceivable question. This has certainly been the case throughout our study of health, and stress is no exception.

According to Genesis 1 and 2, God's original design for man included an ideal environment. In the Garden of Eden, there was no disease, no death, and no stress. Adam and Eve enjoyed perfect harmony, love, and transparency with one another. Furthermore, there was no sin barrier—human beings had intimate fellowship with their Creator, who even took walks with the first man and woman in the cool of the day (Genesis 3:8).

The term *stress* is actually an engineering term and refers to the work capacity of a given product. Every product has certain "design limitations." As long as the product is used in accordance with its design, it functions properly. The desk upon which my computer rests is experiencing no stress whatever, since the weight that is upon it is well within its design. If a product's design limitations are exceeded, then it will experience stress, and damage may result.

A certain amount of stress, however, is necessary to life.

When we say someone is "under stress," we actually mean under excessive stress or distress, just as the statement "he is running a temperature" refers to an abnormally high temperature, that is, fever. Some heat production is essential to life. . . . Complete freedom from stress is death.[1]

In the Garden of Eden, man did not just lie around all day doing nothing. He was given the responsibility of "keeping" the garden. This meant work, but it was something he no doubt enjoyed; it was not stressful.

So how did stress, as we use the term today, begin? It began when Adam and Eve exceeded God's design limitations for them. They ate of the forbidden fruit, violating the only restriction that He had placed upon them. As a direct result, they experienced stress for the first time in their lives in at least five ways.

Isolation from One Another

Man's first response to sin was to make clothing to cover himself. This is significant, especially in light of the fact that there were no other human beings on earth. Who were they hiding from? Each other. Suddenly both felt a sense of need to protect themselves from each other. They had lost their ability to be honest, transparent, and trusting—all of which are critical to intimacy. We see further evidence of this isolation in that Adam blamed Eve for his mistake. And, just a few years later, their firstborn son, Cain, murdered his one and only brother, which obviously caused immeasurable stress and pain for Adam and Eve.

God designed us to love and to be genuinely loved by one another. Whenever we fail to do that, through evil words, attitudes, or actions, we introduce stress in each other's lives. This will be manifested as pain, hurt, bitterness, anger, discouragement, and so on.

> For all the law is fulfilled in one word, even in this; Thou shalt love thy neighbour as thyself. (Galatians 5:14)

Isolation from God

Rather than walk with God, man hid from Him. Gone was openness, trust, and intimacy with the Creator. In fact, Adam indirectly blamed God for his failure (as we often do today) when he said, "The woman *whom Thou gavest* to be with me, she gave me of the tree, and I did eat" (Genesis 3:12, italics added).

God designed us for intimate fellowship with Him. When we are distant from Him, we exceed our design limitations, and stress is the result.

Disease and Death

Have you ever considered the fact that the bodies we possess were designed never to die? Indeed, our glorified bodies shall not taste death. But as a result of the Fall, disease and death are the rule for every one of us now. Sickness and death are major stressors for all of us.

Burdensome Work

Due to the cursing of the ground, man's work would now become a greater burden, as he would have to earn his survival by the "sweat of [his] face" (Genesis 3:17–19). Work and financial pressures are major sources of stress to us.

Eviction from His Home

Finally, God removed man from his magnificent utopian home, the Garden of Eden. Stress is so much a part of our lives today that we hardly recognize it. But what a blow this must have been for the First Parents. They had experienced the bliss of a stress-free life, only to lose it all.

Like Adam and Eve, we too experience stress whenever we, or those around us, violate God's design limitations. The question is, Can we at least partially experience what life was like prior to the Fall? After all that was lost in the Garden, is rest possible for the soul? The answer to that question is found in the book of Hebrews.

> *To day if ye will hear his voice, harden not your hearts, as in the provocation, in the day of temptation in the wilderness: when your fathers tempted me, proved me, and saw my works forty years. Wherefore I was grieved with that generation, and said, They do always err in their heart; and they have not known my ways. So I sware in my wrath, They shall not enter into my rest. . . . So we see that they could not enter in because of unbelief. . . . There remaineth therefore a rest to the people of God. For he that is entered into his rest, he also hath ceased from his own works, as God did from his. Let us labour therefore to enter into that rest, lest any man fall after the same example of unbelief. (Hebrews 3:7–11, 19; 4:9–11)*

Yes, we have hope—there is still rest for the soul! This passage speaks of salvation, but it also suggests four critical steps we must take in order to experience the rest from stress that God desires to give to us. We will deal with the first two in this chapter.

STEP #1: LABOR TO ENTER INTO GOD'S REST

Conquering stress is going to take effort. Do you *really* want to deal with stress properly? Are you willing to pay the price to do so? Do you *really* want to be well? Or will you wait for worse health or other consequences before becoming truly motivated? It won't be easy. It will involve some tough choices. But it is more than worth the effort. Start now by purposing in your heart to conquer this Trojan horse.

STEP #2: CEASE FROM YOUR OWN LABORS

"Time Management" is a buzzword in the West today. I myself attended seminars, read books, and listened to audiotapes, each with the hope that I would at long last learn the secret of how I could get everything done that I need to do. Yet, despite all of that input from the experts, I still found that my "To Do List" always substantially exceeded the time available to do it. At the end of the day, there were usually far more unchecked items than there were items marked "completed."

As I struggled to gain mastery over time, one Scripture verse both awed and humbled me. It was part of a conversation that Jesus Christ had with His heavenly Father as our Lord was nearing the end of His life.

I have glorified thee on the earth: I have finished the work which thou gavest me to do. (John 17:4)

What an incredible statement! Jesus must have been an expert time manager. How else can you explain His ability to fulfill the most incredible assignment ever given? He was responsible to develop a mastery of the Scriptures, live a sinless life, and proclaim the coming of the kingdom of God. At the same time, He had to carefully select a small group of men, transform their hearts, then train and equip them with a message that would sustain the animosity of every power on the face of the earth. Their mission would require such commitment and devotion that those He selected had to be willing to sacrifice their very lives for it. From the human standpoint, God's plan of the ages would rest upon the shoulders of twelve men: it would be up to them to spread His message to the world. And the Lord had only three years to get them ready. But He did it. And there are several reasons for His being able to do it.

He Spurned His Own Agenda

First of all, He was able to "finish the work" because He had no agenda of His own. He "ceased from His own labors." His ambition was only to do the will of His heavenly Father.

For I came down from heaven, not to do mine own will, but the will of him that sent me. (John 6:38)

Likewise, commit yourself to complete obedience to God's will. This is essential to living within His design limitations for you. Submit to His plan, to His purposes. Get rid of your own agenda and expectations. Apart from Him, they won't amount to anything worthwhile anyway.

He Fulfilled His Mission Only

Second, Jesus was able to accomplish His mission because He was absolutely clear on what it was. He knew what was His responsibility and what was not. Therefore, He was able to stay focused on His calling despite being surrounded by overwhelming needs that were still unmet at the time of His departure.

When Jesus said, "I have finished the work which thou gavest me to do," there were still many sick who had not been healed, and most of the people on the face of the earth had still not heard the gospel. Yet He knew that He had done exactly what God had expected of Him. In other words, He understood His *jurisdiction.*

Live within your jurisdiction. Every city has city limits. Within those city limits, the mayor of the city has jurisdiction, or rule. Outside the city limits, the mayor is just another citizen, with no special authority. Similarly, the deed to our land has a property description that draws the legal boundaries within which I have rights of jurisdiction.

In the same way, each believer has certain God-given responsibilities, as well as a sphere of authority for accomplishing them. That is his or her *jurisdiction.*

Are you an employee? Then you have the jurisdictional responsibility to work heartily and serve your employer "as unto the Lord" (see Ephesians 6; Colossians 3). On the other hand, you probably do not have the jurisdiction to evaluate and change company policy.

Are you a husband? Then you have the responsibility to love, cherish, and protect your wife, to live with her in an understanding way, and to disciple her through the Word (Ephesians 5; 1 Peter 3). On the other hand, you do not have jurisdiction to dump on her your responsibility for handling financial pressures, for dealing with creditors, or for the spiritual leadership of the family.

Are you a father? Then you are given the mission of training your children in the fear and admonition of the Lord and of properly providing for their spiritual as well as physical needs (Deuteronomy 6:6–7; Ephesians 6:4). However, you cannot make certain key decisions for them, such as their believing in the Savior.

Let me give you an example of how living within your jurisdiction lowers your level of stress. Years ago, my wife and I chose to have our children taught at home. My wife, who carries most of the teaching workload, gave counsel to me and worked with me on that decision, but the decision was ultimately my responsibility.

During the first few years, many questioned the wisdom of our decision to homeschool. Invariably they would address their concerns to my wife, and she experienced a great deal of stress trying to defend us.

Finally, I asked her to no longer discuss that decision with others but to refer any such concerns to me. This relieved a great deal of unnecessary pressure on her, for she had been carrying a burden (the responsibility for defending our family policy on the education of our children) that was not hers to carry. Once she was able to confine herself to her own jurisdiction, her "burden" was lightened considerably. (Interestingly, I do not recall anyone ever bothering to address those concerns to me!)

For many years now, my wife has avoided discussing home policy issues outside our family. (These kinds of discussions tend to take place most often at today's equivalent to Mars Hill—the church nursery.) She realizes that family policy decisions are within my jurisdiction and are therefore my responsibility to discuss or defend. Yes, she still has conversations about home schooling with her friends but only within the context of her jurisdiction. For example, she often seeks the advice of others on various curriculum options, such as which math or science books to use. But she does not seek their advice on whether or not to homeschool. That is a policy decision that rests upon my shoulders.

When wives overstep their jurisdiction and take on burdens that God designed only for the husband, they experience substantial unnecessary stress. Since it is the husband's responsibility for education, financial provision, protection, and so on, it is an act of faith for a woman to entrust those areas of concern into the hands of God, believing that He will take care of those needs through her husband. That trust in God is what teenagers need if they are to avoid the rebellion toward parents that so many experience.

Live within your jurisdiction. That is a key principle in helping you understand God's will and calling for you, and it will greatly simplify your life.

Come unto me, all ye that labor and are heavy laden, and I will give you rest. Take my yoke upon you, and learn of me; for I am meek and lowly in heart: and ye shall find rest unto your souls. For my yoke is easy, and my burden is light. (Matthew 11:28–30)

Live within your unique ability. Another key to understanding and fulfilling your mission is recognizing what specific abilities God has given you. What is it that you do best? What do you do that no one else can do? In his series *How the Best Get Better,* consultant Dan Sullivan challenges listeners to identify, develop, and focus their time and efforts on their own distinctive ability, that which is rare and unique about them.[2]

Jesus had the unique ability to lead a sinless life and offer Himself as the Sacrificial Lamb, an acceptable sacrifice, on the cross for us. There was no one else who could step in and take His place. Had He neglected His unique ability, calling, and mission, mankind would still be lost and without hope.

God has given me, as an associate pastor and physician, a special ministry to the sick in our church. This is especially appreciated when I accompany our pastors to the hospital, where I am able to dialogue with physicians and nursing staff and assist the sick in understanding their illness. God has placed me in a unique church ministry setting. If I neglect it, there is no one else to step in and meet that need.

Even more important, I have a unique ability as a husband and father. No other man can fulfill the responsibilities I have toward my own wife and children. If I neglect them, they lose out—there is no one else to fulfill my God-given responsibilities.

Understanding your unique ability to meet the needs of those around you will give you invaluable insight into ceasing from your own works and in fulfilling the unique mission for which God has created you.

He Knew His Limitations

Third, Jesus knew His human limitations and obtained physical rest when it was needed. Yes, there were long days, and, yes, there were times of fatigue. But they did not destroy Him. When He was pushed to His limits, He withdrew to a quiet place, where He took time to "recharge His batteries," not only through getting physical rest but especially through intimate fellowship with His heavenly Father. Likewise, know your limitations and regularly withdraw for periods of physical and spiritual rest.

Counsel for the Type A Personality

Learning to stay within God's design limitations is a major challenge for those with strong Type A tendencies. But Psalm 127:2 says, "It is vain for you to rise up early, to sit up late, to eat the bread of sorrows: for so he giveth his beloved sleep." Here are several steps that Type A's should consider taking:

Take on only that which is your jurisdiction. Understanding jurisdiction and staying within it is a critical first step. Type A's have a great tendency to overcommit themselves.

Set boundaries. Especially set boundaries around work hours and activity, which otherwise tend to spill over and devour personal and family time. This is particularly difficult for those who own their own business and/or work out of their homes. Someone once said, "Home businesses usually don't work. Either the home does not provide the resources to make the business successful, or the business takes over the home environment, or both."

Since I often work out of an office in my home, I have found that I must establish certain days of the week and certain hours of the day in which I am "at work." At 5:30 P.M., I need to "leave" the office and join my family for the evening activities. If I do not have clear-cut time boundaries, I find that work activity dominates my home and family life.

Accept incompleteness and imperfection. Compulsive people tend to be perfectionists. In such cases, one's self-image is often closely tied with performance. Certainly, we are to strive for excellence. But we also need to realize our own limitations. Jesus was a great example for us, accepting the "incompleteness" of many still lost and hurting people but knowing His ministry and time on earth were done. Do not force unrealistic expectations on yourself. Remember, Jesus' yoke is easy, and His burden is light.

Improve time management. One way to improve is actually very simple: be punctual. Type A's tend to squeeze every minute out of the day. Because we try to work up to the very last minute, we are frequently late for appointments and activities.

My son's Sunday school teacher, Phil Collins, is never late for anything. He told his class to try to be not merely on time but "comfortably early." I decided to apply his advice and have found it to be very helpful, as well as stress relieving. Now I set my schedule for local appointments so that I can easily arrive at least fifteen minutes in advance. For longer trips, I arrange for a greater cushion of time. This allows us to travel and arrive without time pressure—and it shows that we have respect for the time of those who will be awaiting us. Being on time is said to be one of the four personal habits that causes others to recommend a person's business services.[3]

Regardless of your behavior type, it is always a challenge to improve one's *utilization* of time. On a regular basis, set aside times for prayerful review and planning. Each day should be started not only with a list of the items that need to be done but with their God-determined priority, so that you are actually spending your time doing that which is most important.

Think about only one thing at a time. Type A's tend to jump from one topic or thought to another. Just as you need to set boundaries around your time, you must also restrict your thoughts to the subject at hand. Are you home from work? Then think about the needs of your family. Forget the office until you are back at work. Daydreaming rarely bears good fruit. Instead, it generally squanders time that could be more useful for other purposes.

Take an extended vacation or sabbatical. When I counsel smokers on quitting their cigarettes, I always encourage them to schedule a vacation to coincide with their stop date. This allows them to remove themselves from their normal routine, of which their cigarettes have become a natural part.

For some people, it is almost impossible to get out of the rut and correct their stressful environment while in it. Instead, they need to get away for a long enough period of time to step back from their normal routine, get the "big picture," and develop a new set of habits.

Take time to step out of the whirlwind of life, let the dust settle, and find joyful rest in the company of your family. Many a preacher has said that men on their deathbeds never regret the work that they did not get accomplished, but only that they did not take more time for others, especially their family. Take time out for the things that *need* to be done in order to avoid having such regrets.

John Wesley certainly had a busy life. During his fifty-three years of ministry, he traveled more than a quarter of a million miles on horseback, preached 42,000 sermons, and rose at four each morning for devotions. Yet regarding his labors, he said, "Though I am always in haste, I am never in a hurry, because I never undertake more work than I can do with calmness of spirit."[4]

THE DIFFERENCE BETWEEN STRESSORS AND STRESS

Before proceeding further, we need to make an important, though subtle, distinction in terms. Most of the discussion thus far has actually been focusing not on stress but on *stressors*. What's the difference? Stressors are external changes or events that are common to others. But how *external* stressors affect me depends upon my perception of the stressors. Therefore stress is an *internal* event; it is unique to me.

Two people can be going through the same circumstances (stressors) but with totally different responses. Let's say two people are caught in a traffic jam. One person might experience severe stress because the delay is keeping him from getting to important projects at work. Another, realizing that he can't do anything about the situation, may be grateful for the time just to sit and rest and enjoy the reprieve from those same pressures.

The degree to which stressors have an impact upon me depends upon my *internal* condition. My ability to withstand stress is determined by the condition of my soul.

As we discussed in chapters 14 and 15, the adrenal glands have been typically referred to as the body's stress organs. Actually, Scripture indicates that it is not the adrenal organs that are the principal stress organ but rather the *"heart"*—the inner person. Recently, science has had to agree.

All the days of the afflicted are evil: but he that is of a merry heart hath a continual feast. (Proverbs 15:15)

CONCLUSION

If you are ever going to conquer stress and stress-related illness, you must learn the ultimate key to entering into God's rest—how to "keep the heart."

So far, we have identified two steps to rest for the soul: (1) labor to enter into God's rest, and (2) cease from your own labors. In the next chapter, we will address the last two steps.

17

HOW TO
KEEP YOUR HEART

In order for you to understand the final two steps to finding rest from stress, I need to digress a little here to introduce you to a fascinating area of heart research. Once this is understood, you will realize the enormous implications it has on learning how to "keep your heart."

Several years ago, I attended a seminar on stress physiology, where I began an interesting journey of learning the effects of stress on the human body. During the course of the seminar, I was introduced to some fascinating technology that is now being used to measure certain physiological parameters of the heart. This in turn led me to the most fascinating Bible study that I have ever undertaken: the study of the heart (soul; inner man) in Scripture. What I learned showed me that the heart is the key to properly responding to stress.

All our perceptions, our responses, and our reactions to stress are initiated during the first few seconds of a stress encounter. What we do during the next sixty seconds determines how our body will deal with that encounter and whether or not we succeed in developing habits that help us manage stress in a way that minimizes illness and disease.[1]

Proverbs 23:7 says, "For as [a man] thinketh in his heart, so is he." And Proverbs 4:23 says, "Keep thy heart with all diligence; for out of it are the issues of life." Prior to this, I had applied these Scriptures only in a spiritual context, but now I see that they apply to the physical realm as well.

With this new technology mentioned above, an electrocardiogram (EKG) monitors the rate of each individual beat. The normal heart does not beat at a constant fixed rate. Instead, it oscillates. That is, someone who has a pulse that averages 70 beats per minute will tend to fluctuate between two rates, one faster than 70 and one slower, so that the average comes out to 70. From one beat to the next, the heart rate may speed up to 75. Then it may slow down to 65, and so on.

This varying beat-to-beat pattern is referred to as heart rate variability (HRV).

HEART RATE VARIABILITY

There are two basic HRV patterns. The first is the pattern that was just mentioned. This is considered a normal, healthy pattern. The other is an erratic pattern, in which there is no consistency to the HRV. This latter pattern is considered unhealthy, since it is associated with an increased rate of sudden death from heart disease. In fact, a poor HRV is the most accurate physiologic predictor of death from heart attack that we have.[2]

But what is most interesting is that research has now connected one's heart rate variability pattern with his or her *emotional state.* Individuals who have emotions that are characterized by terms such as caring, compassion, or appreciation tend to have "healthy" HRV patterns. Conversely, those who are experiencing anger or frustration tend to have the erratic pattern, and that places them at much greater risk of fatal heart attack. Individuals who can change their emotional pattern from negative to positive are able to improve their HRV pattern and thereby reduce their risk of sudden cardiac death.[3]

Research has linked the emotions with other physiological effects as well. For example, secretory IgA is an antibody secreted as a first line of defense against infection. It is found in various body fluids, including saliva. Individuals who experienced an episode of intense anger or frustration for just five minutes were found to have secretory IgA levels that dropped 55 percent in the first hour. These levels were still below normal six hours later —after only five minutes of anger or frustration.

On the other hand, individuals who experienced an episode of deep appreciation or love for five minutes saw their IgA levels rise to 40 percent above normal and stay elevated for more than six hours.[4]

Research confirms that "a merry heart doeth good like a medicine, but a broken spirit drieth the bones" (Proverbs 17:22). For example, severe depression is now considered a major predictor of heart disease—stronger, in fact, than smoking, high blood pressure, or poor diet. In one study, recovering heart patients who were depressed because of having suffered a heart attack were eight times more likely to die suddenly than those who were hopeful and happy that they had survived. Similarly, men who were characterized as "high anxiety" (fear, worry, insecurity) were at six times the risk of sudden cardiac death than men identified as optimistic.

Finally, there are two Type A behaviors that have now been associated with heart disease. The first is time pressure frustration. The hardworking Type A who sets lots of goals and accomplishes them is not necessarily at increased risk for heart disease. Rather, it is the one who sets goals but gets overwhelmed or frustrated when they are not completed on his time schedule. The other Type A behavior that is associated with heart disease is unresolved conflict. This individual harbors underlying anger, resentment, or bitterness toward others.[5]

ENTRAINMENT[6]

There are several oscillating systems in the body in addition to the heart:

- The brain: whose electrical activity is measured with EEG
- The lungs: which are automatically electrically triggered to inspire twelve to sixteen times per minute
- The arteries: which rhythmically pulse, moving blood along
- The intestines: which move food and waste through rhythmic contractions

But of all the oscillators, the heart is by far the most powerful. It has forty to sixty times the electrical strength of the brain. This becomes important because of a process referred to as *entrainment*.

Suppose that you were to mount a number of pendulum clocks on a wall, each keeping its own time. Within a fairly brief period, all of the pendulums will be swinging synchronously, with the heaviest one setting the pace. This is called entrainment: it is a law of nature. The underlying reason for it is that it is easier to "go with the flow" than against it. In this case, subtle air movement induced by the swinging pendulums eventually results in their all moving together.

Since the heart is the strongest oscillator in the body, the heart sets the pace for the others. Thus, when the heart has a good HRV pattern, the brain, lungs, and intestines all function optimally. That is why people who are in a panic (i.e., whose "hearts are troubled") tend to make poor decisions. We have all heard what we should do in an emergency: slow down, take some deep breaths, gather your thoughts, then decide what to do. The heart's ability to entrain the other organs, including the brain, gives us a *physiological* basis for this ancient advice.

THE HEART:
SEAT OF THE INTELLECT, EMOTIONS, MOTIVES, AND WILL

That the heart (soul) is the seat of the intellect, emotions, motives, and will is consistent with a scriptural view of the heart. The first two mentions of "heart" in the Bible occur in Genesis.

*And God saw that the wickedness of man was great in the earth, and that every **imagination** of the **thoughts** of his **heart** was only evil continually. And it repented the Lord that he had made man on the earth, and it **grieved** him at his **heart**.* (Genesis 6:5–6, emphasis added)

*And the Lord smelled a sweet savour; and the Lord said in his **heart**, I **will not** again curse the ground any more for man's sake; for the **imagination** of man's **heart** is evil from his youth; nei-*

ther will I again smite any more every thing living, as I have done. (Genesis 8:21, emphasis added)

According to the law of first mention, these Scriptures indicate that the heart (soul) has several key functions:

- It is the seat of our motives.
- It is the seat of our intellect.
- It is the seat of our emotions.
- It is the seat of our will.

Remember that human beings are spirit, soul, and body. Our spirit is what enables us to communicate with our heavenly Father. With our soul, also commonly referred to as our mind, will, and emotions, we have personality. Our personalities make us unique and allow us to interact with one another. Our physical body is what houses these two.

Both spirit and soul have an effect on the body.

For the Lord thy God hardened his spirit, and made his heart obstinate, that he might deliver him into thy hand. (Deuteronomy 2:30)

The sacrifices of God are a broken spirit: a broken and a contrite heart, O God, thou wilt not despise. (Psalm 51:17)

A merry heart maketh a cheerful countenance: but by sorrow of the heart the spirit is broken. (Proverbs 15:13)

But he is a Jew, which is one inwardly; and circumcision is that of the heart, in the spirit, and not in the letter. (Romans 2:29)

Forasmuch as ye are manifestly declared to be the epistle of Christ ministered by us, written not with ink, but with the Spirit of the living God; not in tables of stone, but in fleshy tables of the heart. (2 Corinthians 3:3)

For the word of God is quick, and powerful, and sharper than any two-edged sword, piercing even to the dividing asunder of soul and spirit, and of the joints and marrow, and is a discerner of the thoughts and intents of the heart. (Hebrews 4:12)

The heart's motives can be pure, sincere, centered on others, Christlike, or they can be self-centered or tending toward evil. The heart will either be led by the Spirit toward that which is good and positive, or we will allow it to be led by our carnal nature (what Scripture refers to as our "flesh") into that which is detrimental.

In addition, we also see that our heart has "thoughts." Now, as a scientist, I was trained that it is the mind that does all the thinking. The physical heart merely serves as a pump for blood. But in one sense the heart does think. It certainly responds to the mind's thoughts. Obviously, we have all experienced situations in which something that we have heard or seen has troubled our spirit or soul and has had an effect upon the physical heart. We even say that our hearts "sank" when we heard bad news. Science is beginning to recognize that the heart does indeed have a significant function connected to the intellect.

> The heart is a highly intelligent system that plays a far more central role in perception, mental/emotional balance and stress than previously believed. When people self-generate feelings of sincere love, care or appreciation a corresponding coherence pattern appears in the frequency spectrum of their ECG [electrocardiogram]. It is as though the heart, brain, and rest of the body were designed to function best when we experience positive emotional states.[7]

HOW THE HEART THINKS

Showing emotion tends to be disdained today. For example, we criticize people as being too "emotional" or "driven by their feelings." However, Scripture does not criticize feelings —except when we do not have any! This unfeeling condition is often referred to in Scripture as "hardness of heart." When I reviewed references in the King James Version, I discovered only two occasions in which the word "feeling" was used. The first occurs in Ephesians 4:19:

> *Who being past feeling [i.e., apathetic] have given themselves over unto lasciviousness, to work all uncleanness with greediness.*

Revelation 3:15–16 says:

> *I know thy works, that thou art neither cold nor hot: I would thou wert cold or hot. So then because thou are lukewarm, and neither cold nor hot, I will spew thee out of my mouth.*

God does not desire that we have no feelings. In fact, He would rather we have strongly negative feelings than no feelings at all. Someone who has no feelings simply does not care. He is hardened and apathetic.

Since we now have both biblical and scientific evidence that the heart "thinks," how can we tell what it is thinking? To answer this, I would like to propose something that is extremely important to understanding this serious problem of stress and how it affects us physically.

Your feelings, or emotions, will tell you what your heart is thinking at any given moment in time. And the electrical function of the physical heart will change with your emotional state. Your emotions will also tell you what your heart believes is true at any given moment in time.

Now, truth is not determined by your feelings. Rather, truth is fixed and unchanging. Furthermore, Scripture indicates that the heart can be deceived.

He that trusteth in his own heart is a fool: but whoso walketh wisely, he shall be delivered. (Proverbs 28:26)

So the heart needs an outside standard, and that standard is the Word of God:

For the word of God is quick, and powerful, and sharper than any two-edged sword, piercing even to the dividing asunder of soul and spirit, and of the joints and marrow, and is a discerner of the thoughts and intents of the heart. (Hebrews 4:12)

Therefore, although my feelings do not tell me what the truth is, they do tell me whether or not I believe the truth at any given moment. Now then, we are ready to introduce the final two steps to finding rest for the soul.

STEP #3: REFRAIN FROM HARDENING YOUR HEART

We can harden our hearts in different ways. For example, has God spoken to you about a particular matter, but you have not obeyed?

Harden not your heart, as in the provocation, and as in the day of temptation in the wilderness. (Psalm 95:8)

The heart can become hardened through the deceitfulness of sin:

But exhort one another daily, while it is called To day; lest any of you be hardened through the deceitfulness of sin. (Hebrews 3:13)

One of the consequences of a hardened heart is foolish decisions:

Happy is the man that feareth alway: but he that hardeneth his heart shall fall into mischief. (Proverbs 28:14)

He is wise in heart, and mighty in strength: who hath hardened himself against him, and hath prospered? (Job 9:4)

People's hardness of heart was why Moses allowed divorce:

He saith unto them, Moses because of the hardness of your hearts suffered you to put away your wives: but from the beginning it was not so. (Matthew 19:8)

God's wrath is being stored up against hearts that are hard and unrepentant:

Or despisest thou the riches of his goodness and forbearance and longsuffering; not knowing that the goodness of God leadeth thee to repentance? But after thy hardness and impenitent heart

*treasurest up unto thyself wrath against the day of wrath and revelation of the righteous judg-
ment of God; who will render to every man according to his deeds.* (Romans 2:4–6)

You can harden your heart toward a fellow human being in need:

*If there be among you a poor man of one of thy brethren within any of thy gates in thy land which
the Lord thy God giveth thee, thou shalt not harden thine heart, nor shut thine hand from thy
poor brother: But thou shalt open thine hand wide unto him, and shalt surely lend him sufficient
for his need, in that which he wanteth. Beware that there be not a thought in thy wicked heart,
saying, The seventh year, the year of release, is at hand; and thine eye be evil [stingy] against
thy poor brother, and thou givest him nought; and he cry unto the Lord against thee, and it be
sin unto thee. Thou shalt surely give him, and thine heart shall not be grieved when thou givest
unto him: because that for this thing the Lord thy God shall bless thee in all thy works, and in
all that thou puttest thine hand unto.* (Deuteronomy 15:7–10)

Thankfully, Jesus Christ did not harden His heart to the needs of those around Him.

*But when he saw the multitudes, he was moved with compassion on them, because they fainted,
and were scattered abroad, as sheep having no shepherd.* (Matthew 9:36)

*And Jesus, moved with compassion, put forth his hand, and touched him, and saith unto him . . .
be thou clean.* (Mark 1:41)

*For we have not an high priest which cannot be touched with the feeling of our infirmities; but
was in all points tempted like as we are, yet without sin.* (Hebrews 4:15)

When someone has offended you or hurt you, it is very easy to respond by hardening
your heart toward that person. Jesus said that, instead, forgiveness must come from the heart.

*So likewise shall my heavenly Father do also unto you, if ye from your hearts forgive not every
one his brother their trespasses.* (Matthew 18:35)

Christians sometimes make the mistake of believing that they have forgiven someone
simply by saying, "I forgive you." Nevertheless, they still *feel* anger, resentment, bitterness,
or coldness toward the individual whom they have supposedly forgiven. If you have truly
forgiven, then the thoughts of your heart will be positive toward the person. You will have
positive feelings toward him because you will no longer be considering his offense.

Ephesians 4:26–27, in the context of avoiding persistent anger, warns us not to "give
place" to the devil. Someone who has failed to forgive his offenders becomes imprisoned
with bitterness. His life becomes characterized by a lack of the fruit of the Spirit (Galatians
5:22–23). If your life is characterized by fruit that is not of the Spirit, perhaps you have allowed Satan a foothold in your life.

I have been there. Ten years ago the Lord crossed my path with that of biblical counselor
Jim Logan. He showed me from God's Word how to reclaim the ground I had surrendered
to the adversary, and I experienced for the first time what it meant to be totally free. If you

see a similar need in your life, I encourage you to obtain Jim Logan's book and apply it. If you do, your life will never be the same.[8]

STEP #4: KEEP THE FAITH

Faith (trust) also comes from the heart.

Take heed, brethren, lest there be in any of you an evil heart of unbelief, in departing from the living God. (Hebrews 3:12)

From the human standpoint, faith from the heart is what brings about conversion.

That if thou shalt confess with thy mouth the Lord Jesus, and shalt believe in thine heart that God hath raised him from the dead, thou shalt be saved. For with the heart man believeth unto righteousness; and with the mouth confession is made unto salvation. (Romans 10:9–10)

Faith is being fully persuaded or convinced of something. It is having complete, unshakable confidence in something to the extent that you place your full trust in and base your thoughts and actions upon it.

For example, you are probably sitting in a chair right now. When you came to sit in that chair and read this book, you did not test out the chair in a variety of ways to make sure that it would hold you. You simply believed that it was strong enough. You had faith in the strength of the chair, and you confidently sat on it. Likewise, your faith in God will affect not only your thoughts but also your emotions and actions.

Let's say that God has directly commanded you to go to the other side of town and take a meal to a needy family. In order to do so, you have to walk down a dark alley. Let's also say that you are aware that last night a murder took place in that very same alley. But in obedience, you start down that dark alley to your destination.

While you are walking, you quote various Bible verses to yourself.

Yea, though I walk through the valley of the shadow of death, I will fear no evil: for thou art with me; thy rod and thy staff they comfort me. (Psalm 23:4)

The Lord is my light and my salvation; whom shall I fear? the Lord is the strength of my life; of whom shall I be afraid? (Psalm 27:1)

For God hath not given us the spirit of fear; but of power, and of love, and of a sound mind. (2 Timothy 1:7)

Despite the fact that your mind is reciting these verses, you are *feeling* afraid. This is telling you something very important. Your mind is speaking one thing, but your heart is not convinced. This is an example of scriptural double-mindedness.

But let him ask in faith, nothing wavering. For he that wavereth is like a wave of the sea driven with the wind and tossed. . . . A double minded man is unstable in all his ways. (James 1:6–8)

God's standard for you is not that you just accept a truth with your mind, but that you believe it "in your heart" (act upon it). An evidence of a truth's being a reality to you is whether or not your feelings are consistent with it. If God actually told you to walk down a dark alley, I believe that He desires that you be able to walk down that alley with your heart completely at peace—no sweaty palms, no racing heart, no rapid breathing—because you are totally convinced that He is with you and will take care of you.

This, unfortunately, seems to be a rare kind of faith. How often have I seen that what is in my own heart is not consistent with what God expects of me. This is always a very humbling experience. Once again it has opened my eyes to the truth that we are all totally dependent upon the grace of God, who says:

God resisteth the proud, but giveth grace unto the humble. (James 4:6)

CONCLUSION

Do you have rest for your soul? Take the "Hebrews Stress Test."

- Have you purposed in your heart that you will labor to enter into God's rest?
- Have you ceased from your own labors, gotten rid of your own agenda, and taken on the yoke of Jesus Christ?
- Have you repented of a hardened heart and allowed Him to make it tender toward Him and others?
- Are you even now entering into God's rest by trusting Him?

Thou wilt keep him in perfect peace whose mind is stayed on thee: because he trusteth in thee. (Isaiah 26:3)

Trust is a function of the heart. A mind at perfect peace will not be possible without a heart that truly trusts in God.

18

STEPS TO TAKE
WHEN YOU BECOME ILL

What should you do if you become sick? The tendency of most Christians when they fall ill is immediately to make an appointment with their doctor, get his diagnosis, and follow his prescribed treatment regimen. But that isn't the picture we get when we look at the Word. In fact, going to a doctor did not seem to be highly regarded in Bible times.

Ordinarily, the ancient Hebrews did not go to physicians when they were sick. It is quite probable that any physicians referred to in these days were foreigners, and not Jews of the land.[1]

The reason the Hebrews rarely used physicians was that the doctors of their day were not trained in a manner that was consistent with Scripture. Therefore, it is reasonable to assume that the Hebrews believed a physician would not be able to tell them the root cause of their sickness—that is, give them an accurate diagnosis. Pagan doctors would not be thinking of whether or not the individual had fallen short of God's promises for health and long life. They would not be aware of the six root causes of sickness as given in the Word. Instead, pagan physicians were trained in concepts that were clearly unbiblical. Understandably, this led to bizarre theories, diagnoses, and treatments.

Dig seven pits, and burn in them some vine branches not yet four years old. Then let the woman, carrying a cup of wine in her hand, come up to each pit in succession, and sit down by the side of it, and each time let the words be repeated: "Be free from thy sickness."[2]

Every ancient civilization had a medical system that was developed from and compatible with its religion. One flowed naturally from the other. Ancient Taoism proposed that a man's life originated from and was sustained by a life force known as *chi* ("chee"), which permeates the universe and flows through man along a dozen or so invisible channels, or "meridians." Therefore, Chinese doctors reasoned that all disease was due to an imbalance of *chi*. It was natural then for a Taoist-trained physician to diagnose a sick person as having a meridian blocked and to use acupuncture, pressure, diet, herbs, or meditation to remove the blockage and restore proper flow. Our modern-day direct descendants of this pagan theory include iridology, reflexology, and certain aspects of applied kinesiology.

The Babylonians and Egyptians believed in a spirit world in which there were many gods. The goal of man was to live in harmony with those gods, so ancient Babylonian and Egyptian medicine is filled with sorcery, magic, and divination. No wonder the Jewish people had a problem with physicians.

To be a medical doctor and study the Word about my profession is a humbling thing. Aside from Luke, who was known as "the beloved physician," there just isn't much good said about us. The first mention of a doctor in Scripture (Genesis 50:2) indicates that we were really good at embalming dead people (perhaps former patients?). The next reference indicates that King Asa made a big mistake in not seeking the Lord but only going to doctors (2 Chronicles 16:12). Job said his friends were "all physicians of no value" (Job 13:4). Finally, Jesus hit us in a sensitive area when He was able to heal a hemorrhaging woman by her mere touch of His garment after she had spent "all that she had," having "suffered many things of many physicians" (Mark 5:26; see also Luke 8:43).

So what does the Word say we should do when illness strikes? In today's language, the answer is to get the proper diagnosis. In other words, first determine the root cause of the illness. Now, establishing the diagnosis is the goal of every Western-trained doctor as well. The problem is that he is usually focused on *only* the physical realm. But Scripture gives three legitimate avenues to pursue in establishing the diagnosis: (1) Seek the Lord. (2) Call for the elders. (3) Recognize when there is need for a physician.

SEEK THE LORD

Seeking the Lord is foremost. After all, the Inventor and Master Engineer of the human being knows why you are sick. You want His perspective on things. Don't make the mistake of King Asa, who, although he had walked with God nearly all his life, failed to seek Him at a time of serious illness. Consult with the Great Physician. He knows your true diagnosis, and His office charges are very reasonable.

CALL FOR THE ELDERS

Calling for the elders is really part of "seeking the Lord." In the book of James, our Lord's brother gave us clear instructions for what to do when one becomes ill.

Is any sick among you? let him call for the elders of the church; and let them pray over him, anointing him with oil in the name of the Lord: And the prayer of faith shall save the sick, and the Lord shall raise him up; and if he have committed sins, they shall be forgiven him. Confess your faults one to another, and pray one for another, that ye may be healed. The effectual fervent prayer of a righteous man availeth much. (James 5:14–16)

It is fairly common for a member of our church who is ill to request prayer from the pastors and deacons. Whenever we meet for this purpose, the pastor requests that one of us read the above passage from James 5. Then he asks if anyone would like to speak. That is an opportunity for each of us to examine himself and acknowledge before God and those present anything that is contrary to His will. We then consider:

- Have the conditions for God's promises of health been met?
- Has the sick person honored his parents, been honest in business, guarded his tongue, and so on?
- Has God given any discernment into the root cause(s) of the illness?
- Does this illness appear to be related purely to the physical? If so, then have physical laws been violated that would naturally result in this illness?

Often, the person requesting prayer will confess fear or some other spiritual need. Quite commonly, one of the pastors or deacons will also acknowledge a particular need, so that, by judging himself, he will not be a hindrance to the healing that is desired for the one under the church's spiritual oversight.

The pastor then explains that the oil for anointing is just olive oil. Purchased at the local grocery store, it has no inherent healing power. What we are doing is putting our faith in God through humbling ourselves before Him, asking His will to be done, and making ourselves available for whatever that is. The sick individual is anointed on the forehead with a drop of olive oil, while the pastor says, "I anoint you in the name of the Lord." We conclude by kneeling in prayer together for the ill person.

In response to anointing and prayer, there have been times when the individual simply felt at peace with proceeding with the prescribed medical treatment. At other times, we have noted healing take place quite dramatically. One couple who had experienced a long period of infertility conceived a child. After being prayed for and anointed with oil, my own niece, who was born with congenital glaucoma of one eye, experienced normalization of eye pressure and was able to avoid surgery. God has chosen to work both through medicine and through the simple faith of very ordinary people who are committed to serving Him.

It is interesting to note that two different Greek words are used for "anoint." *Creo* is used strictly in a ceremonial sense, whereas *aleipho* may be used ceremonially or to indicate the application of medicine. This passage in James uses *aleipho*, indicating that the anointing is not necessarily a ceremonial one and is not necessarily done by the elders themselves. The emphasis in this passage is on the elders *praying* for the sick individual. The anointing (*aleipho*) with "oil" may have already been initiated in the process of receiving medical treatment.[3]

RECOGNIZE WHEN THERE IS NEED FOR A PHYSICIAN

Despite all of the "bad press" in Scripture, there are some times when we do need a physician. Even Jesus said so.

They that are whole need not a physician; but they that are sick. (Luke 5:31)

Generally, you should consider seeing a health care professional in at least two situations.

When a Medical Emergency Exists

Obviously, when a medical emergency exists, you should not delay in seeking help. Today, with heart disease afflicting almost one of every two Americans, more than a third die before they even reach the emergency room. Learn to recognize the warning signs of an impending heart attack, stroke, or other life-threatening emergency. But even if an emergency exists, we always have instant access to our heavenly Father through prayer. Keep your spiritual eyes fixed upon Him despite the storm that may be brewing around you. On the other hand, there are occasions when the medical profession tends to make patients *feel* that there is an emergency when actually there is none. In such cases, patients may feel pressured into making quick decisions instead of prayerfully taking the steps outlined above.

When You Continue to Be Sick, Despite Seeking the Lord

Sometimes the Lord will provide us with an answer directly, such as through prayer. More commonly, He tends to answer our prayers for healing through other people.

In chapter 2, I told you the story of how I met Pastor Cornett and how God used a herniated disc in his neck to introduce us to one another. At that time, I had to give him only one prolotherapy injection treatment, and he was well.

Several years later, he reinjured his neck, and, despite prolotherapy three times, he still had severe pain. I did not understand why he was not responding. One day, I received a call from his mother, whom I had also treated. She suggested that I have him do exercises in a tub of hot water. As we talked, I began to wonder if maybe she was right. I'd never had to have a neck patient do that before, but in this case the pastor's pain was so severe that he would not even move his neck, something that was necessary in order for the injections to accomplish their purpose.

I called him up and suggested that to him. The next day, he filled a tub with water as hot as he could stand. After a few minutes of sitting with water up to his chin, he found the water very soothing and was able to move his arms without pain. That night, for the first time in six weeks, he slept pain free. By the next Sunday, with no other treatment other than exercising in hot water, he was back in the pulpit and has had no problem since.

This example illustrates the balance between seeking the Lord, calling for the elders, and consulting with a physician. As in this case, the answer does not always come right away. In fact, it has been my experience that *usually* there is a period of crying out to God before we hear from Him. During that time, He may be addressing needs in our lives that are more important than the physical healing.

Remember Paul's "thorn in the flesh"? It was sent from God but was a "messenger of Satan." Pastor Ron Dunn says, "Good and evil travel on parallel tracks. And they tend to arrive about the same time." What the adversary would like to use to hinder us, God is using for His good purposes. As my friend Gary Fraley says, "You'll never know that Jesus is all you need, until He is all you've got."

THE ROLE OF FAITH IN HEALING

James said, "The prayer of faith shall save the sick" (James 5:15). Is faith necessary in order for us to get well? Probably the answer is that it *depends upon the cause of the illness.* In some cases, the answer would have to be yes. Why else would we see so many connections between faith and healing in Scripture? In several instances, Jesus said specifically that it was faith that made the person well. He said that to the woman who was healed of a hemorrhage (Mark 5:25–34), the Syrophenician woman (Matthew 15:27–28), a blind man (Mark 10:52), and a leper (Luke 17:15–19). He even said that it was the faith of Jairus that allowed his daughter to be raised from the dead (Mark 5:35–42).

Since we don't really recognize the role of faith in medicine, it is sometimes confused with the "placebo effect." Placebo refers to a pill, usually containing sugar, which has no medicinal properties.

People involved in research studies are usually randomly assigned to receive either the actual drug being tested or the placebo, a "fake." In a double-blind study, neither doctor nor patients know what they are getting. Sometimes someone getting the drug will think he is getting a placebo. Conversely, some patients taking the placebo become convinced that they are getting the drug. In a typical study, it is expected that around one-third of the placebo group will actually show as much benefit as if they were on the actual medication. This improvement may be due simply to the positive physical changes that can take place when a person believes that he is getting better.

But faith is not the same as the placebo effect. The placebo effect is based upon presumption (that one is getting the "real" medicine), and a false presumption at that. However, we often confuse presumption with faith. For example, let's say that you desire to purchase a new car with cash. The problem is that your income is just one step above the poverty level, and reality would seem to say it cannot be done. You convince yourself, though, that if you just believe hard enough, God will give you a new car. And somehow it happens: you are able to buy a new car. Now you might say that you got your new car by faith. But that was not faith; it was presumption. *You* are the one who determined the goal, and you presumed that God would assist you in accomplishing it.

Similarly, you can try to "will" yourself into getting well. And doing so might help; you might get better. But that is not faith. That is also presumption. Biblical faith is based upon God's Word. If *God* were to tell you that He is going to give you a new car, then—despite the fact that getting one looks impossible—you should believe Him, because He said He would do it. In the same way, if God speaks to your heart through the use of His written Word and tells you that you are going to be healed, then you should believe Him, no matter what the doctors tell you. If He truly did say it, then He will bring it to pass. Our responsibility is to discern His voice and to believe Him.

The Institute in Basic Life Principles defines faith as "picturing what God intends to do in a given situation, and acting in harmony with it." In other words, faith is being so fully convinced of something *by the Scriptures* that you are willing to base your words, attitudes, and actions upon it, even though the outcome appears humanly impossible. Let me give you a personal example.

Despite the fact that we greatly desired more children, my wife was unable to conceive after our first child was born. We prayed for children for years, asking the Lord to open her womb. One day, while my heart was in considerable anguish over this situation, I was leading my family in devotions when the Holy Spirit broke the six years of silence as I read Psalm 126.

They that sow in tears shall reap in joy. He that goeth forth and weepeth, bearing precious seed, shall doubtless come again with rejoicing, bringing his sheaves with him. (Psalm 126:5–6)

I had read that passage many times before, but this time the verses seemed exactly to identify the troubled feelings of my heart. I experienced a quiet calmness, telling me that this was God's answer for us. The next day as we were praying, I realized that I needed to stop *asking* God for another child but begin *thanking Him by faith* for the promise that He had given. Shortly thereafter, my wife conceived our son Nathan, just as "through faith also Sara herself received strength to conceive seed" (Hebrews 11:11).

Faith is like the clutch on an automobile. It is what engages the engine's power and converts it into motion. You can have under the hood a huge, perfectly tuned 454-horsepower engine that has the capacity to go from 0 to 60 mph in nothing flat. But if you never engage the transmission, you won't move. We have an awesome, all-powerful God, who has the capacity to rule the world from His throne while stooping to hear our silent prayer. But His power and love do not become a reality in the lives of many because of their lack of faith.

And [Jesus] did not many mighty works there because of their unbelief. (Matthew 13:58)

DO YOU HAVE AN IDOL IN YOUR LIFE?

Sometimes we fool ourselves. We think our faith is in God, only to find that, when it is tested, that it is in ourselves or in something or someone else. Without realizing it, we can make something an "idol." How can we know that we have an idol, a false god? Our "god" is the object of our faith—what we look to for our most basic needs. Consider the following:

Purpose

Is my purpose or fulfillment found in my job, my ministry, in following a diet, a program, and so on, or in Christ?

Provision

Who (or what) do I really believe provides for all of my needs? Is it my job, my employer, the government, my spouse? If God were to take my job away tomorrow, would my faith be shaken?

Protection/Security

What has my confidence to protect me from harm or death? Is my confidence in a weapon, in self-defense training, in a home security system? Who or what will protect me from disease? Is it the medical profession, medication, a diet, supplements, or herbs? Or is it the One who made me, the Great Physician?

Except the Lord keep the city, the watchman waketh but in vain. (Psalm 127:1)

Power

Who or what receives the credit for restoring my health? Is it the doctors, a diet program, a drug, a supplement or other product? Or is it the Lord?

My Passion

Where do my thoughts go during idle time? Do they *always* go to something other than the Lord? Do I find myself often preoccupied with concerns over diet, health, and so forth? What is the usual topic of my conversations? These are good indications of where my "treasure" (therefore, my heart) is, for I will "worship" the focus of my passion.

Where your treasure is, there will your heart be also. (Matthew 6:21)

If the object of our faith is anything other than Christ, we will experience fear, because deep down we know that at any time we could have our security taken away. Fear of loss of health or anything else that is temporal is a signal that our faith is not in Christ. Again, a definition from the Institute in Basic Life Principles is noteworthy: Security is "structuring my life around that which is eternal and cannot be destroyed or taken away."

When our lives center on Christ, we will have peace that can withstand all the storms of time, aging, and illness.

Conclusion

Looking at our health from the perspective of the Word literally involves examining every aspect of our lives. Encompassing far more than diet and doctor visits, a biblical view of health and disease includes our relationships with God and others as well as our own personal character. *The Word on Health* has reminded us that:

- The church must be central in laying a biblical foundation for how one should think of health and disease—whether pastor, patient, or physician.
- Compassion for the sick has been closely identified with the message of the gospel since the time of Christ.
- Numerous conditional promises in Scripture relate to health and long life. These range from honoring our parents to being honest in business practices.
- There are six root causes of disease. Many of these have a spiritual basis.
- Into the void created by the church's silence on health and medicine have come erroneous teachings, some claiming to be biblically based. In particular, we are told that God's ideal is for us to be vegetarian.
- If such false teaching is received, it can lead to numerous devastating consequences.
- Although our Lord has given us great liberty in the area of diet, temperance is nevertheless expected in this realm as well as any other.
- Our Creator has given us a proven dietary plan, which is graphically organized into the Biblical Diet Pyramid. A very similar program has demonstrated a drastic reduction in the two leading causes of death in the West, heart disease and cancer.
- Those with food allergies and blood sugar control problems need to make certain adjustments in their diet program.
- Stress, if not dealt with properly, can have disastrous effects upon health.
- Stress management and resolution must involve giving the adrenal glands a rest and finding rest for the soul.
- Rest for the soul can be understood and obtained only through learning how to keep the heart.
- The "thoughts of the heart"—one's feelings (emotions)—are a significant key to a walk of honesty and faith.
- The object of our faith must be Christ alone.

As you pursue optimum health, focus on Christ, with whom you will spend eternity if you have been born again (John 3:16; Romans 10:9–10). Don't make diet, medicine, health, or long life your god. Death is certain for all. God knows your days; He holds you in His strong hand and will keep you—forever.

Look unto me, and be ye saved, all the ends of the earth: for I am God, and there is none else. (Isaiah 45:22)

A

A WORD
ON SCIENCE

Because that, when they knew God, they glorified him not as God, neither were thankful; but became vain in their imaginations, and their foolish heart was darkened. Professing themselves to be wise, they became fools, and changed the glory of the uncorruptible God into an image made like to corruptible man, and to birds, and fourfooted beasts, and creeping things. (Romans 1:21–23)

SCIENCE, MEDICINE, AND THE CHURCH

Over the last several centuries, the church and science have felt very uncomfortable with one another. The reason for this is simple. The church, by proclaiming the revealed Word of the Creator, claims to profess the truth. Science, on the other hand, is by nature constantly challenging the truth to test and verify that it is so. "Science" is defined in *Dorland's Medical Dictionary* as "(1) The systematic observation of natural phenomena for the purpose of discovering laws governing those phenomena (2) The body of knowledge accumulated by such means."

"Such means" refers to what is now known as the *scientific method*, which involves five specific steps:

1. Stating the problem
2. Forming a hypothesis
3. Observing and experimenting
4. Interpreting data
5. Drawing conclusions

History attributes the birth of the scientific method to an English monk named Roger Bacon. Because there were so many errors in thinking, Bacon saw the need to verify one's presumptions through experimentation. He believed that understanding could be obtained without depending upon the ideas of those who were considered authorities in their respective fields. This form of logic became known as *inductive reasoning,* because it supposedly begins with simple observation, rather than being *deduced* from a known principle, as with Aristotle's *deductive* logic. Bacon's views were considered rebellious toward the establishment, and he was imprisoned for them.

Actually, the scientific method is much older than Bacon. In fact, it is as old as mankind and was first employed by Eve in the Garden of Eden. The first Great Experiment of man is recorded in God's Laboratory Manual in Genesis 3.

1. State the problem.

Eve had been commanded not to eat of the Tree of Knowledge of Good and Evil. But she had a problem: the fruit looked tasty and appealing, and she wanted to be wise.

2. Form a hypothesis.

Based upon the information given to her by the serpent, Eve hypothesized that she could partake of the fruit, become wise, and suffer no adverse effect (i.e., she would not die).

3. Observe and experiment.

She then conducted two experiments. She ate of the forbidden fruit, then repeated the experiment by giving it to her husband. Both experiments yielded the same results, showing the reproducibility of her findings.

4. Interpret the data.

She noticed that she was still standing, breathing, thinking, and talking. She also noticed that her husband bore evidence that he was alive as well. Furthermore, there was evidence that her knowledge had increased, because now her "eyes" appeared to be open. For the first time, she noticed that she and her husband were naked.

5. Draw conclusions.

Eve concluded that if she ate of the forbidden fruit that it would taste good, that she would have more knowledge, that she would not die, and that her hypothesis was therefore correct.

But Eve was wrong. She did not become wiser. Instead, she was deceived. Her understanding and ability to reason had become corrupted. Furthermore, she *had* died, although that was not readily observable to her with the instruments that she had available. First of all, she had died spiritually, being instantly cut off from fellowship with her Creator. Second, the moment she consumed the fruit, the process of death had begun in her physical body as well—it would just take time before it revealed itself.

The first test of the scientific method had not revealed the truth to man at all but, instead, a lie. Furthermore, a closer look at this world premiere of science reveals the inherent weaknesses of the scientific method and why it tends to produce conflicting, confusing, and perhaps even totally wrong results.

THE SCIENTIFIC METHOD IS NOT TRULY INDUCTIVE

Eve did not simply reject the authoritative principles of her Creator and start from scratch. Instead, she replaced them with *false presuppositions* from the serpent and used those as the basis for her experiment. The scientific method claims not to reason from known principles (i.e., make deductions from the conclusions of authoritative sources), but this is simply not true. It is virtually impossible for man to function that way. We *always* operate with a set of preconceived ideas.

As the *World Book Encyclopedia* says so well, "The human mind probably does not actually solve problems in a systematic fashion. But, after the problem is solved, the scientist can use the scientific method to explain the problem and its solution in an orderly way."

Therefore, most of the great scientific breakthroughs have not been made through the scientific method (operating through the five steps), but rather they have come quite unexpectedly. Here are just a couple of many examples that could be cited:

- *Rubber.* In 1839, Charles Goodyear accidentally spilled a mixture of sulfur and rubber on a hot stove. The rubber compound was "cured" by the heat and stayed firm in hot or cold temperatures. The process became known as vulcanization and enabled the birth of the rubber industry.
- *Penicillin.* In 1928, Alexander Fleming found that bacteria growing in a culture were being destroyed near a mold that had formed unintentionally.

THE SCIENTIST ALWAYS OPERATES WITHOUT ALL OF THE FACTS

Eve thought she had all the facts she needed in order to form her hypothesis. But she didn't. First of all, she did not know who the serpent was and what his intentions were. Second, she did not know what true wisdom and knowledge were. And third, she did not know what death was. She had never seen it or experienced it. On the other hand, her Creator knew all this information. Therefore, she should have trusted Him and never conducted the experiment at all.

Scientific experimentation is *always* conducted with a limited set of facts. Yes, knowledge is gained through systematic observation, but how does the scientist know that he is properly interpreting his data? And despite all of science's discoveries, one thing is clear: experimentation always reveals that there is much more still to learn. Only God has all the facts.

In whom are hid all the treasures of wisdom and knowledge. (Colossians 2:3)

STARTING PRINCIPLES MUST BE
CONSISTENT WITH GOD'S WORD, REVEALED TRUTH

The revealed word of the Creator must be the basis from which science derives its principles. Actually, the scientific method is basically deductive in nature and is working with a very limited understanding of "the problem." If, like Eve, science ignores revealed truth, it will incorrectly state the problem, form an inaccurate hypothesis, wrongly interpret data, and come to false conclusions.

Let's take bread as an example. A recent newspaper headline read, "Smell of Baked Bread May Be Health Hazard." The article went on to describe how baked bread apparently releases organic compounds into the air that can break down ozone. Sometime later, I received a humorous analysis of the article on my e-mail. Although all our efforts have thus far failed to identify the creative author, he or she is obviously an "authoritative source" on the subject. I quote:

> I was horrified. When are we going to do something about bread-induced global warming? Sure, we attack tobacco companies, but when is the government going to go after Big Bread? Well, I've done a little research, and what I've discovered should make anyone think twice. . . .

> 1. More than 98 percent of convicted felons are bread users.
> 2. Fully HALF of all children who grow up in bread-consuming households score below average on standardized tests.
> 3. In the 18th century, when virtually all bread was baked in the home, the average life expectancy was less than 50 years; infant mortality rates were unacceptably high; many women died in childbirth; and diseases such as typhoid, yellow fever, and influenza ravaged whole nations.
> 4. More than 90 percent of violent crimes are committed within 24 hours of eating bread.
> 5. Bread is made from a substance called "dough." It has been proven that as little as one pound of dough can be used to suffocate a mouse. The average American eats more bread than that in one month!
> 6. Primitive tribal societies that have no bread exhibit a low incidence of cancer, Alzheimer's, Parkinson's disease, and osteoporosis.
> 7. Bread has been proven to be addictive. Subjects deprived of bread and given only water to eat begged for bread after as little as two days.
> 8. Bread is often a "gateway" food item, leading the user to "harder" items such as butter, jelly, peanut butter, and even cold cuts.
> 9. Newborn babies can choke on bread.
> 10. Bread is baked at temperatures as high as 400 degrees Fahrenheit! That kind of heat can kill an adult in less than one minute.

> In light of these frightening statistics, we propose the following bread restrictions:

> 1. No sale of bread to minors.
> 2. A nationwide "Just Say No To Toast" campaign, complete with celebrity TV spots and bumper stickers.

3. A 300 percent federal tax on all bread to pay for all the societal ills we might associate with bread.
4. No animal or human images nor any primary colors (which may appeal to children) may be used to promote bread.
5. The establishment of "Bread-free" zones around schools.

Although this whole discussion on bread has been far-fetched, it still reflects the absurd conclusions that man can come to when his thinking is "set free" from the moorings of revealed truth. Actually, after reading historical accounts of some of the false ideas that have been revered by scientists in the past, some of these observations related to bread don't seem all that far-fetched. Consider a few modern-day examples.

- Science operates on the presupposition that man is an evolved animal and that he came about as the result of a time-and-chance process. Beside that presupposition's being totally contradictory to natural law accepted by science itself, the Word of God clearly indicates that man was designed and given life by a personal, wise, powerful, and loving Creator.
- Science denies the historical account of a worldwide flood, not based upon the evidence (of which there is a great deal to support the Genesis account) but because of faulty presuppositions.
- Science operates on the premise that human life is under man's control and therefore may be prevented or taken at will through contraception, abortion, and even euthanasia.

THE SCIENTIFIC METHOD IS
A POOR APPROACH TO DETERMINING TRUTH

It is the glory of God to conceal a thing: but the honour of kings is to search out a matter. (Proverbs 25:2)

God commanded man to subdue the earth and take dominion over it (Genesis 1:28). It is His intention for us to learn about our world and to master it. As the study of nature (creation), science is an important part of fulfilling that mandate. Look again at the definition of science: "The systematic observation of natural phenomena for the purpose of discovering laws governing those phenomena."

However, just like anything else in life, science can be used properly or improperly; there are rules and restrictions. Science should examine God's world for His laws, but when science tries to refute God's Word, it crosses the line and becomes destructive.

Today, experiments are being conducted in an effort to disprove that which God has already revealed—for example, fossil studies that continue to search for Darwin's "missing links."

For the wrath of God is revealed from heaven against all ungodliness and unrighteousness of men, who hold the truth in unrighteousness, because that which may be known of God is mani-

fest in them; for God hath showed it unto them. For the invisible things of him from the creation of the world are clearly seen, being understood by the things that are made, even his eternal power and Godhead; so that they are without excuse. (Romans 1:18–20)

Remember that the very definition of science is "the systematic observation of natural phenomena for the purpose of discovering laws governing those phenomena." But fixed laws are totally incompatible with an evolutionary worldview. Chance processes do not produce fixed laws. The earth, if it were formed according to evolutionary theory, would be a place of total chaos. Only a Creator with power and intelligence could establish the fixed laws governing the circuits of the planets, the force of gravity, the spinning of the earth with its predictable sunrise and sunset, the gestational periods of humans and the various animals, the cycle of rain, the seasons, and so on. It should come as no surprise that nearly all of the great early scientists (Bacon, Newton, Galileo, etc.) were believers in a divine Creator. To study creation for the discovery of fixed laws would only make sense to such an individual.

Solomon was the wisest man who ever lived, and God gave him his wisdom. But beside the fact that his wisdom was great, the Bible says something else about it:

And Solomon's wisdom excelled the wisdom of all the children of the east country, and all the wisdom of Egypt. For he was wiser than all men . . . and his fame was in all nations round about. And he spake three thousand proverbs: and his songs were a thousand and five. And he spake of trees, from the cedar tree that is in Lebanon even unto the hyssop that springeth out of the wall: he spake also of beasts, and of fowl, and of creeping things, and of fishes. And there came of all people to hear the wisdom of Solomon, from all kings of the earth, which had heard of his wisdom. (1 Kings 4:30–34)

Solomon was a scientist, a student of nature. And his understanding of God's creation gave him great insight into the ways of the Creator. Science should not be feared. Instead, the Christian should embrace it. But science needs to assume its proper place. If it purports to seek to understand the laws of nature, then it must know and be yielded to the Lawgiver, the Creator Himself. To fail to do so will bring the same results that Eve experienced.

HOW CLINICAL STUDIES ARE DESIGNED

Let's say that you want to test a new pill for high blood pressure. In order to do so, you could just give the pill to 100 people and record their blood pressures. This would yield results that gave you some information. Unfortunately, you would not know whether it was the chemical effect of the pill itself that was being of benefit or if the results were due to some other factor, such as the patient's or doctor's belief in the pill's effectiveness.

In order to remove that potential bias, you would give some of the patients a "fake" pill, or placebo. The placebo, often just a sugar pill, serves as a standard against which the effectiveness of the actual drug is measured. The experimental group is made up of patients who receive the real medicine. The "control group" patients are those who receive the fake pill.

Now, since everyone involved in the study would naturally like to be assigned to the group that gets the real thing, you must remove that bias as well. Therefore, you *randomly* assign your 100 patients into two groups. To randomly assign them means that they are arbitrarily placed in one of the two groups without the opportunity for researcher or patients to choose which.

For example, when we conducted a study on heart disease, we put the names of the study participants on slips of paper and placed them in a hat. My four-year-old son drew each name sequentially out of the hat. Prior to each drawing, we determined to which group the next name would be assigned. Since Nathan had no knowledge of which name would be drawn out next, the patients were effectively assigned to either the experimental group or the control group in a randomized fashion. This made the study "randomized and placebo-controlled."

Then, in order to completely remove the possibility of bias, the pills are disguised so that neither researcher nor patient knows whether or not the participant is getting "the real thing." If neither doctor nor patient knows to which group each belongs, the study is referred to as double-blind.

Now, back to testing your pill for high blood pressure. It is expected that approximately one-third of the patients taking the placebo will actually experience a reduction in blood pressure. This "placebo effect" is probably a result of the benefits that occur when one has a positive attitude toward his illness. In other words, these patients, even though they are taking a pill that has no direct benefit on their blood vessels, begin to *believe* that they are taking the real medicine and that their blood pressure is going down. Such an individual can convince himself that he is taking the actual medicine (even though he is not) and get better.

This then is the nature of a double-blind, randomized, placebo-controlled study. It is the gold standard of the scientific medical profession in determining which treatments are most effective. But it is not infallible. Studies examining the same problem often come up with conflicting results. One major reason for this is the fact that people are complex beings. It is very difficult to have exactly the same set of circumstances in different individuals so that one can be sure that it is the true effect of the drug that is being measured. That is why researchers have to control for other factors that might influence the outcome of the study.

People who have high blood pressure tend also to smoke, or to have high intake of salt, or to be male, or to be under a great deal of stress. Researchers would need to examine the two groups to make sure that there was not a high predominance of individuals with one or more of those risk factors in one group as compared to the other. Since new discoveries are being made every day as to the cause and the factors of a disease, it is easy to see how complex these research studies can become—and how difficult it is to authoritatively state one's conclusions.

How much better, whenever possible, to have revealed truth available to you as a starting point. Science is a wonderful profession, and its discoveries have provided us with countless benefits and conveniences. However, science and the scientific method are not to be worshiped. Instead, it is our Creator who is to be worshiped, and scientific study needs to be conducted with a reverent respect for the God who made us.

ADRENAL
STRESS INDEX

As explained in chapter 14, chronic stress taxes the adrenal glands. In response to stress, ordinarily the adrenals release cortisol in increased amounts. If the stress persists, this cortisol release becomes magnified. At the same time, the production of DHEA, an important adrenal hormone that counterbalances the effects of cortisol, falls off. Eventually, chronic stress to the adrenals will cause cortisol output to lessen as well.

So the adrenal glands go through successive stages of maladaptation, fatigue, and eventually exhaustion. The normal healthy adrenal gland produces cortisol in a twenty-four-hour rhythm. Normally, cortisol output is highest in the morning, approximately midvalue throughout the day, and then drops off to a very negligible output during the night.

The pattern in which cortisol is released is just as important as the total amount. This is why doing the typical twenty-four-hour urine collections for cortisol or testing the blood once or twice during the day are inadequate means of determining if the adrenals are cycling through a proper pattern. In order to properly assess adrenal function, at least four specimens should be taken at specific times throughout the day. Any less will result in an unreliable snapshot of adrenal output at a given time, rather than the overall "motion picture" that is necessary to assess this time-integrated organ function.

Since at least 1969, it has been known that adrenal hormones can be measured in the saliva, and salivary measurements of cortisol have been used in stress research for more than ten years.[1] With a home test kit, the patient can collect samples of saliva at multiple points throughout the day, while going about his normal routine. The clinical laboratory that has led the way in making this technology available to the practicing

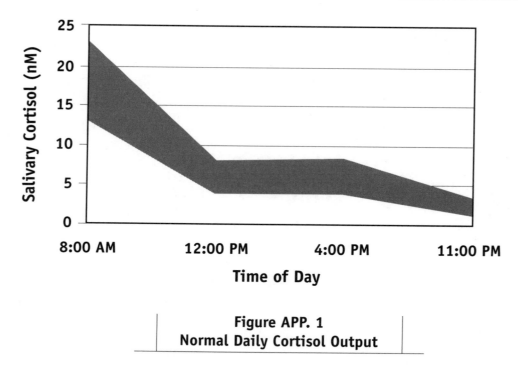

Figure APP. 1
Normal Daily Cortisol Output

physician is Diagnos-Techs, of Kent, Washington. With their Adrenal Stress Index (ASI), saliva samples are collected by the patient at home at approximately 8:00 A.M., 12:00 noon, 4:00 P.M., and 11:00 P.M. A normal cortisol release pattern is seen in figure APP.1.

Under normal conditions, remember, the highest levels of cortisol output occur in the morning, with moderate levels throughout the day, and the lowest levels at night. Since cortisol blocks the function of the immune system and makes us feel good, it is by the Creator's design that it is high during the day and low at night. This allows us to go through the healing phase at night while we are resting, instead of during the daytime. Repair mechanisms are painful and drain us of our energy, and it is a blessing that they take place while we are asleep.

However, in a chronically stressed individual, these mechanisms go haywire, resulting in a variety of Adrenal Stress Index patterns. This Appendix will identify two of the most common patterns.

First, and perhaps most common, is the clinical situation in which the adrenal glands become stressed by low blood sugar, also known as hypoglycemia. In this situation, the individual's blood sugar drops too low or too fast or both. Since the adrenal glands release cortisol and adrenaline in order to boost blood sugar that has fallen too low, an Adrenal Stress Index may show elevated levels of cortisol either in the afternoon, when this most commonly occurs, or possibly on the early morning specimen, since low blood sugar may strike at night while the individual is sleeping. The symptoms of hypoglycemia were identified in chapter 13.

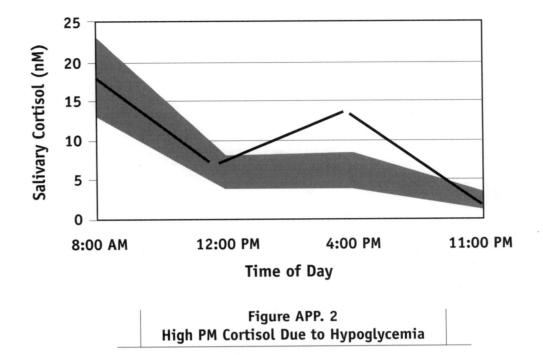

Figure APP. 2
High PM Cortisol Due to Hypoglycemia

The second commonly identified disorder is one in which the patient's cortisol levels are elevated at night. Recall from our discussion that the body needs low cortisol levels at night in order for it to go through proper rest and healing phases. When cortisol levels are elevated at night, the patient is essentially getting adrenal hormone surges, which interfere with his ability to get proper sleep. This results in a variety of problems, most commonly fatigue, difficulty sleeping, depression, and painful or aching joints or muscles. All of these are a direct result of inability to get good quality rest.

Such an individual may not always be aware of the fact that he is not resting properly. He may believe that he is getting plenty of sleep. The problem is that his sleep quality is poor and not accomplishing its purpose. The ASI is an excellent tool for identifying a possible underlying cause to any of these common clinical problems.

The ASI can be obtained with a doctor's order by calling 1-800-878-3787. Test kits are provided at no charge, and laboratory fees are arranged through your ordering physician. The specimens, once collected, are refrigerated until they are shipped first class or express. Research has confirmed that the lab results remain accurate despite shipping. However, it is recommended that the specimens be collected and shipped at the beginning of the week in order to minimize the time in the mail. Diagnos-Techs maintains a technical support team to assist your physician in interpreting and applying the results of your test.

In addition to salivary cortisol levels, the ASI also measures DHEA, secretory IgA (a surface antibody), and anti-gliadin antibodies, for the detection of gluten sensitivity.

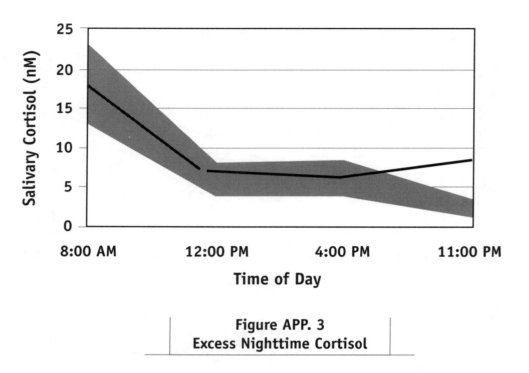

Figure APP. 3
Excess Nighttime Cortisol

NOTES

Chapter 1

1. C. McEvedy, "The Bubonic Plague," *Scientific American* 258, no. 2 (1988): 118–23.

2. W. L. Yule, "A Scottish Doctor's Association with the Discovery of the Plague Bacillus," *Scottish Medical Journal* 40, no. 6 (1995): 184–86.

3. A. W. Sloan, "The Black Death in England," *South African Medical Journal* 59, no. 18 (1981): 646–50.

4. John Travis, "Taking a Bite Out of the Plague," *Science News* (1998): 154.

5. Brian Inglis, *A History of Medicine* (Cleveland: World, 1965), 63; Rex Russell, *What the Bible Says About Healthy Living* (Ventura, Calif.: Regal, 1996), 84.

6. Inglis, *History*, 152–54; Russell, *Healthy Living*, 19–20.

7. Richard Haehl, *Samuel Hahnemann: His Life and Work*, trans. Marie L. Wheeler and W. H. R. Grundy, 2 vols. (New Delhi: B. Jain Publishers Pvt. Ltd., 1995), 1:390–1.

8. Martin Kaufman, *Homeopathy in America: The Rise and Fall of a Medical Heresy* (Baltimore: Johns Hopkins, 1971), 13–15.

9. Haehl, *Samuel Hahnemann*, 1:25.

10. Kaufman, *Homeopathy*, 8.

11. Ibid., 7.

12. Barbara Distel and Ruth Jakusch, *Concentration Camp Dachau 1933–1945: Comite International de Dachau 65, rue de Haerne* (Brussels Lipp GmbH, Munich, 1978).

13. Charles R. Swindoll, *The Tale of the Tardy Oxcart—and 1,501 Other Stories* (Nashville: Word, 1998), 539.

14. Inglis, *History*, 59.

15. Joel S. Levine, "Socioeconomic Forces Shaping American Health Care," *Critical Issues Shaping Medical Practice*, University Hospital Consortium, 1994.

16. A. J. Baumgart, "Hospital Reform and Nursing Labor Market Trends in Canada," *Medical Care* 35, no.10 suppl.: OS124–31, 1997.

17. W. J. Mackillop et al., "Does a Centralized Radiotherapy System Provide Adequate Access to Care?" *Journal of Clinical Oncology* 15, no. 3 (1997): 1261–71; V. Benk et al., "Predictors of Delay in Starting Radiation Treatment for Patients with Early Stage Breast Cancer," International Journal of Radiation Oncology, Biology, Physiology 41, no. 1 (1998): 109–15.

18. G. Cohen et al., "Cost-Effective Provision of Cardiac Services in a Fixed-Dollar Environment," Annals of Thoracic Surgery 62, no. 5, suppl. (1996): S18–21; discussion S31–2.

19. V. Dirnfeld, "The Benefits of Privatization," Canadian Medical Association Journal 155, no. 4 (1996): 407-10; F. de Montigny, "Private Practice: A Choice, but What Challenges!" Canadian Nurse 93, no. 6 (1997): 39–45; 26.

20. F. Lowry, "Larger Private-Sector Role in Health Care Needed Now, Think Tank Warns," Canadian Medical Association Journal 154, no. 4 (1996): 549–51.

Chapter 2

1. Rex Russell, *What the Bible Says About Healthy Living* (Ventura, Calif.: Regal, 1996), 43.

2. *Hebrew Greek Key Study Bible* (King James Version), ed. Spiros Zodhiates, 2d ed. (Chattanooga: AMG, 1991).

3. Personal correspondence, 1999.

4. Personal correspondence, 1998.

5. Personal correspondence, 1999.

6. Henry Wright, telephone conversation, 1998.

7. Ibid.

8. Rollin McCraty, "Stress and Emotional Health" (paper read at Steroid Hormones Clinical Correlates: Therapeutic and Nutritional Considerations, Chicago, February 1996).

Chapter 3

1. Alfred M. Rehwinkel, *The Flood* (Saint Louis: Concordia, 1951), 7.

2. Laura Myers, "Scientists Link Cardiovascular Disease to Cell Aging," *Cincinnati Enquirer,* 1996.

3. Rehwinkel, *The Flood,* 22.

Chapter 4

1. Ben M. Edidin, *Jewish Customs and Ceremonies* (New York: Hebrew Publishing Company, 1941), 35.

2. Jay P. Green Sr., *The Interlinear Bible* (Peabody, Mass.: Hendrickson Publishers, 1986).

3. *Character Sketches,* ed. Institute in Biblical Life Principles, 4 vols. (Institute of Basic Life Principles, 1976), 1:14–15.

4. James Logan, "Victory at the Cross" (paper read at Spiritual Warfare Basics, Indianapolis Training Center, March 14, 1997).

Chapter 5

1. Ben M. Edidin, *Jewish Customs and Ceremonies* (New York: Hebrew Publishing Company, 1941), 42.

2. A. C. Guyton, "Behavioral and Motivational Mechanisms of the Brain—The Limbic System and Hypothalamus," *Textbook of Medical Physiology* (Philadelphia: W. B. Saunders, 1991), 248–58.

3. Neil T. Anderson and Dave Park, *The Bondage Breaker,* Youth Edition (Eugene, Ore.: Harvest House, 1993), 126, 130–31.

4. Jim Logan, *Reclaiming Surrendered Ground* (Chicago: Moody Press, 1995), 158.

5. Edidin, *Jewish Customs,* 35.

6. Guyton, "Dietary Balances; Regulation of Feeding; Obesity and Starvation," in *Textbook of Medical Physiology* (Philadelphia: W. B. Saunders, 1991), 648–58.

7. D. A. Pan, A. J. Hulbert, and L. H. Storlien, "Dietary Fats, Membrane Phospholipids and Obesity," *Textbook, Journal of Nutrition* 124, no. 9 (1994): 1555–65.

8. L. R. Landsberg et al., "Obesity, Blood Pressure and the Sympathetic Nervous System, *Annals of Epidemiology* 1, no. 4 (1991): 295–303.

9. J. E. Hall, "Renal and Cardiovascular Mechanisms of Hypertension in Obesity," *Hypertension* 23, no. 3 (1994): 381–94.

10. L. Christensen, "Effects of Eating Behavior on Mood: A Review of the Literature," *International Journal of Eating Disorders* 14, no. 2 (1993): 171–83.

11. Marshall Mandell and Lynne Walker Scanlon, "Compulsive Eating and Drinking," *5-Day Allergy Relief System* (New York: Harper & Row, 1988), 106–32; Marshall Mandell and F. G. Mandell, *It's Not Your Fault You're Fat Diet* (Cambridge: Harper & Row, 1983).

Chapter 6

1. Rex Russell, *What the Bible Says About Healthy Living* (Ventura, Calif.: Regal, 1996), 29.

2. Bob L. Smith, "Organic Foods vs. Supermarket Foods: Elemental Levels," *Journal of Applied Nutrition* 45 (November 1993): 35–39.

Chapter 7

1. Fred H. Wight, *Manners and Customs of Bible Lands* (Chicago: Moody Press, 1953), 44, 59.

2. Ibid., 45, 48.

3. Ibid.

4. Charles R. Swindoll, *The Tale of the Tardy Oxcart—and 1,501 Other Stories* (Nashville: Word, 1998), 611.

5. "Dietary Phytochemical Research Demonstrates Potential for Major Role in Cancer Prevention," *Primary Care and Cancer* 16, no. 7 (1996): 6–7.

6. G. Block, B. Patterson, and A. Subar, "Fruit, Vegetables, and Cancer Prevention: A Review of the Epidemiological Evidence," *Nutrition and Cancer* 18, no. 1 (1992): 1–29.

7. J. D. Potter and K. A. Steinmetz, "Vegetables, Fruits, and Phytoestrogens as Protective Agents," *IARC Scientific Publication* 139 (1996): 61–90.

8. "Cancer and Tomatoes," *Nutrition Week* (1995): 7.

9. Alicja Wolk et al., "Nutrition and Renal Cell Cancer," *Cancer Causes and Control* 7 (1996): 5–18.

10. Gosta Axelsson et al., "Dietary Factors and Lung Cancer Among Men in West Sweden," *International Journal of Epidemiology* 25, no. 1 (1996): 32–39.

11. Silvia Franceschi et al., "Intake of Macronutrients and Risk of Breast Cancer," *Lancet,* 18 May 1996 and 347: 1351–56.

12. J. D. Potter and K. A. Steinmetz, "Vegetables, Fruit, and Cancer Prevention: A Review," *Journal of American Dietetic Association* 96, no. 10 (1996): 1027–39.

13. Nigel Plummer, "Human Microflora, Probiotics and Intestinal Recolonization Strategies" (paper read at Clinical Aspects of Adrenal and Sex Steroids, Chicago, Ill., February 24–25, 1996.

14. American Women of Amman, *Sahtain Wa Hana Cookbook,* 5th ed. (Amman, Jordan: National Press, 1984).

Chapter 8

1. A. C. Guyton, "States of Brain Activity—Sleep; Brain Waves; Epilepsy; Psychoses," in *Textbook of Medical Physiology* (Philadelphia: W. B. Saunders, 1991), 659–66.

2. G. C. Curhan et al., "Beverage Use and Risk for Kidney Stones in Women," *Annals of Internal Medicine* 128, no. 7 (1998): 534–40.

3. F. Batmanghelidj, *Your Body's Many Cries for Water,* 2d. ed. (Falls Church, Va.: Global Health Solutions, 1995), 23.

4. C. W. Armstrong et al., "Outbreak of Fatal Arsenic Poisoning Caused by Contaminated Drinking Water, *Archives Environmental Health* 39, no. 4 (1984): 276–79.

5. R. D. Morris, "Drinking Water and Cancer," *Environmental Health Perspective* 103, no. 8, suppl. (1995): 225–31.

6. A. H. Smith et al., "Cancer Risks from Arsenic in Drinking Water," *Environmental Health Perspective* 97 (1992): 259–67.

7. "New Arsenic Standards for US Drinking Water," *Reuters Health* (March 1999).

8. Joe Harrison, Water Quality Association, 1999. Personal communication.

9. Ibid.

10. K. P. Cantor, "Drinking Water and Cancer," *Cancer Causes Control* 8, no. 3 (1997): 292–308.

11. Harrison, Water Quality Association, ibid.

12. Mary H. Ward et al., "Drinking Water Nitrate and the Risk of Non-Hodgkin's Lymphoma," *Epidemiology* 7, no. 5 (1996): 465–71.

13. "Shigella Sonnei Outbreak Associated with Contaminated Drinking Water—Island Park, Idaho, August 1995," from the Centers for Disease Control and Prevention, *Journal of the American Medical Association* 275, no. 14 (1996): 1071.

14. A. B. Bloch et al., "Recovery of Hepatitis A Virus from a Water Supply Responsible for a Common Source Outbreak of Hepatitis A," *American Journal of Public Health* 80, no. 4 (1990): 428–30.

15. A. Ferroni et al., "Outbreak of Nocomial Urinary Tract Infections Due to Pseudomonas Aeruginosa in a Paediatric Surgical Unit Associated with Tap-Water Contamination," *Journal of Hospital Infection* 39, no. 4 (1998): 301–7.

16. F. Bert et al., "Multiresistant Pseudomonas Aeruginosa Outbreak Associated with Contaminated Tap Water in a Neurosurgery Intensive Care Unit," *Journal of Hospital Infection* 39, no. 1 (1998): 53–62.

17. H. V. Smith and P. G. Smith, "Parasitic Protozoa in Drinking Water," *Endeavour* 14, no. 2 (1990): 74–79.

18. E. B. Hayes et al., "Large Community Outbreak of Cryptosporidiosis Due to Contamination of a Filtered Public Water Supply," *New England Journal of Medicine* 320, no. 21 (1989): 1372–6.

19. Jeremy M. McAnulty et al., "A Community-wide Outbreak of Cryptosporidiosis Associated with Swimming at a Wave Pool," *Journal of the American Medical Association* 272, no. 20 (1994): 1597–1600.

20. "Outbreak of Cryptosporidiosis Associated with a Water Sprinkler Fountain—Minnesota," *Morbidity and Mortality Weekly Report* 47, no. 40 (1997): 856–60.

21. S. T. Goldstein et al., "Cryptosporidiosis: An Outbreak Associated with Drinking Water Despite State-of-the-Art Water Treatment," *Annals of Internal Medicine* 124, no. 5 (1996): 459–68. Published erratum appears in *Annals of Internal Medicine* 125, no. 2 (1996): 158.

22. M. S. Dworkin et al., "Cryptosporidiosis in Washington State: An Outbreak Associated with Well Water," *Journal of Infectious Diseases* 174, no. 6 (1996): 1372–6.

23. W. R. MacKenzie et al., "A Massive Outbreak in Milwaukee of Cryptosporidium Infection Transmitted Through the Public Water Supply," *New England Journal of Medicine* 331, no. 3 (1994): 161–67. Published erratum appears in *New England Journal of Medicine* 3311, no. 15 (1994): 1035.

24. K. P. Cantor, "Drinking Water and Cancer," *Cancer Causes and Control* 8, no. 3 (1997): 292–308; D. T. Wigle, "Safe Drinking Water: A Public Health Challenge," *Chronic Diseases in Canada* 19, no. 3 (1998): 103–7; Ann Aschengrau et al., "Cancer Risk and Tetrachloroethylene-Contaminated Drinking Water in Massachusetts," *Archives of Environmental Health* 48, no. 5 (1993): 284–97.

25. D. G. Addiss et al., "Reduction of Risk of Watery Diarrhea with Point-of-Use Water Filters During a Massive Outbreak of Waterborne Cryptosporidium Infection in Milwaukee, Wisconsin," *American Journal of Tropical Medicine and Hygiene* 54, no. 6 (1996): 659–63.

26. "Feds Issue Warning for Some to Boil Tap Water," *Nutrition Week* 14, no. 24 (1995): 7.

27. Joe Harrison, Water Quality Association, personal communication, 1999.

28. S. H. Jee et al., "The Effect of Chronic Coffee Drinking on Blood Pressure: A Meta-Analysis of Controlled Clinical Trials" *Hypertension* 33, no. 2 (1999): 647–52.

29. Bong Sung et al., "Caffeine Elevates Blood Pressure Response to Exercise in Mild Hypertensive Men," *American Journal of Hypertension* 8 (1995): 1194–88.

30. R. L. Donnerstein et al., "Acute Effects of Caffeine Ingestion on Signal-Averaged Electrocardiograms," *American Heart Journal* 136, no. 4, pt. 1 (1998): 643–46.

31. Arthur Klatsky et al., "Coffee Use Prior to Myocardial Infarction Restudied: Heavier Intake May Increase the Risk," *American Journal of Epidemiology* (1990): 479–88; Diederick E. Grobbee et al., "Coffee, Caffeine and Cardiovascular Disease in Men," *The New England Journal of Medicine* 323, no. 15 (1990): 1026–32.

32. G. M. Etherton and M. S. Kochar, "Coffee: Facts and Controversies," *Archives of Family Medicine* 2, no. 3 (1993): 317–22.

33. Elizabeth M. Puccio et al., "Clustering of Atherogenic Behaviors in Coffee Drinkers," *American Journal of Public Health* 80, no. 11 (1990): 1310–13.

34. Hiroshi Nagasawa et al., "Suppression by Coffee Cherry of Spontaneous Mammary Tumors in SHN Mice," *Anticancer Research* 16 (1996): 151–53.

35. Inger Stensvold and Bjarne K. Jacobsen, "Coffee and Cancer: A Prospective Study of 43,000 Norwegian Men and Women," *Cancer Causes and Control* 5 (1994): 401–8.

36. Elizabeth E. Hatch and Michael B. Bracken, "Association of Delayed Conception with Caffeine Consumption," *American Journal of Epidemiology* 138, no. 12 (1993): 1082–92.

37. Larry Dlugosz et al., "Maternal Caffeine Consumption and Spontaneous Abortion: A Prospective Cohort Study," *Epidemiology* 7, no. 3 (1996): 250–55.

38. Astrid Nehlig and Gerard Debry, "Consequences on the Newborn of Chronic Maternal Consumption of Coffee During Gestation and Lactation: A Review," *Journal of the American College of Nutrition* 13, no. 1 (1994): 6–21.

39. R. P. Ford et al., "Heavy Caffeine Intake in Pregnancy and Sudden Infant Death Syndrome," New Zealand Cot Death Study Group, *Archives of Disease in Childhood* 78, no. 1 (1998): 9–13.

40. L. Fenster et al., "Caffeinated Beverages, Decaffeinated Coffee, and Spontaneous Abortion," *Epidemiology* 8, no. 5 (1997): 515–23.

41. Susan S. Harris and Bess Dawson-Hughes, "Caffeine and Bone Loss in Postmenopausal Women," *American Journal of Clinical Nutrition* 60 (1994): 573–78; Mauricio Hernandez-Avila et al., "Caffeine and Other Predictors of Bone Density Among Pre- and Perimenopausal Women," *Epidemiology* 4, no. 2 (1993): 128–34.

42. Eric C. Strain et al., "Caffeine Dependence Syndrome: Evidence from Case Histories and Experimental Evaluations," *Journal of the American Medical Association* 272, no. 13 (1994): 1043–48.

43. "Dietary Phytochemical Research Demonstrates Potential for Major Role in Cancer Prevention," *Primary Care and Cancer* 16, no. 7 (1996): 6–7.

44. J. S. Shim et al., "Chemopreventive Effect of Green Tea (Camellia Sinesis) Among Cigarette Smokers," *Cancer Epidemiology, Biomarkers and Prevention* 4 (1995): 387–91; Yoshiyuki Ohno et al., "Tea Consumption and Lung Cancer Risk: A Case-Controlled Study in Okinawa, Japan," *Japanese Journal of Cancer Research* 86 (1995): 1027–34; Taik-Koo Yun and Soo-Yong Choi, "Preventive Effect of Ginseng Intake Against Various Human Cancers: A Case-Control Study on 1,987 Pairs," *Cancer Epidemiology, Biomarkers and Prevention* 4 (1995): 401–8; Guo-Pei Yu et al., "Green Tea Concumption and Risk of Stomach Cancer: A Population-Based Case-Controlled Study in Shanghai, China," *Cancer Causes and Control* 6 (1995): 532–38.

45. R. Alexandra Goldbohn et al., "Consumption of Black Tea and Cancer Risk: A Prospective Cohort Study," *Journal of the National Cancer Institute* 88, no. 2 (1996): 93–100.

46. Jerry Avorn et al., "Reduction of Bacteriuria and Pyuria After Ingestion of Cranberry Juice," *Journal of the American Medical Association* 271, no. 10 (1994): 751–54.

47. Ronald L. Prior, "Total Antioxidant Capacity of Fruits," *Journal of Agricultural and Food Chemistry* 44 (1996): 701–5.

48. C. S. Burchat et al., "The Distribution of Nine Pesticides Between the Juice and Pulp of Carrots and Tomatoes After Home Processing," *Food Additives and Contaminants* 15, no. 1 (1998): 61–71.

49. D. T. Y. Pang et al., "Fluoride Intake from Beverage Consumption in a Sample of North Carolina Children," *Journal of Dental Research* 71, no. 7 (1992): 1382–88.

50. A. S. Papas et al., "Dietary Models for Root Caries," *Journal of Dental Research* 71 (1992): 243, 1100.

51. "Juice," *Nutrition Week* (March 18, 1994): 7.

52. C. Kneepkens and J. Hoekstra, "Fruit Juice and Chronic Nonspecific Diarrhea," *Journal of Pediatrics* 122, no. 3 (1992): 499.

53. The grapefruit juice effect [news report], *Harvard Health Letter* 22, no. 12 (1997): 8; Robert E. Benton et al., "Grapefruit Juice Alters Terfenadine Pharmacokinetics, Resulting in Prolongation of Repolarization on the Electrocardiogram," *Clinical Pharmacology and Therapeutics* 59, no. 4 (1996): 383–88.

Chapter 9

1. Seppa Nathan, "Cow's Milk, Diabetes Connection Bolstered," *Science News* (1999), 404–5.

2. Linnea Anderson et al., *Nutrition in Health and Disease,* 17th ed. (Philadelphia: Lippincott, 1982), 311–18; Frank A. Oski, *Don't Drink Your Milk: New Frightening Facts About the World's Most Overrated Nutrient* (Brushton, N.Y.: Teach Services, 1996), 1–26.

3. Oski, *Don't Drink Your Milk,* 11.

4. Fred H. Wight, *Manners and Customs of Bible Lands* (Chicago: Moody Press, 1953), 49–50.

5. John Robbins, *Diet for a New America* (Walpole, N.H.: Stillpoint Publishing, 1987), 105–21.

6. A. Sanchez et al., "A Hypothesis on the Etiological Role of Diet on Age of Menarche," *Medical Hypotheses* 7, no. 11 (1981): 1339–45.

7. K. A. Oster, "Role of Plasmalogen in Heart Disease," *Recent Advances in Studies on Cardiac Structure and Metabolism* 1 (1972): 803–13.

8. C. Y. Ho and A. J. Clifford, "Digestion and Absorption of Bovine Milk Xanthine Oxidase and Its Role as an Aldehyde Oxidase," *Journal of Nutrition* 106, no. 11 (1976): 1600–1609; M. E. Mangino and J. R. Brunner, "Homogenized Milk: Is It Really the Culprit in Dietary-Induced Atherosclerosis?" *Journal of Dairy Science* 59, no. 8 (1976): 1511–12.

9. A. J. Clifford et al., "Homogenized Bovine Milk Xanthine Oxidase: A Critique of the Hypothesis Relating to Plasmalogen Depletion and Cardiovascular Disease," *American Journal of Clinical Nutrition* 38, no. 2 (1983): 327–32; H. C. Deeth, "Homogenized Milk and Atherosclerotic Disease: A Review," *Journal of Dairy Science* 66, no. 7 (1983): 1419–35.

10. P. Rank, "Milk and Arteriosclerosis," *Medical Hypotheses* 20, no. 3 (1986): 317–38.

11. Rex Russell, *What the Bible Says About Healthy Living* (Ventura, Calif.: Regal), 218.

12. J. E. Ford, et al., "Influence of the Heat Treatment of Human Milk on Some of Its Protective Constituents," *Journal of Pediatrics* 90, no. 1 (1977): 29–35; C. L. Hicks, J. Bucy, and W. Stofer, "Heat Inactivation of Superoxide Dismutase in Bovine Milk," *Journal of Dairy Science* 62, no. 4 (1979): 529–32; T. R. Henderson, T. N. Fay, and M. Hamosh, "Effect of Pasteurization on Long Chain Polyunsaturated Fatty Acid Levels and Enzyme Activities of Human Milk," *Journal of Pediatrics* 132, no. 5 (1998): 876–78; J. M. Wardell et al., "Bile Salt-Stimulated Lipase and Esterase Activity in Human Milk After Collection, Storage, and Heating: Nutritional Implications," *Pediatric Research* 18, no. 4 (1984): 382–86.

13. E. Lerebours, "Yogurt and Fermented-Then-Pasteurized Milk: Effects of Short-Term and Long-Term Ingestion on Lactose Absorption and Mucosal Lactase Activity in Lactase-Deficient Subjects," *American Journal of Clinical Nutrition* 49, no. 5 (1989): 823–27.

14. N. Desmasures, F. Bazin, and M. Gueguen, "Microbiological Composition of Raw Milk from Selected Farms in the Camembert Region of Normandy," *Journal of Applied Microbiology* 83, no. 1 (1997): 53–58; N. Desmasures and M. Gueguen, "Monitoring the Microbiology of High Quality of Milk by Monthly Sampling over 2 Years," *Journal of Dairy Research* 64, no. 2 (1997): 271–80.

15. S. J. Knabel et al., "Effects of Growth Temperature and Strictly Anaerobic Recovery on the Survival of Listeria Monocytogenes During Pasteurization," *Applied Environmental Microbiology* 56, no. 2 (1990): 370–76.

16. C. O. Tacket et al., "A Multistate Outbreak of Infections Caused by Yersinia Enterocolitica Transmitted by Pasteurized Milk," *Journal of the American Medical Association* 251, no. 4 (1984): 483–86.

17. *Morbidity and Mortality Weekly Report* 48 (16 March, 1999): 228-29.

18. S. B. Werner, G. L. Humphrey, and I. Kamei, " Association Between Raw Milk and Human Salmonella Dublin Infection," *British Medical Journal* 2, no. 6184 (1979): 238–41.

19. G. A. Richwald et al., "Assessment of the Excess Risk Associated with the Use of Certified Raw Milk," *Public Health Reports* 103, no. 5 (1988): 489–93.

20. P. R. Taylor, W. M. Weinstein, and J. H. Bryner, "Campylobacter Fetus Infection in Human Subjects: Association with Raw Milk," *American Journal of Medicine* 66, no. 5 (1979): 779–83; M. E. Potter et al., "Human Campylobacter Infection Associated with Certified Raw Milk," *American Journal of Epidemiology* 117, no. 4 (1983): 475–83; Rachel Wood et al., "Campylobacter Enteritis Outbreaks Associated with Drinking Raw Milk During Youth Activities: A Ten-Year Review of Outbreaks in the United States," *Journal of the American Medical Association* 268, no. 22 (1992): 3228–30.

21. W. E. Keene et al., "A Prolonged Outbreak of Escherichia Coli O157: H7 Infections Caused by Commercially Distributed Raw Milk," *Journal of Infectious Disease* 176, no. 3 (1997): 815–18.

22. Anita Bleem, "EscherichiaColi O157: A7 in Raw Milk: A Review," *Animal Health Insight* (Spring/Summer 1994): 1–9; A. E. Heuvelink et al., "Occurrence and Survival of Verocytotoxin-Producing Escherichia Coli O157 in Raw Cow's Milk in the Netherlands," *Journal of Food Protection* 61, no. 12 (1998): 1597–601; S. S. Dineen et al., "Persistence of Escherichia Coli O157: H7 in Dairy Fermentation Systems,"*Journal of Food Protection* 61, no. 12 (1998): 1602–8.

23. M. L. Headrick et al., "The Epidemiology of Raw Milk—Associated Foodborne Disease Outbreaks Reported in the United States, 1973 Through 1992," *American Journal of Public Health* 88, no. 8 (1998): 1219–21.

24. Herbert L. Dupont, "How Safe Is the Food We Eat?" *Journal of the American Medical Association* 268, no. 22 (1992): 3240; M. E. Potter et al., "Unpasteurized Milk: The Hazards of a Health Fetish," *Journal of the American Medical Association* 252, no. 15 (1984): 2048–52.

25. Bonnie Liebman, "Lactose: Truth or Intolerances," *Nutrition Action Health Letter* (April 1991): 8–9; D. A. Savaiano et al., "Lactose Malabsorption from Yogurt, Pasteurized Yogurt, Sweet Acidophilus Milk, and Cultured Milk in Lactase-Deficient Individuals," *American Journal of Clinical Nutrition* 40, no. 6 (1984): 1219–23.

26. Wight, *Manners and Customs of Bible Lands*, 51.

27. Ghazalia Boudraa et al., "Effect of Feeding Yogurt Versus Milk in Children with Persistent Diarrhea," *Journal of Pediatric Gastroenterology and Nutrition* 11 (1990): 509–12.

28. K. Thoreux et al., "Diet Supplemented with Yogurt or Milk Fermented with Lactobacillus Casei DN—114 001 Stimulates Growth and Brush-Border Enzyme Activities in Mouse Small Intestine," *Digestion* 59, no. 4 (1998): 349–59.

29. Eileen Hilton et al., "Ingestion of Yogurt Containing Lactobacillus Acidophilus as Prophylaxis for Candidal Vaginitis," *Annals of Internal Medicine* 116, no. 5 (1992): 353–57.

30. P. van't Peer et al., "Consumption of Fermented Milk Products and Breast Cancer: A Case-Control Study in the Netherlands," *Cancer Research* 49, no. 14 (1989): 4020–23.

31. Ben M. Edidin, *Jewish Customs and Ceremonies* (New York: Hebrew Publishing Company, 1941), 38.

Chapter 10

1. Ben M. Edidin, *Jewish Customs and Ceremonies* (New York: Hebrew Publishing Company, 1941), 36.

2. Ibid., 37.

3. Rex Russell, *What the Bible Says About Healthy Living* (Ventura, Calif.: Regal, 1996), 153.

4. Ibid., 157.

5. Paul Recer, "Source of 1918 Flu Epidemic Found," *Cincinnati Enquirer,* 21 March 1997.

6. "Malaysia to Kill 1 Million Pigs in Fight Against Virus," *Cincinnati Enquirer,* 30 March 1999.

7. Achim Schneider et al., "Pork Intake and Human Papilloma Virus-Related Disease," *Nutrition and Cancer* 13 (1990): 209–11.

8. P. Dore et al., "Lipoid Nephrosis Secondary to Food Allergy, Report of Two Cases," *Revue Francaise D Allergologie* 29, no. 3 (1989): 133–37.

9. J. Laurent and G. Lagrue, "Dietary Manipulation for Idiopathic Nephrotic Syndrome: A New Approach to Therapy," *Allergy* 44 (1989): 599–603.

10. Diana L. Wells et al., "Swine Flu Virus Infections: Transmission from Ill Pigs to Humans at a Wisconsin Agricultural Fair and Subsequent Probable Person-Person Transmission," *Journal of the American Medical Association* 465, no. 4 (1991): 478–81.

11. L. Gail Darlington, "Nutrition and Rheumatic Diseases, Rheumatic Disease Clinics of North America," *Dietary Therapy for Arthritis* 17, no. 2 (1991):273–85.

12. W. Y. Choi et al., "Foodborne Outbreaks of Human Toxoplasmosis," *Journal of Infectious Diseases* 175, no. 5 (1997): 1280–82.

13. S. M. Landry et al., "Trichinosis: Common Source Outbreak Related to Commercial Pork," *Southern Medical Journal* 85, no. 4 (1992): 428–29.

14. D. Trout et al., "Outbreak of Brucellosis at a United States Pork Packing Plant," *Journal of Occupational and Environmental Medicine* 37, no. 6 (1995): 697–703.

15. P. M. Schantz et al., "Neurocysticercosis in an Orthodox Jewish Community in New York City," *New England Journal of Medicine* 327, no. 10 (1992): 692–95.

16. Z. Davanipour et al., "A Case-Control Study of Creutzfeldt-Jakob Disease: Dietary Risk Factors," *American Journal of Epidemiology* 122, no. 3 (1985): 443–51.

17. Russell, *Healthy Living,* 154–55.

18. "Pork Chopped," *Nutrition Week* (5 April 1995).

19. David Macht, "An Experimental Pharmacological Appreciation of Leviticus XI and Deuteronomy XIV," *Bulletin of Historical Medicine* 47, no. 1 (1953): 444–50.

20. Laura's Lean Beef, *Nutritional Facts,* 1998. Brochure.

21. Dean Ornish et al., "Can Lifestyle Changes Reverse Coronary Heart Disease?" *Lancet* 336 (July 21, 1990): 129–33.

22. Edidin, *Jewish Customs,* 38.

23. "Fecal Contamination for Meat Approved by USDA," *Nutrition Week* (April 26, 1996): 3.

24. Russell, *Healthy Living,* 148.

25. Fred H. Wight, *Manners and Customs of Bible Lands* (Chicago: Moody Press, 1953), 51.

26. Ibid., 52.

27. J. A. T. Pennington, *Food Values of Portions Commonly Used,* 15th ed. (New York: Harper & Row, 1987).

28. H. N. Ginsberg et al., "Increases in Dietary Cholesterol Are Associated with Modest Increases in Both LDL and HDL Cholesterol in Healthy Young Women," *Arteriosclerosis, Thrombosis, and Vascular Biology* 15, no. 2 (1995): 169–78.

29. P. Schnohr et al., "Egg Consumption and High-Density-Lipoprotein Cholesterol," *Journal of Internal Medicine* 235 (1994): 249–51.

30. Hester H. Vorster et al., "Egg Intake Does Not Change Plasma Lipoprotein and Coagulation Profiles," *American Journal of Clinical Nutrition* 55 (1992): 400–410; Hester H. Vorster et al., "Dietary Cholesterol—The Role of Eggs in the Prudent Diet," *South Africa Medical Journal* 85, no. 4 (1995): 253–56.

31. Xavier Pelletier et al., "Effect of Egg Consumption in Healthy Volunteers: Influence of Yolk, White or Whole-Egg on Gastric Emptying and on Glycemic and Hormonal Responses," *Annals of Nutrition and Metabolism* 40 (1996):109–15.

32. S. E. Scheideler and G. W. Froning, "The Combined Influence of Dietary Flaxseed Variety, Level, Form, and Storage Conditions on Egg Production and Composition Among Vitamin E-Supplemented Hens," *Poultry Science* 75, no. 10 (1996): 1221–26.

33. Les K. Ferrier et al., "Alpha-Linolenic Acid and Docosahexaenoic Acid-Enriched Eggs from Hens Fed Flaxseed: Influence on Blood Lipids and Platelet Phospholipid Fatty Acids in Humans," *American Journal of Clinical Nutrition* 62 (1995): 81–86.

34. D. J. Farrell, "Enrichment of Hen Eggs with N-3 Long-chain Fatty Acids and Evaluation of Enriched Eggs in Humans," *American Journal of Clinical Nutrition* 68, no. 3 (1998): 538–44.

35. M. S. Haddadin et al., "The Effect of Lactobacillus Acidophilus on the Production and Chemical Composition of Hen's Eggs," *Poultry Science* 75, no. 4 (1996): 491–94; S. M. Abdulrahim et al., "The Influence of Lactobacillus Acidophilus and Bactricin on Layer Performance of Chickens and Cholesterol Content of Plasma and Egg Yolk," *British Poultry Science* 37, no. 2 (1996): 341–46; B Mohan et al., "Effect of Probiotic Supplementation on Serum/Yolk Cholesterol and on Egg Shell Thickness in Layers," *British Poultry Science* 36, no. 5 (1995): 799–803.

36. D. DeBoissieu et al., "Allergy to Nondairy Proteins in Mother's Milk as Assessed by Intestinal Permeability Tests," *Allergy* 49 (1994): 882–84.

Chapter 11

1. Laura's Lean Beef, *Nutritional Facts,* 1998. Brochure.

2. W. Martin, "The Combined Role of Atheroma, Cholesterol, Platelets, the Endothelium and Fibrin in Heart Attacks and Strokes," *Medical Hypotheses* 15, no. 3 (1984): 305–22.

3. Udo Erasmus, *Fats and Oils* (Burnaby, B.C.: Alive Books, 1986), 96–102.

4. L. Kohlmeier et al., "Adipose Tissue Trans Fatty Acids and Breast Cancer in the European Community Multicenter Study on Antioxidants, Myocardial Infarction, and Breast Cancer," *Cancer Epidemiology Biomarkers and Prevention* 6, no. 9 (1997): 705–10.

5. S. Yanagi et al., "Comparative Effects of Milk, Yogurt, Butter, and Margarine on Mammary Tumorigenesis Induced by 7, 12—Dimethylbenz (a) Anthracene in Rats," *Cancer Detection and Prevention* 18, no. 6 (1994): 415–20.

6. Margo Denke, "Dietary Fatty Acids and Atherosclerosis," *Lipids and Atherogenesis* 1, no. 1 (1991): 4–7.

7. Rebecca Troisi, Walter C. Willett, and Scott T. Weiss, "Trans-fatty Acid Intake in Relation to Serum Lipid Concentrations in Adult Men," *American Journal of Clinical Nutrition* 56 (1992): 1019–24.

8. A. Ascherio et al., "Trans-fatty Acids Intake and Risk of Myocardial Infarction," *Circulation* 89, no. 1 (1994): 94–101.

9. A. Tavani et al., "Margarine Intake and Risk of Nonfatal Acute Myocardial Infarction in Italian Women," *European Journal of Clinical Nutrition* 51, no. 1 (1997): 30–32.

10. W. C. Willett et al., "Intake of Trans Fatty Acids and Risk of Coronary Heart Disease Among Women," *Lancet* 341, no. 8845 (1993): 581–85.

11. P. G. Shields et al., "Mutagens from Heated Chinese and U.S. Cooking Oils," *Journal of the National Cancer Institute* 87, no. 11 (1995): 836–41.

12. C. Merz et al., "The Secondary Prevention of Coronary Artery Disease," *American Journal of Medicine* 102 (1997): 572–81.

13. A. C. Guyton, "Lipid Metabolism," *Textbook of Medical Physiology* (Philadelphia: W. B. Saunders, 1991).

14. Ancel Keys, "Mediterranean Diet and Public Health: Personal Reflections," *American Journal of Clinical Nutrition* 61, suppl. (1995): 1321S–23S.

Chapter 12

1. Fred H. Wight, *Manners and Customs of Bible Lands* (Chicago: Moody Press, 1953), 43.

2. Ancel Keys, "Coronary Heart Disease in Seven Countries," *Circulation* 41, no. 1, suppl. (1970): 1–211.

3. Ancel Keys, "Mediterranean Diet and Public Health: Personal Reflections," *American Journal of Clinical Nutrition* 61, suppl. (1995): 1321S–23S.

4. Serge Renaud et al., "Cretan Mediterranean Diet for Prevention of Coronary Heart Disease," *American Journal of Clinical Nutrition* 61, suppl. (1995): 1360S–1370S.

5. M. de Lorgeril et al., "Mediterranean Diet, Traditional Risk Factors, and the Rate of Cardiovascular Complications After Myocardial Infarction: Final Report of the Lyon Diet Heart Study," *Circulation* 99, no. 6 (1999): 779–85.

6. M. de Lorgeril et al., "Mediterranean Dietary Pattern in a Randomized Trial: Prolonged Survival and Possible Reduced Cancer Rate," *Archives of Internal Medicine* 158, no. 11 (1998): 1181–87.

7. W. C. Willett et al., "Mediterranean Diet Pyramid: A Cultural Model for Healthy Eating," *American Journal of Clinical Nutrition* 61, no. 6, suppl. (1995): 1402S–406S; Michael Mason, "The Man Who Has a Beef with Your Diet: Harvard's Walter Willett Thinks the Usual Warnings About Fatty Foods Are Wrong," *Hippocrates* (May 1994): 31–37.

Chapter 13

1. L. Businco, N. Benincori and A. Cantani, "The Spectrum of Food Allergy in Infancy and Childhood," *Annals of Allergy* 57 (1986): 213–17; Marshall Mandell and G. Rose, "May Emotional Reactions Be Precipitated by Allergens?" *Connecticut Medicine* 32, no. 4 (1968): 300; Marshall Mandell, "Ecologic Mental Illness: Cerebral and Physical Reactions in Allergic Patients," *New Dynamics of Preventive Medicine,* ed. L. R. Pomeroy (New York: Intercontinental Medical Book Corp.,1974) 200–30; Richard Wilkinson, "Comprehensive vs. Symptomatic Approach—Chemical Sensitivity, Immune System, Endocrine System" (paper presented at World Med '96, Washington, D. C., May 26, 1996); Gary Oberg, "Principles and Practice of Environmental Medicine" (paper presented at World Med '96, Washington D. C., May 26, 1996); Andrew Cant, R. A. Marsden, and P. J. Kilshaw, "Egg and Cow's Milk Hypersensitivity in Exclusively Breast Fed Infants with Eczema, and Detection of Egg Protein in Breast Milk," *British Medical Journal* 291 (5 October 1985): 932–35; M. L. McCann, "Update on Treatment of Food Protein Allergy: Pancreatic Enzyme Supplements" unpublished; J. Egger, "Oligoantigenic Diet Treatment of Children with Epilepsy and Migraine," *Journal of Pediatrics* 114, no. 1 (1989): 51–58; J. Egger, "Is Migraine Food Allergy?: A Double-Blind Controlled Trial of Oligoantigenic Diet," *Lancet* (29 October 1984): 719–21; D. Ratner, E. Shoshani, and B. Dubnov, "Milk Protein-Free Diet for Nonseasonal Asthma and Migraine in Lactase-Deficient," *Israel Journal of Medical Sciences* 19, no. 9 (1983): 806–9; Paganelli et al, "Isotypic Analysis of Antibody Response to a Food Antigen in IBD," *International Archives of Allergy and Applied Immunology* 78 (1985): 81–85.

2. Marshall Mandell and Lynne Walker Scanlon, *5-Day Allergy Relief System, Perennial Library* (New York: Harper & Row, 1988).

3. Elias Ilyia, Objective Evaluation of Stress and Pertinent Clinical Correlates, Chicago: June 1, 1996 Seminar.

Chapter 14

1. Archibald D. Hart, *Adrenalin and Stress* (Waco: Word, 1986), 67.

2. G. Triadafilopoulos, R. W. Simms, and D. L. Goldenberg, "Bowel Dysfunction in Fibromyalgia Syndrome," *Digestive Diseases and Sciences* 36, no. 1 (1991): 59–64.

3. Rollin McCraty, "Stress and Emotional Health" (paper read at Steroid Hormones Clinical Correlates: Therapeutic and Nutritional Considerations, Chicago: February 25, 1996.

4. Andrew G. Goliszek, *Breaking the Stress Habit* (Winston-Salem: Carolina Press, 1987), 20.

5. Hans Selye, *Stress Without Distress* (Philadelphia and New York: J. B. Lippincott, 1974), 43.

6. Hans Selye, "A Syndrome Produced by Diverse Nocuous Agents" (1936, classic article), *Journal of Neuropsychiatry and Clinical Neurosciences* 10, no. 2 (1998): 230–31.

7. Hans Selye, *The Stress of Life* (New York: McGraw-Hill, 1956), 78.

8. Hart, *Adrenalin and Stress,* 36.

9. Selye, *Stress Without Distress,* 46.

10. Selye, *Stress of Life,* 87–89; *Stress Without Distress,* 39.

11. R. M. Sapolsky, L. C. Krey, and B. S. McEwen, "Glucocorticoid-sensitive Hippocampal Neurons Are Involved in Terminating the Adrenocortical Stress Response," *Proceedings of the National Academy of Sciences of the United States of America* 81, no. 19 (1984): 6174–77; Elias Ilyia, Objective Evaluation of Stress and Pertinent Clinical Correlates, Chicago: June 1, 1996 Seminar.

12. Selye, *Stress Without Distress,* 46.

13. Selye, *Stress of Life,* 43, 181; G. Riezzo et al, "Effects of Different Psychophysiological Stressors on the Cutaneous Electrogastrogram in Healthy Subjects," *Archives of Physiology and Biochemistry* 104, no. 3 (1996): 282–86.

14. N. Aoyama et al, "Peptic Ulcers After the Hanshin-Awaji Earthquake: Increased Incidence of Bleeding Gastric Ulcers," *American Journal of Gastroenterolgy* 93, no. 3 (1998): 311–16.

15. Y. Suzuki et al., "Pathogenesis of Water-Immersion Stress-Induced Gastric Ulcers in Rats with Renal Failure," *Scandinavian Journal of Gastroenterology, Supplement* 162 (1989):127–30.

16. A. Morrone et al., "Catecholamines and Vitiligo," *Pigment Cell Research* 5, no. 2 (1992): 65–69.

17. P. Nazzaro, A. Valente, and A. Pirrelli, "Borderline Hypertension: A Psychophysiologic Approach," *Journal Cardiovascular Pharmacology* 8, no. 5, suppl. (1986): S131–33.

18. B. S. Jonas, P. Franks, and D. D. Ingram, "Are Symptoms of Anxiety and Depression Risk Factors for Hypertension? Longitudinal Evidence from the National Health and Nutrition Examination Survey I Epidemiologic Follow-up Study," *Archives of Family Medicine* 6, no. 1 (1997): 43–49.

19. Meyer Friedman and Ray Rosenman, as quoted in Hart, *Adrenalin and Stress,* 39.

20. Hart, *Adrenalin and Stress,* 38, 98.

21. Van Doornen and K. Orlebeke, *Journal of Human Stress* (December 1982), 25–26. As quoted in Hart, 101.

22. Hart, *Adrenalin and Stress,* 97.

23. P. K. Shah, "Plaque Disruption and Coronary Thrombosis: New Insight into Pathogenesis and Prevention," *Clinical Cardiology* 20, no. 11, suppl. 2 (1997): 38–44.

24. W. P. Leary and A. J. Reyes, "Magnesium and Sudden Death," *South Africa Medical Journal* 64, no. 18 (1983): 697–98; Mildred S. Seelig, "Interrelationship of Magnesium and Estrogen in Cardiovascular and Bone Disorders, Eclampsia, Migraine and Premenstrual Syndrome," *Journal of American College of Nutrition* 12, no. 4 (1993): 442–58.

25. F. Morady et al., "Epinephrine-Induced Reversal of Verapamil's Electrophysiologic and Therapeutic Effects in Patients with Paroxysmal Supraventricular Tachycardia," *Circulation* 79, (1989): 783–90.

26. L. Toivonen, K. Helenius, and M. Viitasalo, "Electrocardiographic Repolarization During Stress from Awakening on Alarm Call, *Journal of American College of Cardiology* 30, no. 3 (1997): 774–79.

27. A. Sun et al., "Restraint Stress Changes Heart Sensitivity to Arrhythmogenic Drugs," *Chung Kuo Yao Li Hsueh Pao* 16, no. 5 (1995): 455–59; V. Elharrar et al., "Adrenergically Mediated Ventricular Fibrillation in Probucol-Treated Dogs: Roles of Alpha and Beta Adrenergic Receptors," *Pacing Clinical Electrophysiology* 2, no. 4 (1979): 435–43.

28. D. Lecomte, P. Fornes, and G. Nicolas, "Stressful Events as a Trigger of Sudden Death: A Study of 43 Medico-Legal Autopsy Cases," *Forensic Science International* 79, no. 1 (1996): 1–10; M. H. Huang, J. Ebey, and S. Wolf, "Responses of the QT Interval of the Electrocardiogram During Emotional Stress," *Psychosomatic Medicine* 51, no. 4 (1989): 419–27.

29. R. M. Carney et al., "Major Depression, Panic Disorder, and Mitral Valve Prolapse in Patients Who Complain of Chest Pain," *American Journal of Medicine* 89, no. 6 (1990): 757–60.

30. I. Basha et al., "Atypical Angina in Patients with Coronary Artery Disease Suggests Panic Disorder," *International Journal of Psychiatry in Medicine* 19, no. 4 (1989): 341–46.

31. Diagnostechs Lab Manual (Kent, Wash.: Diagnos-Techs, Inc.,1991). Telephone: (800) 878-3787; Ilyia, Objective Evaluation of Stress.

32. J. F. Sheridan et al., "Psychoneuroimmunology: Stress Effects on Pathogenesis and Immunity During Infection," *Clinical Microbiology Review* 7, no. 2 (1994): 200–212; A. A. Stone and D. H. Bovbjerg, "Stress and Humoral Immunity: A Review of the Human Studies," *Advances in Neuroimmunolgy* 4, no. 1 (1994): 49–56.

33. S. Cohen, D. A. Tyrrell, and A. P. Smith, "Psychological Stress and Susceptibility to the Common Cold," *New England Journal of Medicine* 325, no. 9 (1991): 606–12.

34. Selye, *Stress of Life,* 204.

35. S. A. Dahanukar et al, "The Influence of Surgical Stress on the Psychoneuro-Endocrine-Immune Axis," *Journal of Postgraduate Medicine* 42, no. 1 (1996): 12–14.

36. Selye, *Stress of Life,* 205.

37. A. L. Goldberg et al., "Hormonal Regulation of Protein Degradation and Synthesis in Skeletal Muscle. *Federation Proceedings* 39, no. 1 (1980): 31–36.

38. Selye, *Stress of Life,* 185.

39. L. J. Crosby, "Stress Factors, Emotional Stress and Rheumatoid Arthritis Disease Activity," *Journal of Advanced Nursing* 13, no. 4 (1988): 452–61.

40. Ilyia, Objective Evaluation of Stress.

41. Ibid.

42. H. Kida et al., "Facilitation of Tumor Metastasis to the Lung by Operative Stress in the Rat—Influence of Adrenocortical Hormones and Preoperative Administration of OK—432 (Abstract)," *Nippon Geka Gakkai Zasshi* 89, no. 10 (1988): 1692–98.

43. A. J. Dunn, "Nervous System-Immune System Interactions: An Overview," *Journal of Receptor Research* 8, nos. 1–4 (1988): 589–607.

44. H. J. Baltrusch, W. Stangel, and I. Titze, "Stress, Cancer and Immunity. New Developments in Biopsychosocial and Psychoneuroimmunologic Research," *Acta Neurologica (Napoli)* 13, no. 4 (1991): 315–27.

45. T. R. Miller, "Psychophysiologic Aspects of Cancer: The James Ewing Lecture," *Cancer* 39, no. 2 (1977): 413–18.

46. C. D. Lehman et al, "Impact of Environmental Stress on the Expression of Insulin-Dependent Diabetes Mellitus," *Behavioral Neuroscience* 105, no. 2 (1991): 241–45.

47. Ilyia, Evaluation of Stress.

48. Ibid.

49. Selye, *Stress of Life,* 176; Y. Tache, J. Tache, and Hans Selye, "Antifertility Effect of CS—1 in the Rat," *Journal of Reproduction and Fertility* 37, no. 2 (1974): 257–62; K. H. Cui, "The Effect of Stress on Semen Reduction in the Marmoset Monkey (Callithrix Jacchus)," *Human Reproduction* 11, no. 3 (1996): 568–73; R. Alonso-Uriarte, I. Sojo-Aranda, and V. Cortes-Gallegos, "Role of Stress in Male Fertility," *Archives de Investigacion Medica (Mexico)* 22, no. 2 (1991): 223–28.

50. P. C. Arck et al., "Stress-Triggered Abortion: Inhibition of Protective Suppression and Promotion of Tumor Necrosis Factor-Alpha (TNF-Alpha) Release as a Mechanism Triggering Resorptions in Mice," *American Journal of Reproductive Immunology* 33, no. 1 (1995): 74–80.

51. A. M. Magarinos, J. M. Verdugo, and B. S. McEwen, "Chronic Stress Alters Synaptic Terminal Structure in Hippocampus," *Proceedings of National Academy of Science USA* 94, no. 25 (1997): 14002–8.

52. Selye, *Stress of Life,* 174.

53. Hart, *Adrenalin and Stress,* 71.

Chapter 15

1. Reprinted from: *Breaking the Stress Habit* by Andrew G. Goliszek (Winston-Salem: Carolina Press, 1987). Used by permission.

2. Hans Selye, *The Stress of Life* (New York: McGraw-Hill, 1956), 265.

3. Archibald D. Hart, *Adrenalin and Stress* (Waco, Tex.: Word, 1986), 89.

4. Ibid., 119.

5. Ibid., 126.

6. Goliszek, 40.

7. Hart, 92.

8. R. M. Sapolsky, L. C. Krey, and B. S. McEwen, "Glucocorticoid-sensitive Hippocampal Neurons Are Involved in Terminating the Adrenocortical Stress Response," *Proceedings of the National Academy of Science of the United States of America* 81, no. 19 (1984): 6174–77; Elias Ilyria, Objective Evaluation of Stress and Pertinent Clinical Correlates, Chicago: June 1, 1996 (seminar).

9. Selye, *Stress of Life,* 159.

10. J. Kjeldsen-Kragh et al., "Controlled Trial of Fasting and One-Year Vegetarian Diet in Rheumatoid Arthritis," *Lancet* 338, no. 8772 (1991): 899–902.

11. Selye, *Stress of Life,* 264.

12. Hart, *Adrenalin and Stress.*

13. Ibid, 150.

14. A.C. Guyton, "States of Brain Activity—Sleep; Brain Waves; Epilepsy; Psychoses," *Textbook of Medical Physiology* (Philadelphia: W. B. Saunders, 1991), 659–66; W. C. Stern, "The Relationship Between REM Sleep and Learning: Animal Studies," *International Psychiatry Clinics* 7, no. 2 (1970): 249–57.

15. Hart, *Adrenalin and Stress,* 160–61.

Chapter 16

1. Charles R. Swindoll, *The Tale of the Tardy Oxcart—and 1,501 Other Stories* (Nashville: Word, 1998), 535.

2. Dan Sullivan, *How the Best Get Better* (Toronto: The Strategic Coach, 1996). Audio cassette and booklet.

3. Ibid.

4. *Wisdom Booklet,* Institute in Basic Life Principles (Oak Brook, Ill.: IBLP, 1990).

Chapter 17

1. Andrew G. Goliszek, *Breaking the Stress Habit* (Winston-Salem, NC: Carolina Press), 14.

2. Robert E. Kleiger et al., "Decreased Heart Rate Variability and Its Association with Increased Mortality After Acute Myocardial Infarction," *American Journal of Cardiolgy* 59 (1987): 256–62.

3. William A. Tiller, Rollin A. McCraty, and Mike Atkinson, "Cardiac Coherence: A New Noninvasive Measure of Autonomic Nervous System Order," *Alternative Therapies* 2, no. 1 (1996): 52–65; Rollin McCraty et al., "The Effects of Emotions on Short-Term Power Spectrum Analysis of Heart Rate Variability," *American Journal of Cardiology* 76, no. 14 (1995): 1089–93.

4. Research Update, Institute of HeartMath (Boulder Creek, Colo.: Institute of HeartMath, 1995).

5. Rollin McCraty, "Stress and Emotional Health" (paper read at Steroid Hormones Clinical Correlates: Therapeutic and Nutritional Considerations, Chicago: February 25, 1996).

6. Rollin McCraty, William A. Tiller, and Mike Atkinson, *Head-Heart Entrainment: A Preliminary Survey* (Boulder Creek, Colo.: Institute of HeartMath, 1996).

7. Research Update, Institute of HeartMath.

8. Jim Logan, *Reclaiming Surrendered Ground* (Chicago: Moody Press, 1995).

Chapter 18

1. Fred H. Wight, *Manners and Customs of Bible Lands* (Chicago: Moody Press, 1953), 43–54.

2. Ibid.

3. *Hebrew Greek Key Study Bible* (King James Version), ed. Spiros Zodhiates, 2d ed. (Chattanooga: AMG Publishers, 1991).

Appendix B

1. Shannon, I. L., "Movement of Cortisol from the Bloodstream to Parotid Fluid," *Texas Reports on Biology and Medicine* 25, no. 3 (1967): 437–45; F. H. Katz and I. L. Shannon, "Adrenal Corticosteroids in Submaxillary Fluid," *Journal of Dental Research* 48, no. 3 (1969): 448–51; F. H. Katz and I. L. Shannon, "Parotid Fluid Cortisol and Cortisone," *Journal of Clinical Investigation* 48, no. 5 (1969): 848–55; C. Kirschbaum and D. H. Hellhammer, "Salivary Cortisol in Psychbiological Research: An Overview," *Neuropsychobiology* 22, no. 3 (1989): 150–69.

INDEX OF SUBJECTS

Tables and figures are indicated by italic page numbers.

INDEX OF SCRIPTURE

Moody Press, a ministry of Moody Bible Institute,
is designed for education, evangelization, and edification.
If we may assist you in knowing more about Christ and the Christian life,
please write us without obligation: Moody Press, c/o MLM, Chicago, IL 60610.